Natsume's
BOOK of FRIENDS

Shojo Beat

Natsume's BOOK of FRIENDS

STORY and ART by
Yuki Midorikawa

VOLUME 25

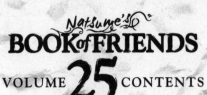

Natsume's BOOK of FRIENDS

VOLUME 25 CONTENTS

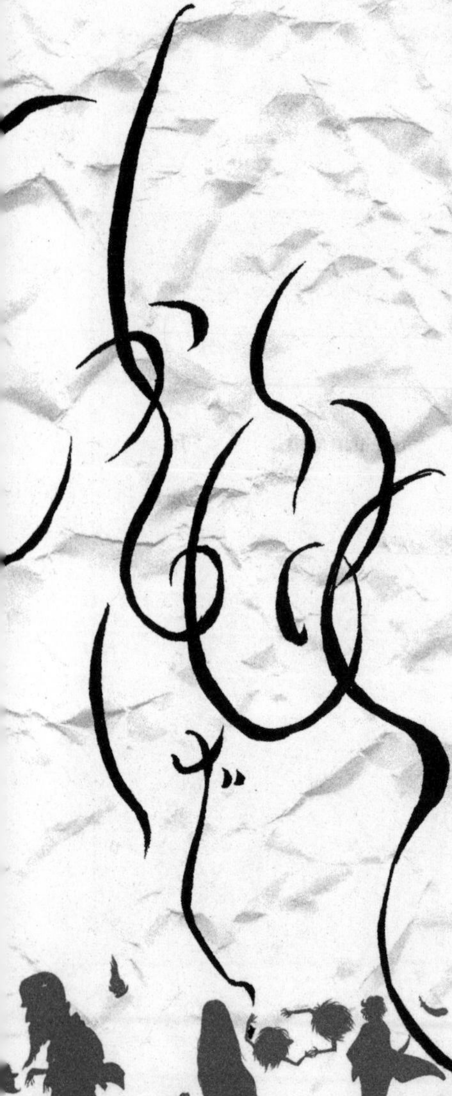

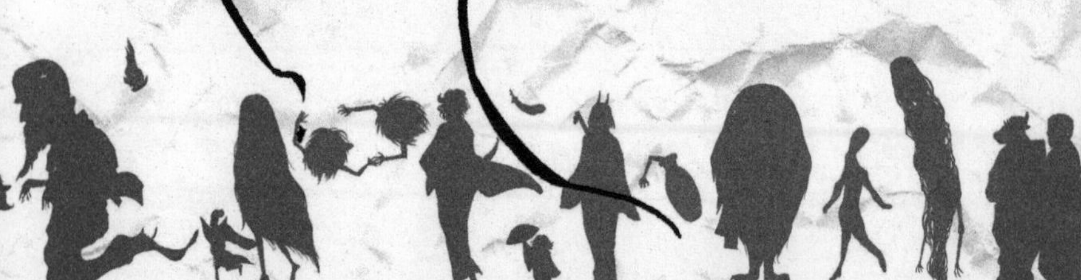

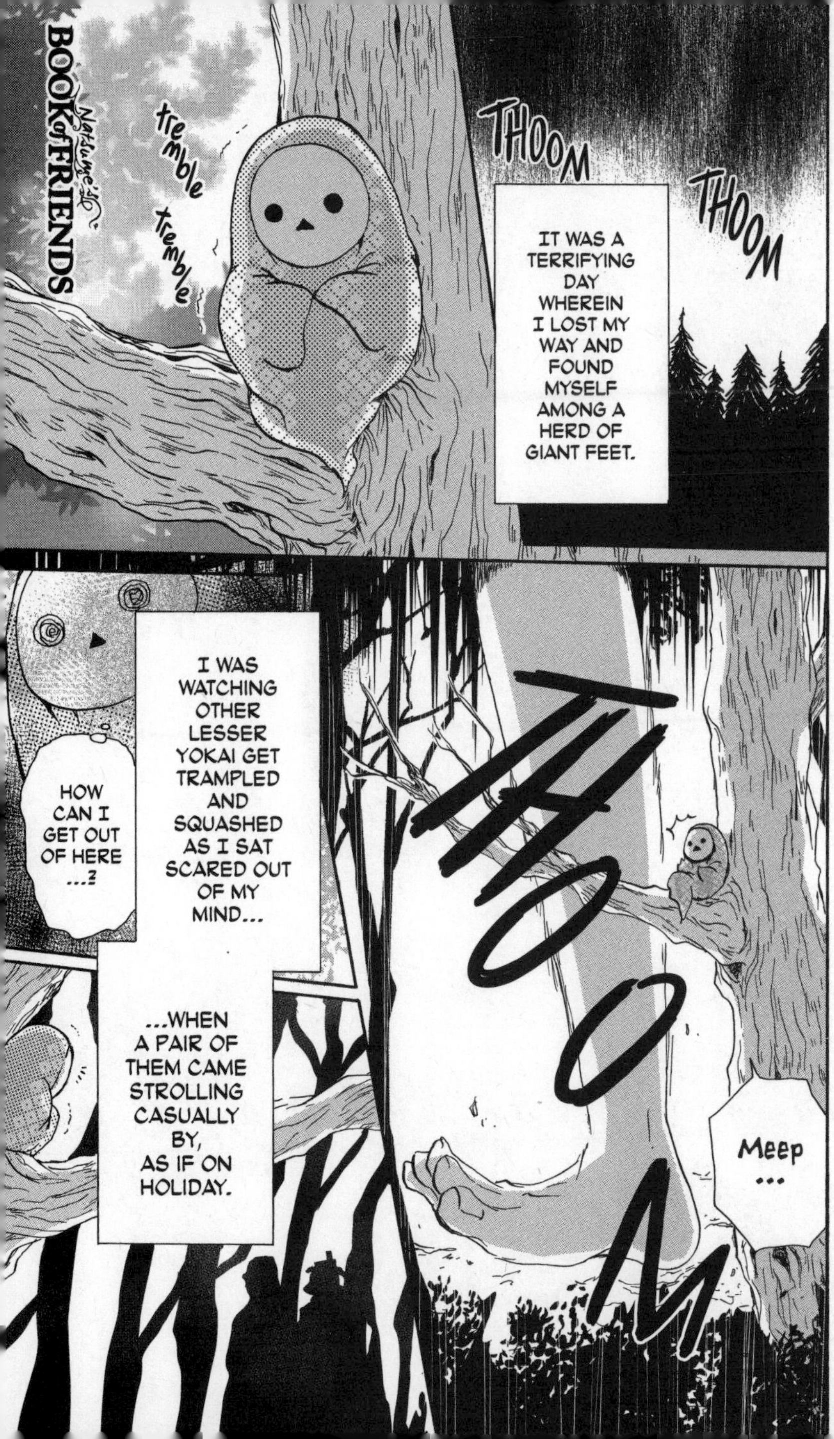
THOOM
THOOM
IT WAS A TERRIFYING DAY WHEREIN I LOST MY WAY AND FOUND MYSELF AMONG A HERD OF GIANT FEET.
tremble tremble
Natsume's BOOK of FRIENDS
THOOOM
Meep...
I WAS WATCHING OTHER LESSER YOKAI GET TRAMPLED AND SQUASHED AS I SAT SCARED OUT OF MY MIND...
HOW CAN I GET OUT OF HERE...?
...WHEN A PAIR OF THEM CAME STROLLING CASUALLY BY, AS IF ON HOLIDAY.

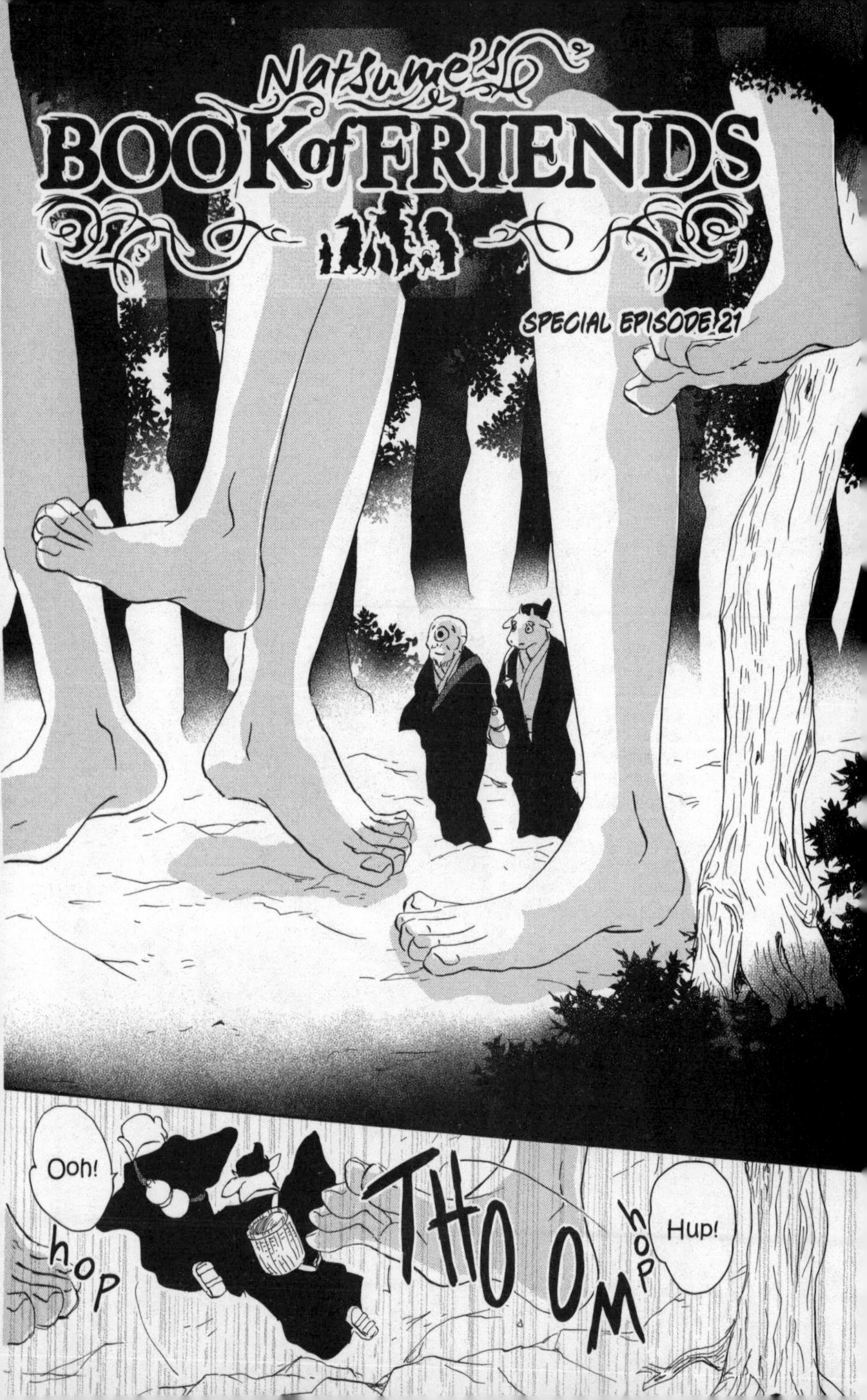
Natsume's
BOOK of FRIENDS
SPECIAL EPISODE 21
Hup!
hop
THOOM
Ooh!
hop

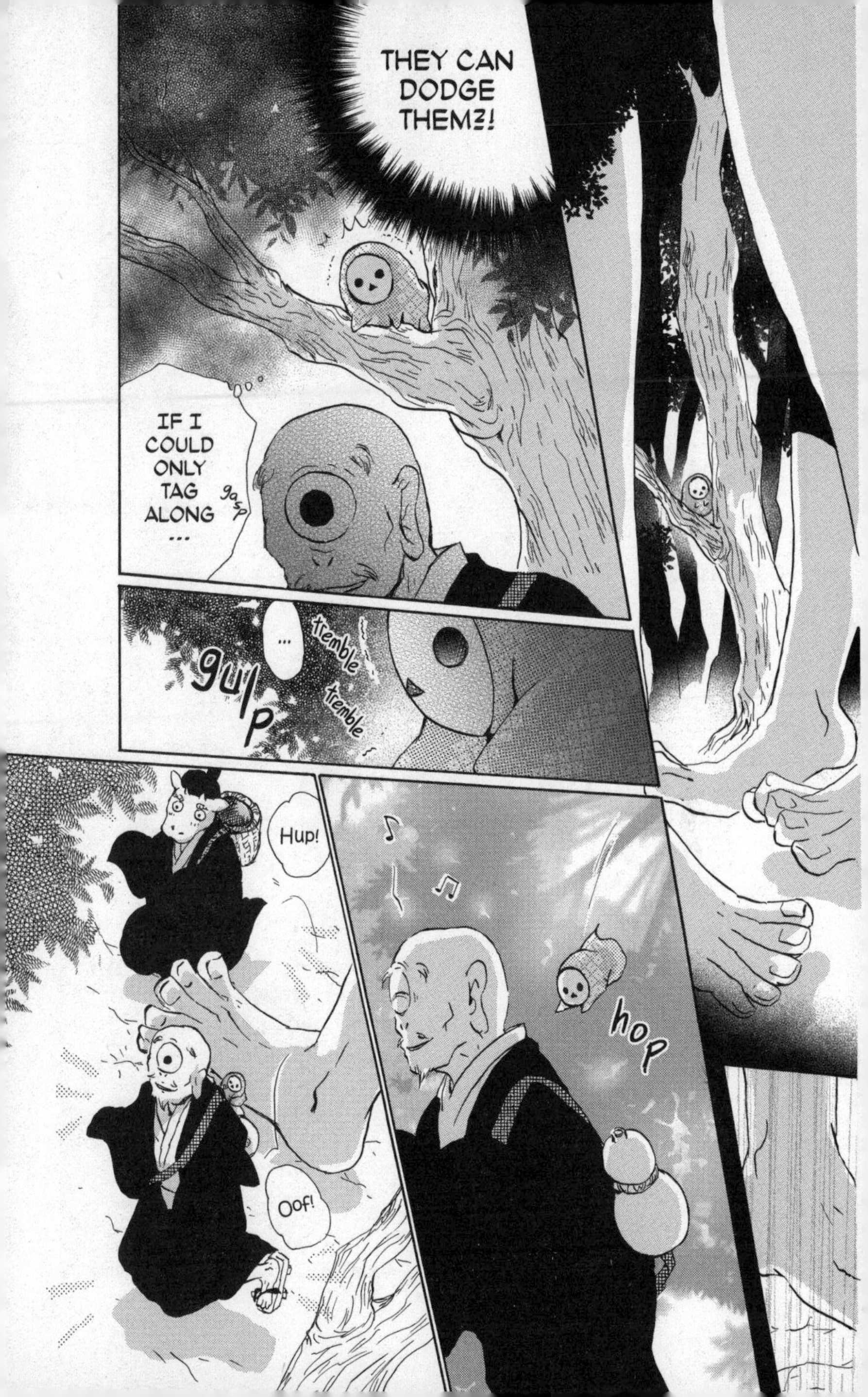
THEY CAN DODGE THEM?!
IF I COULD ONLY TAG ALONG...
gasp
...
tremble
tremble
gulp
♪ ♫
hop
Hup!
Oof!

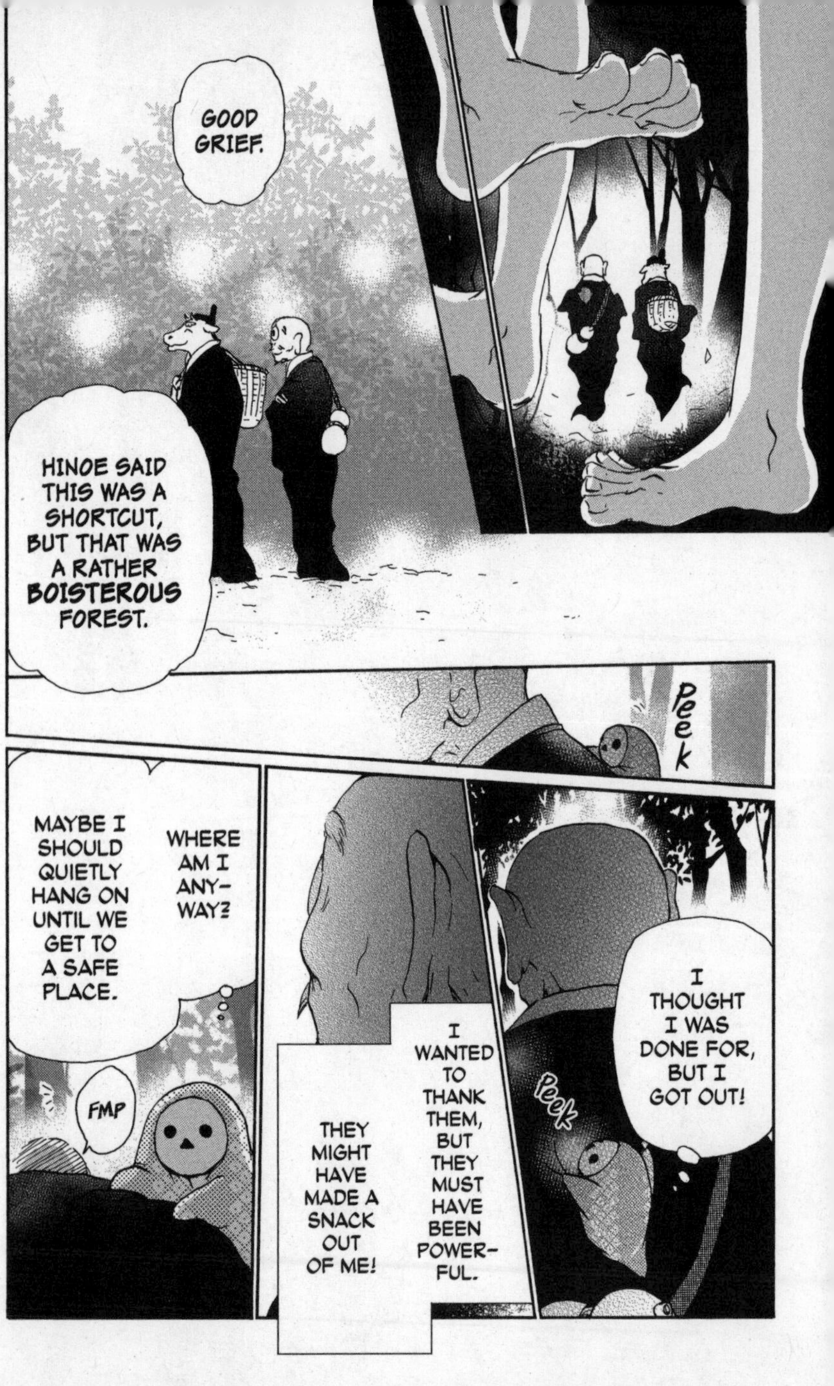
GOOD GRIEF.
HINOE SAID THIS WAS A SHORTCUT, BUT THAT WAS A RATHER **BOISTEROUS** FOREST.
Peek
I THOUGHT I WAS DONE FOR, BUT I GOT OUT!
Peek
I WANTED TO THANK THEM, BUT THEY MUST HAVE BEEN POWER-FUL.
THEY MIGHT HAVE MADE A SNACK OUT OF ME!
WHERE AM I ANY-WAY?
MAYBE I SHOULD QUIETLY HANG ON UNTIL WE GET TO A SAFE PLACE.
FMP

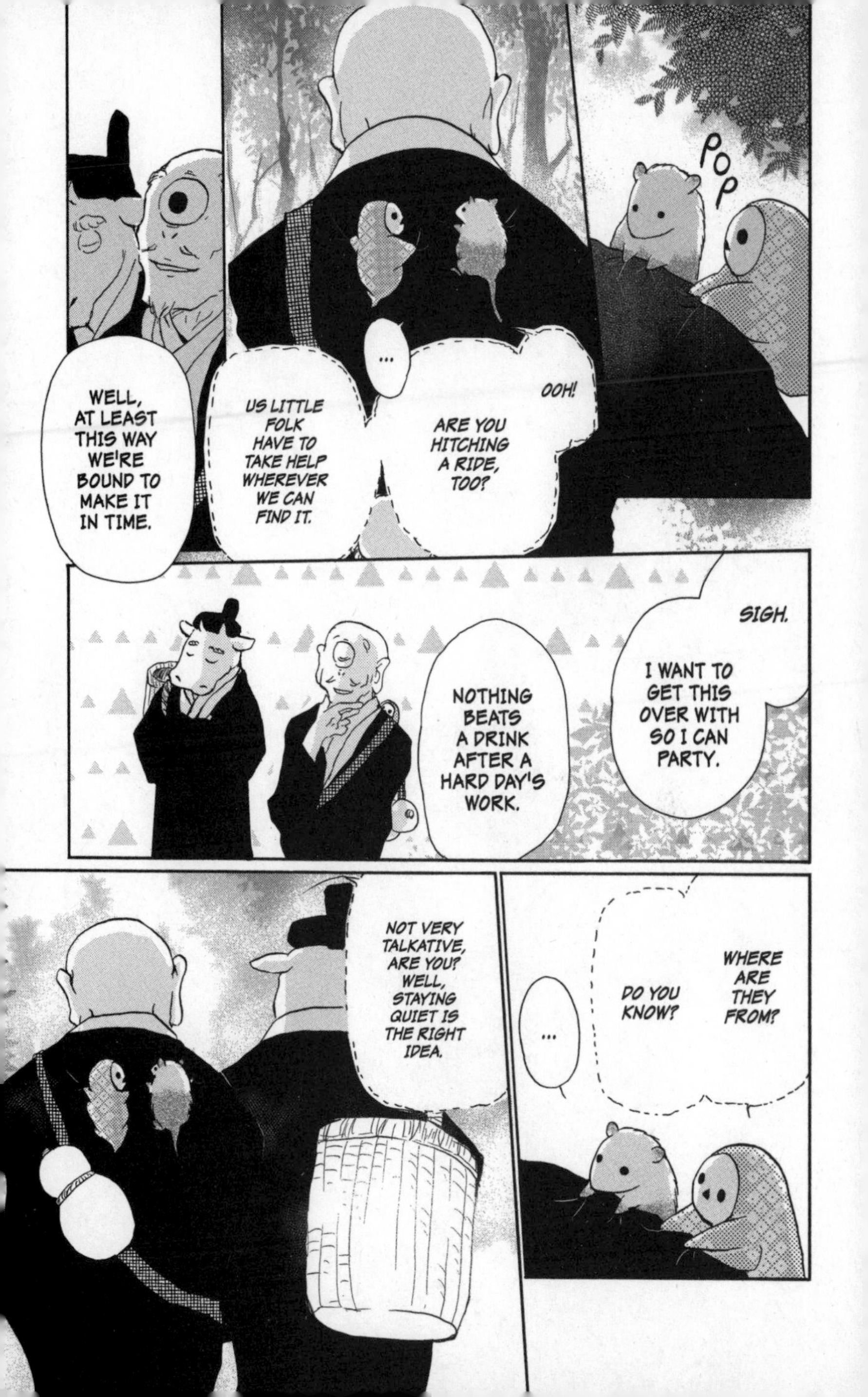
POP POP
OOH! ARE YOU HITCHING A RIDE, TOO?
...
US LITTLE FOLK HAVE TO TAKE HELP WHEREVER WE CAN FIND IT.
WELL, AT LEAST THIS WAY WE'RE BOUND TO MAKE IT IN TIME.
SIGH. I WANT TO GET THIS OVER WITH SO I CAN PARTY.
NOTHING BEATS A DRINK AFTER A HARD DAY'S WORK.
WHERE ARE THEY FROM? DO YOU KNOW?
...
NOT VERY TALKATIVE, ARE YOU? WELL, STAYING QUIET IS THE RIGHT IDEA.

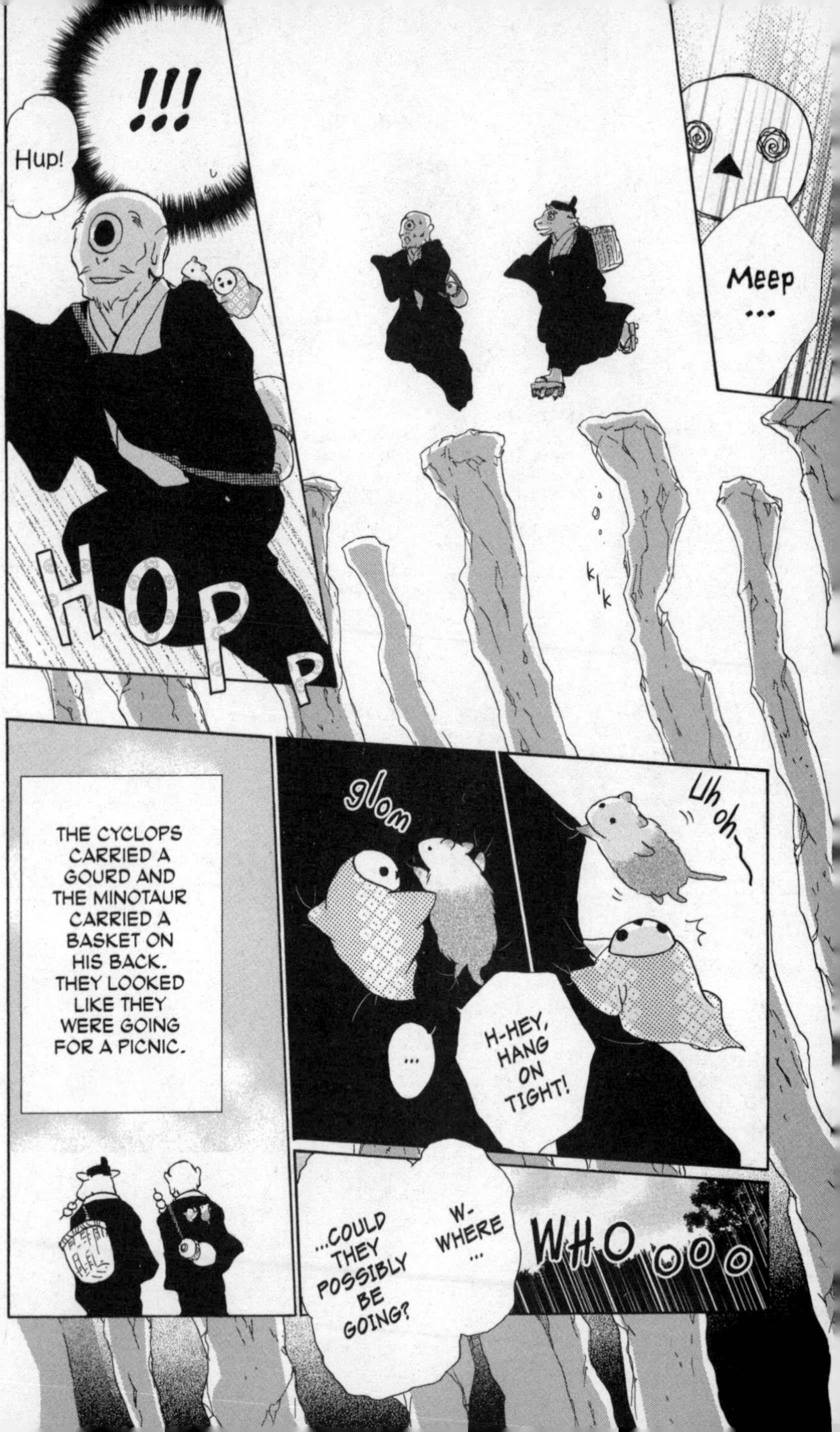
Meep ...
klk
Hup!
!!!
HOPP
Uh oh~
H-HEY, HANG ON TIGHT!
glom
...
WHOOOOO
W-WHERE ...
...COULD THEY POSSIBLY BE GOING?
THE CYCLOPS CARRIED A GOURD AND THE MINOTAUR CARRIED A BASKET ON HIS BACK. THEY LOOKED LIKE THEY WERE GOING FOR A PICNIC.

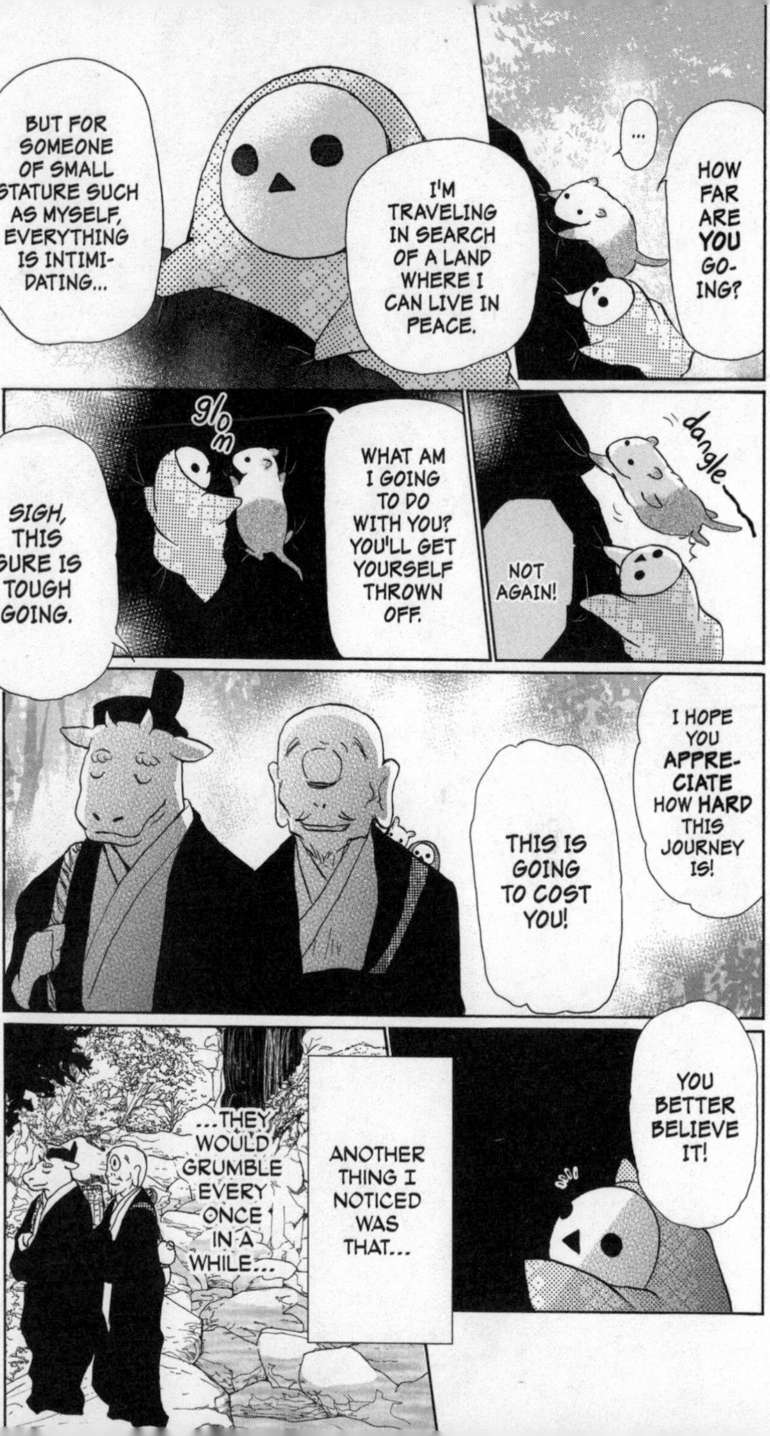
...
HOW FAR ARE YOU GOING?
I'M TRAVELING IN SEARCH OF A LAND WHERE I CAN LIVE IN PEACE.
BUT FOR SOMEONE OF SMALL STATURE SUCH AS MYSELF, EVERYTHING IS INTIMIDATING...
dangle
NOT AGAIN!
glom
WHAT AM I GOING TO DO WITH YOU? YOU'LL GET YOURSELF THROWN OFF.
SIGH, THIS SURE IS TOUGH GOING.
I HOPE YOU APPRECIATE HOW HARD THIS JOURNEY IS!
THIS IS GOING TO COST YOU!
YOU BETTER BELIEVE IT!
ANOTHER THING I NOTICED WAS THAT...
...THEY WOULD GRUMBLE EVERY ONCE IN A WHILE...

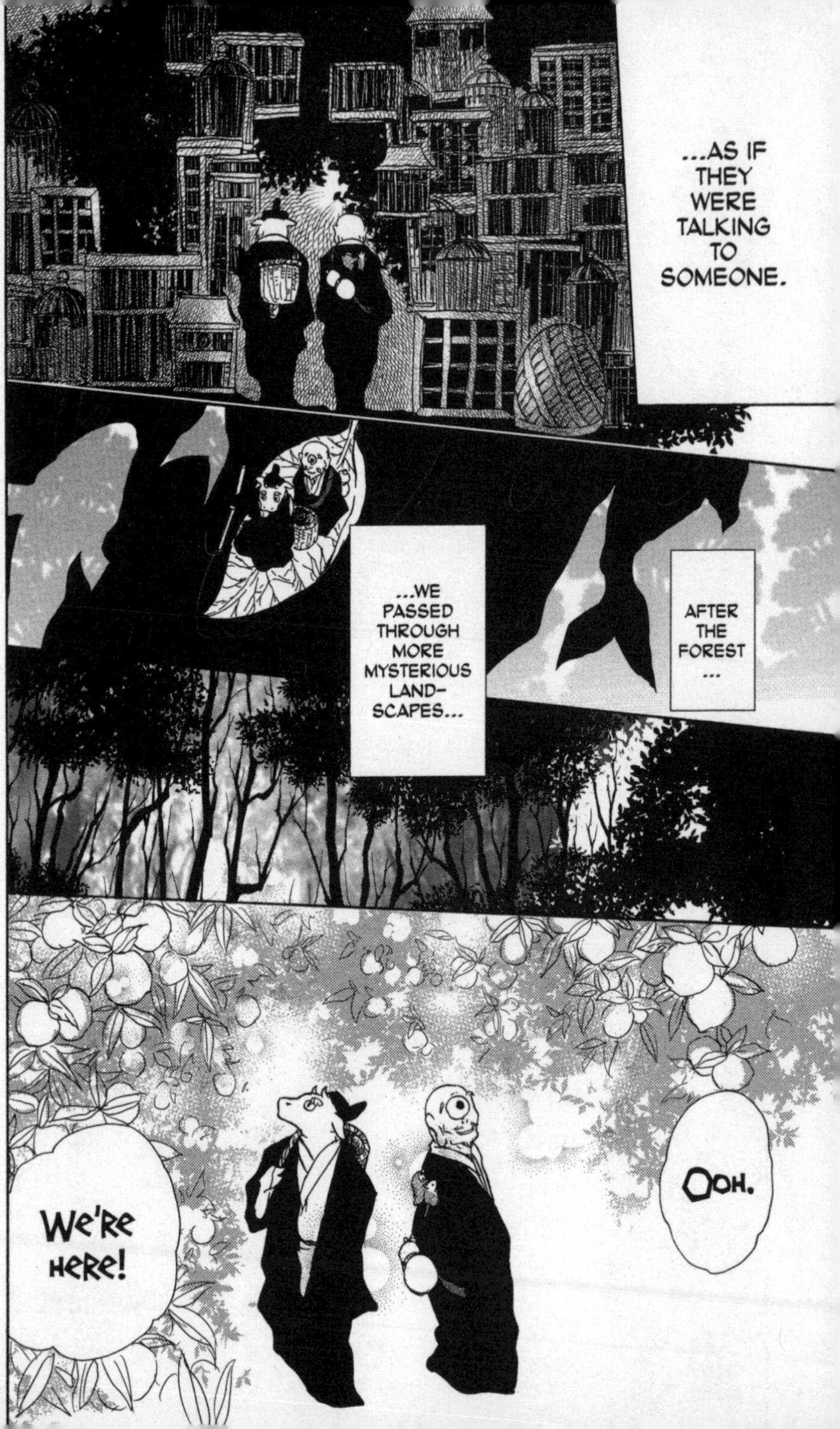
...AS IF THEY WERE TALKING TO SOMEONE.
AFTER THE FOREST...
...WE PASSED THROUGH MORE MYSTERIOUS LAND-SCAPES...
OOH.
We're here!

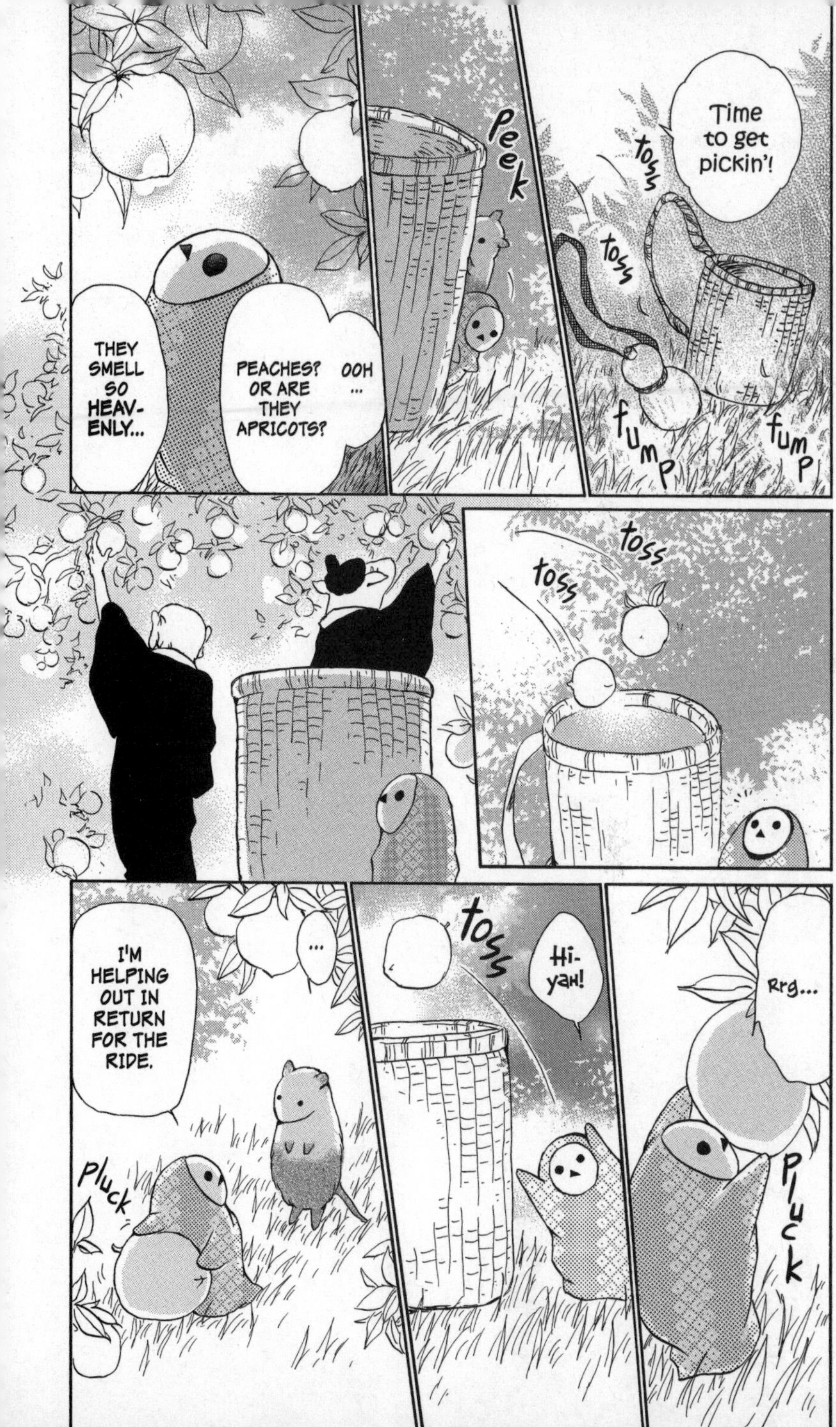
Time to get pickin'!
toss
toss
fump
fump
Peek
OOH ...
PEACHES? OR ARE THEY APRICOTS?
THEY SMELL SO HEAVENLY...
toss
toss
Rrg...
Pluck
toss
Hi-yah!
...
I'M HELPING OUT IN RETURN FOR THE RIDE.
Pluck

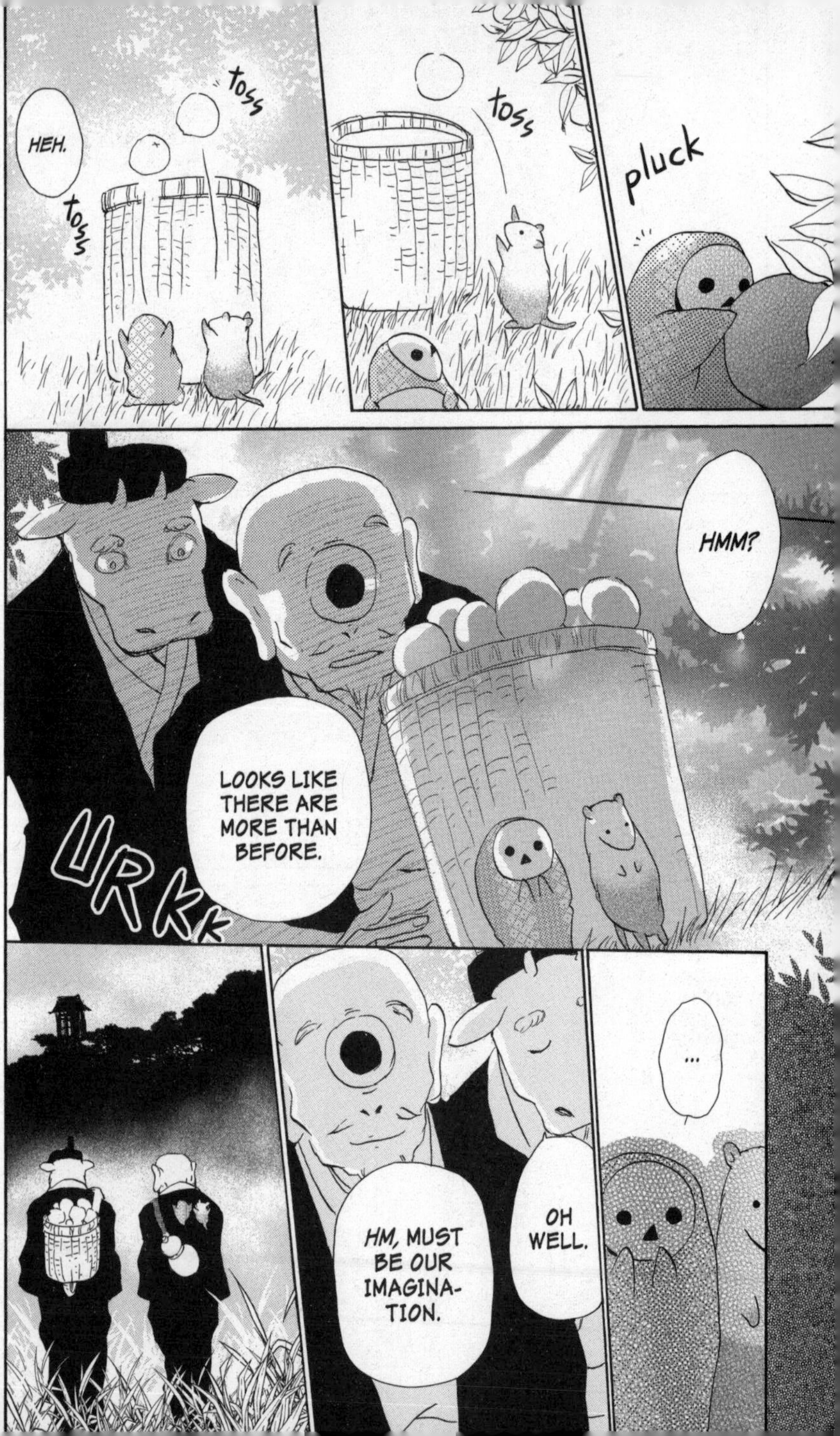
pluck
toss
toss
HEH.
toss
HMM?
LOOKS LIKE THERE ARE MORE THAN BEFORE.
URKK
...
OH WELL.
HM, MUST BE OUR IMAGINATION.

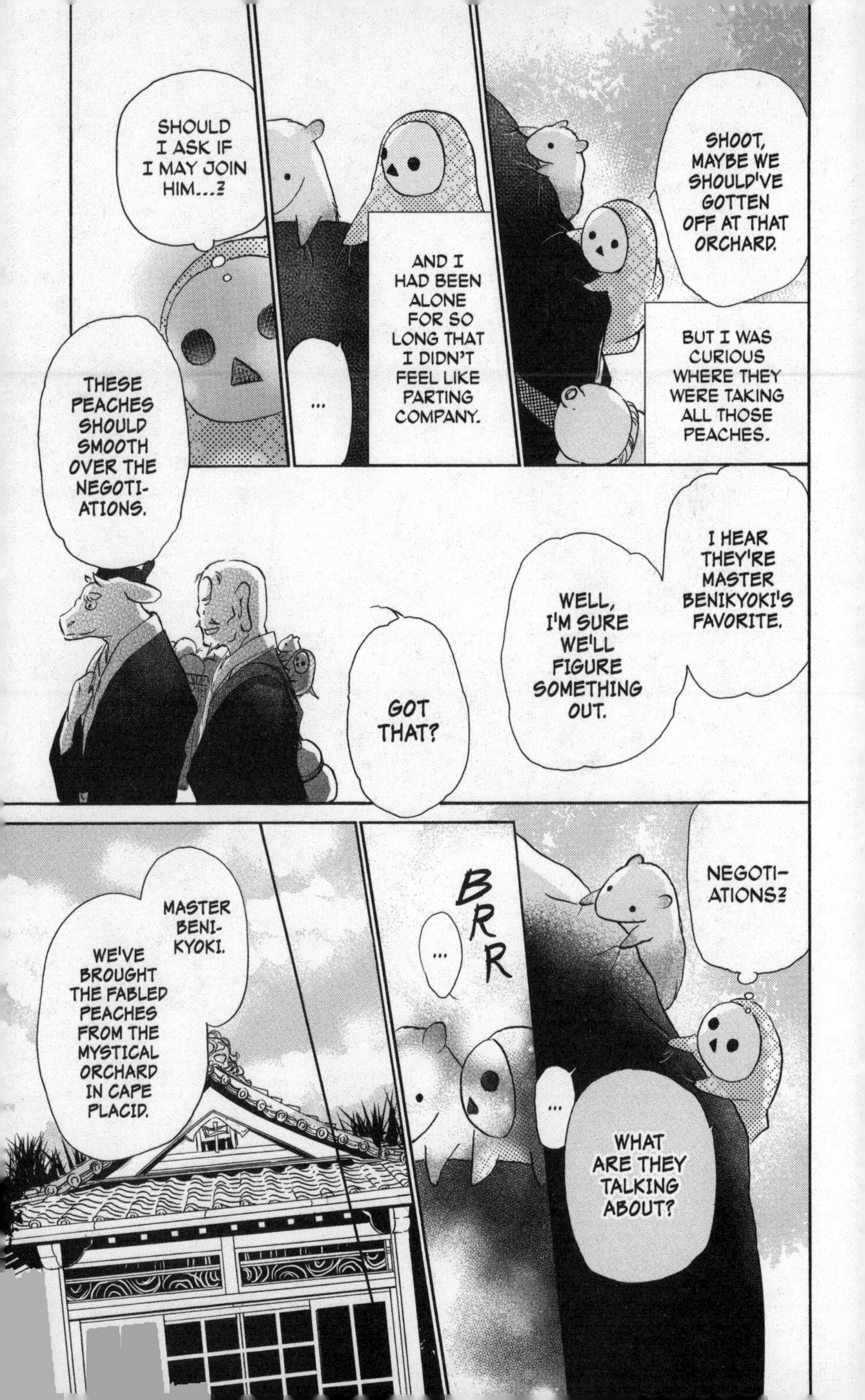
SHOOT, MAYBE WE SHOULD'VE GOTTEN OFF AT THAT ORCHARD.
BUT I WAS CURIOUS WHERE THEY WERE TAKING ALL THOSE PEACHES.
AND I HAD BEEN ALONE FOR SO LONG THAT I DIDN'T FEEL LIKE PARTING COMPANY.
...
SHOULD I ASK IF I MAY JOIN HIM...?
THESE PEACHES SHOULD SMOOTH OVER THE NEGOTIATIONS.
I HEAR THEY'RE MASTER BENIKYOKI'S FAVORITE.
WELL, I'M SURE WE'LL FIGURE SOMETHING OUT.
GOT THAT?
NEGOTIATIONS?
WHAT ARE THEY TALKING ABOUT?
...
BRRR
...
MASTER BENIKYOKI.
WE'VE BROUGHT THE FABLED PEACHES FROM THE MYSTICAL ORCHARD IN CAPE PLACID.

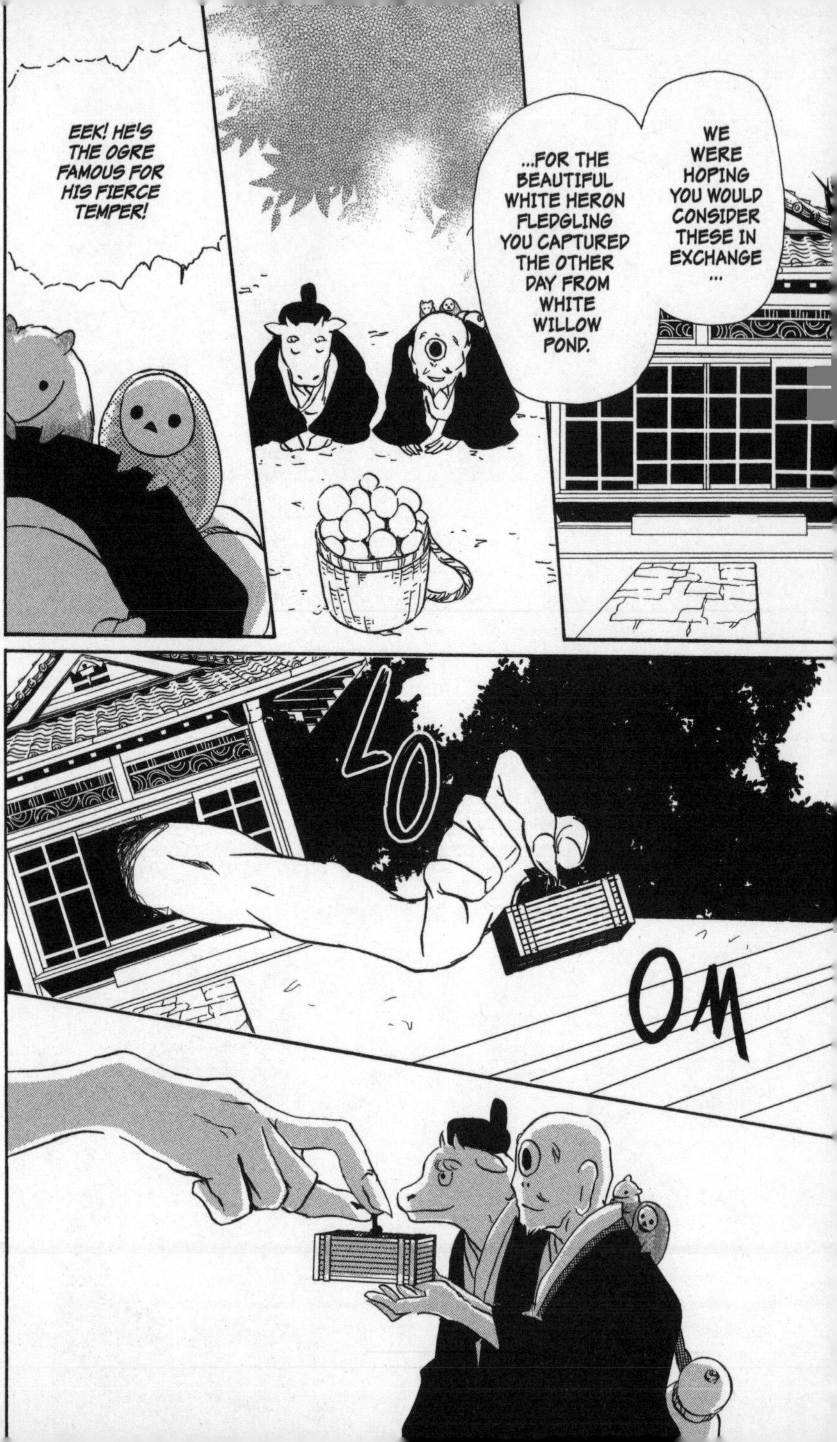
WE WERE HOPING YOU WOULD CONSIDER THESE IN EXCHANGE ...
...FOR THE BEAUTIFUL WHITE HERON FLEDGLING YOU CAPTURED THE OTHER DAY FROM WHITE WILLOW POND.
EEK! HE'S THE OGRE FAMOUS FOR HIS FIERCE TEMPER!
LO
OM

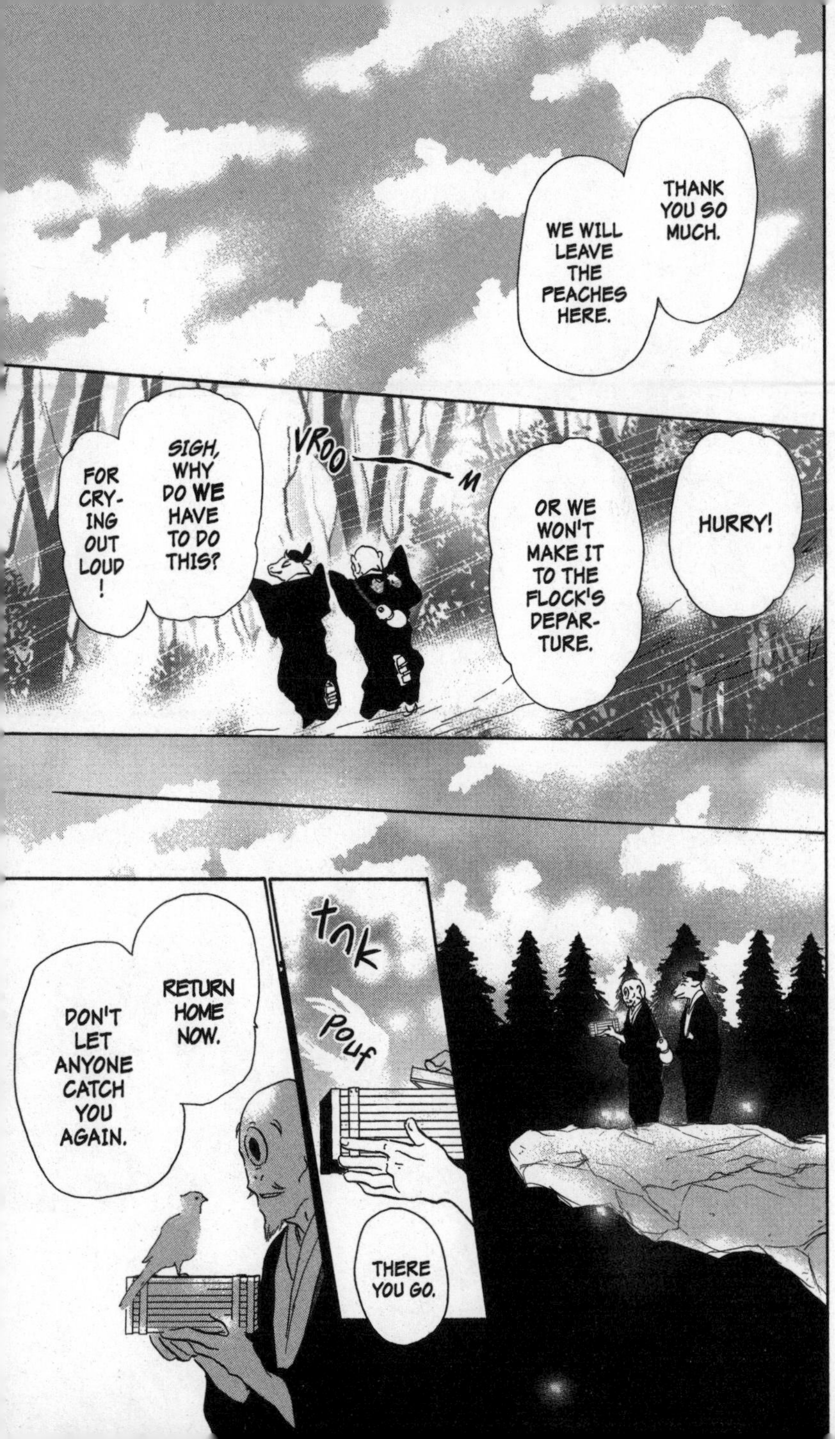
THANK YOU SO MUCH.
WE WILL LEAVE THE PEACHES HERE.
HURRY!
OR WE WON'T MAKE IT TO THE FLOCK'S DEPARTURE.
VROOOM
SIGH, WHY DO WE HAVE TO DO THIS?
FOR CRYING OUT LOUD!
tnk
Pouf
THERE YOU GO.
RETURN HOME NOW.
DON'T LET ANYONE CATCH YOU AGAIN.

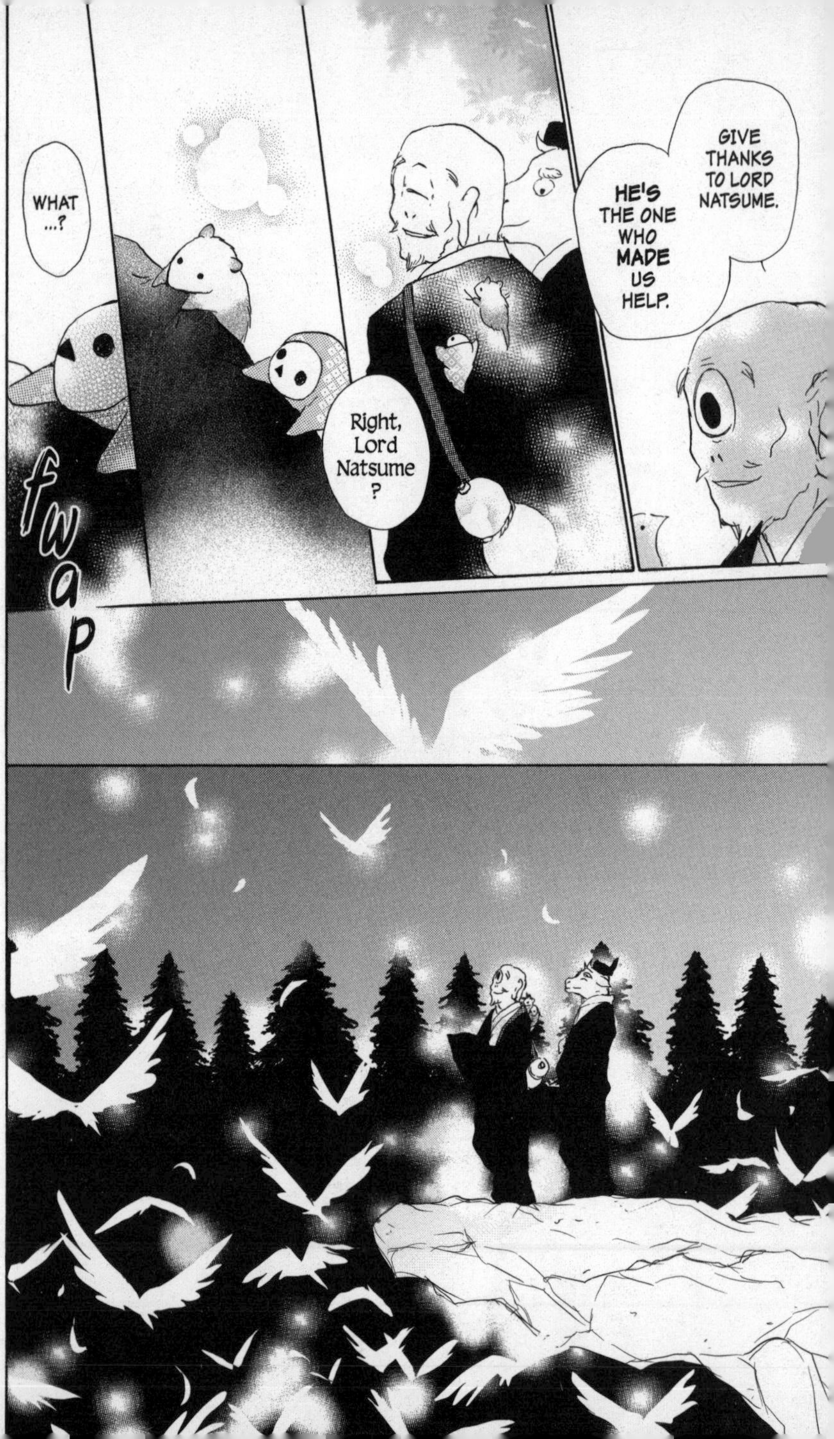
GIVE THANKS TO LORD NATSUME.
HE'S THE ONE WHO MADE US HELP.
Right, Lord Natsume?
WHAT ...?
fwap

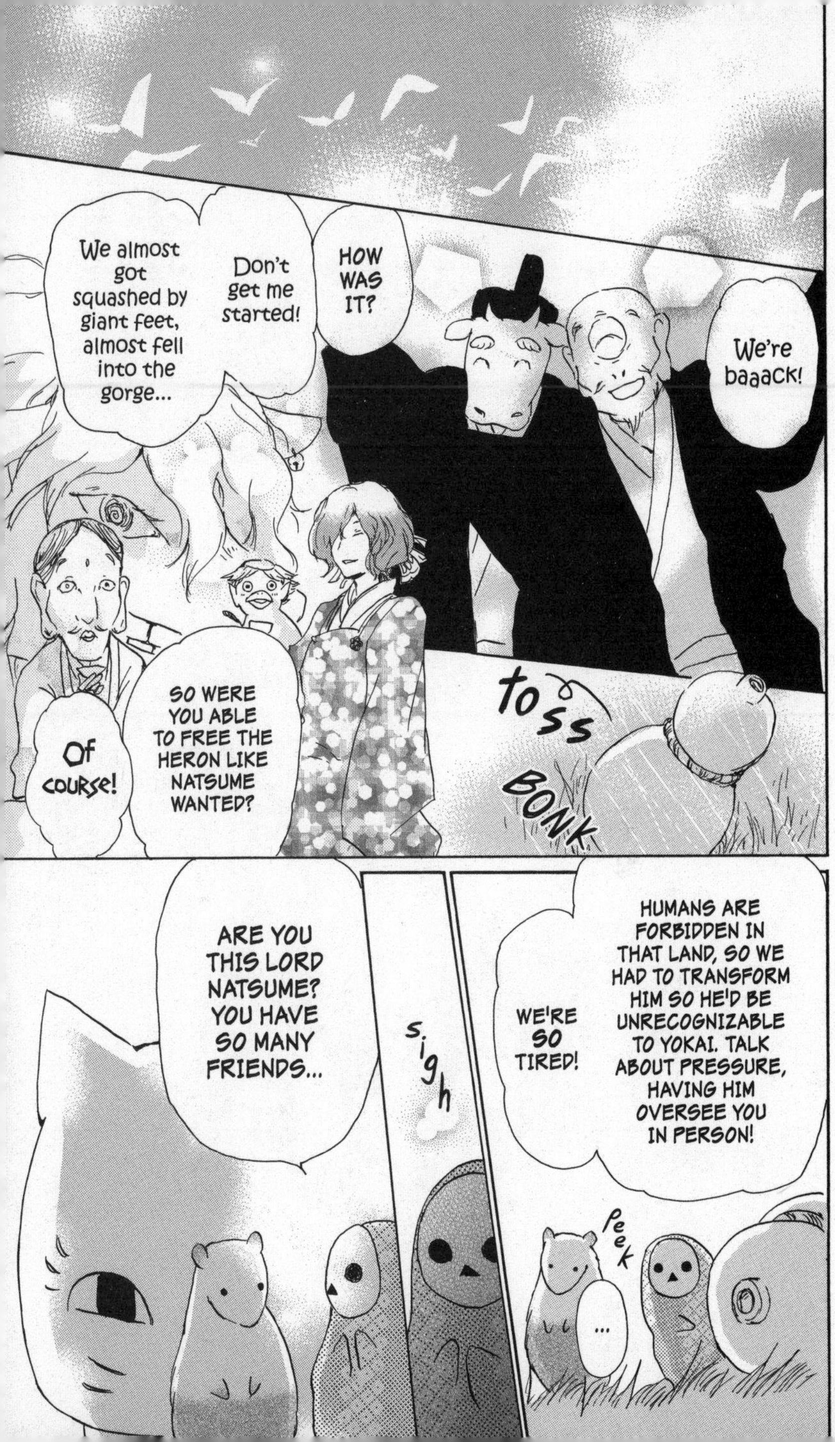
We're baaack!
HOW WAS IT?
Don't get me started!
We almost got squashed by giant feet, almost fell into the gorge...
toss
BONK
SO WERE YOU ABLE TO FREE THE HERON LIKE NATSUME WANTED?
Of course!
HUMANS ARE FORBIDDEN IN THAT LAND, SO WE HAD TO TRANSFORM HIM SO HE'D BE UNRECOGNIZABLE TO YOKAI. TALK ABOUT PRESSURE, HAVING HIM OVERSEE YOU IN PERSON!
WE'RE SO TIRED!
Peek
...
sigh
ARE YOU THIS LORD NATSUME? YOU HAVE SO MANY FRIENDS...

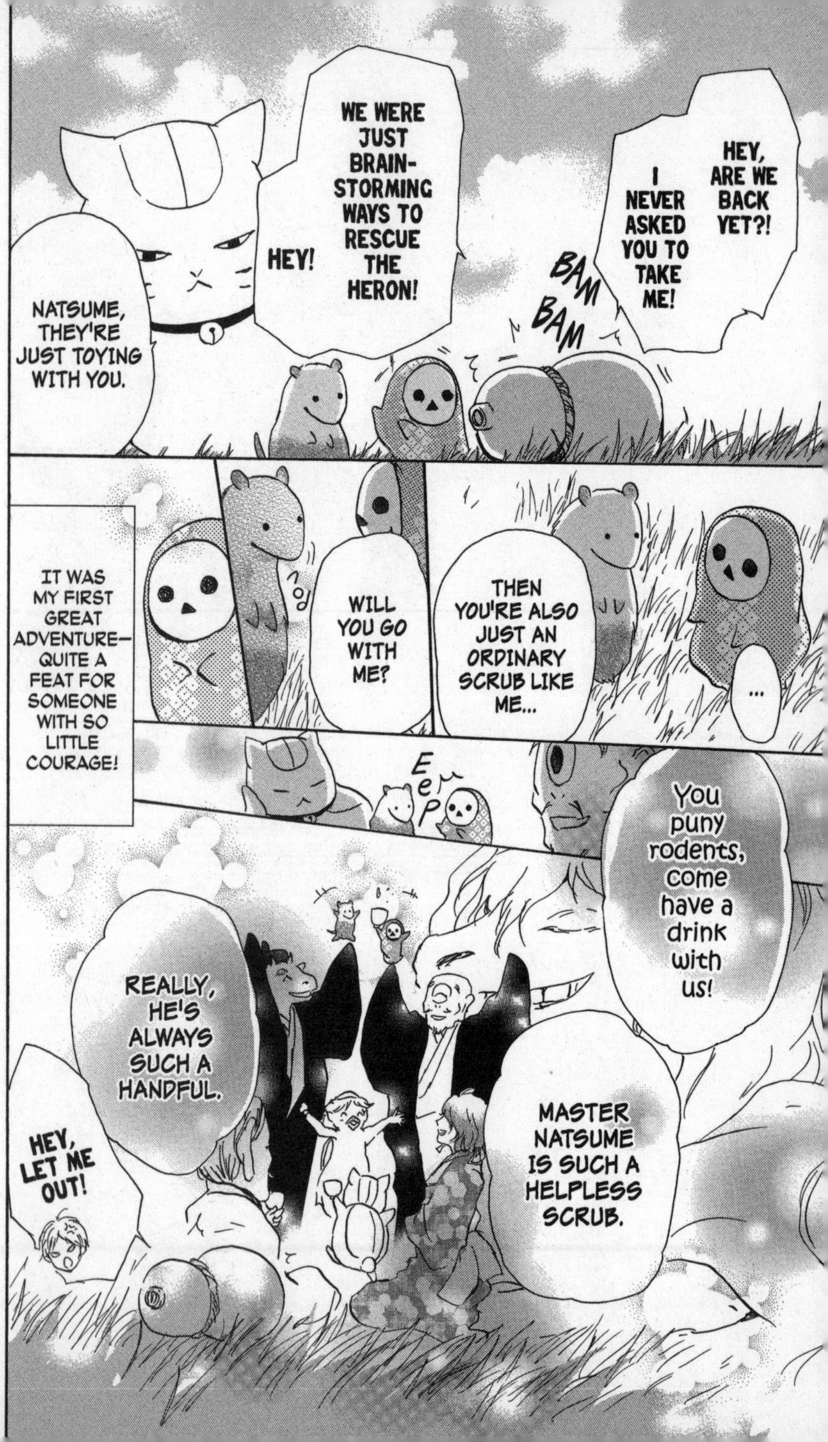
HEY, ARE WE BACK YET?!
I NEVER ASKED YOU TO TAKE ME!
BAM BAM
WE WERE JUST BRAIN-STORMING WAYS TO RESCUE THE HERON!
HEY!
NATSUME, THEY'RE JUST TOYING WITH YOU.
...
THEN YOU'RE ALSO JUST AN ORDINARY SCRUB LIKE ME...
WILL YOU GO WITH ME?
IT WAS MY FIRST GREAT ADVENTURE—QUITE A FEAT FOR SOMEONE WITH SO LITTLE COURAGE!
EeP
You puny rodents, come have a drink with us!
MASTER NATSUME IS SUCH A HELPLESS SCRUB.
REALLY, HE'S ALWAYS SUCH A HANDFUL.
HEY, LET ME OUT!

CHAPTER 100

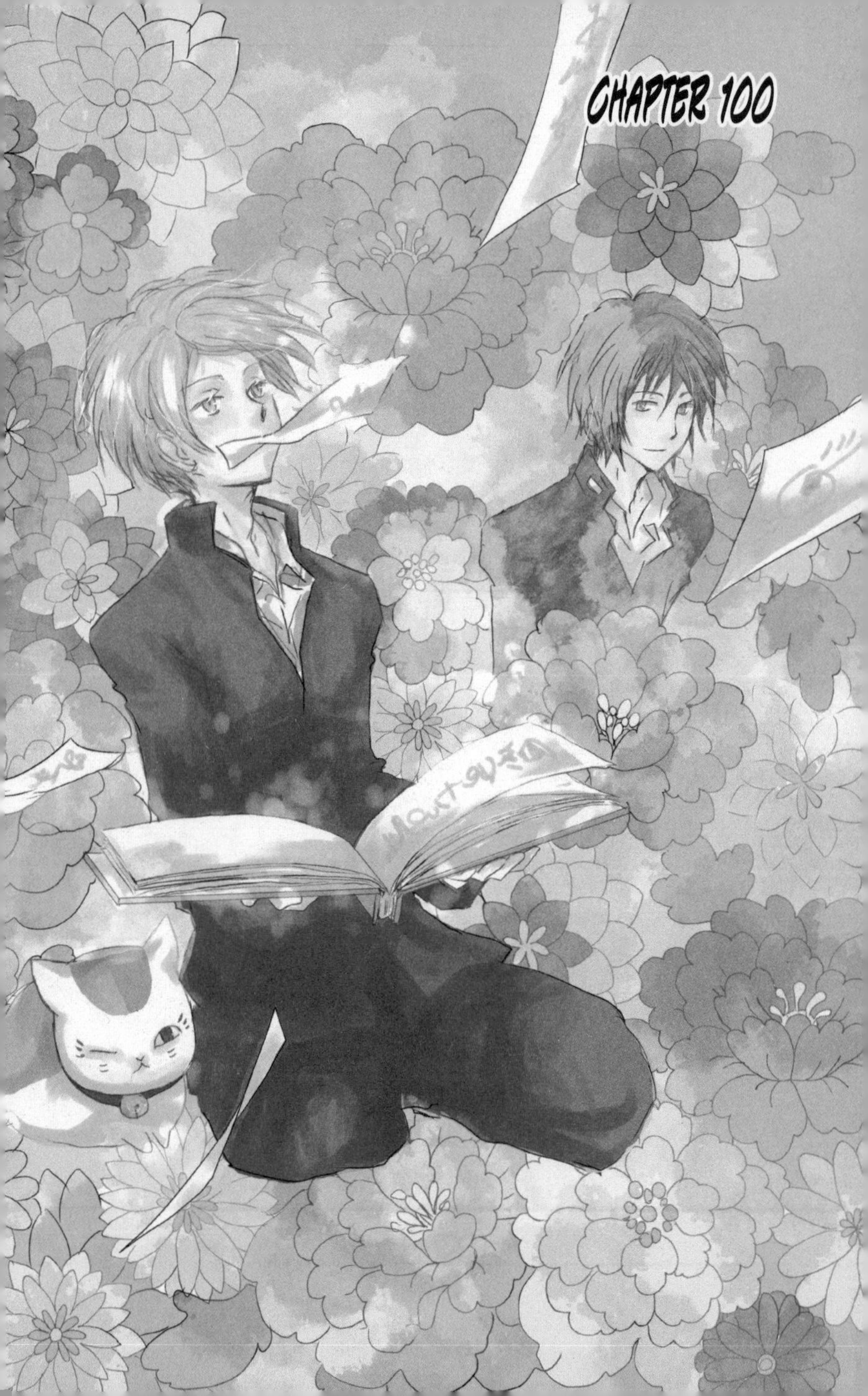

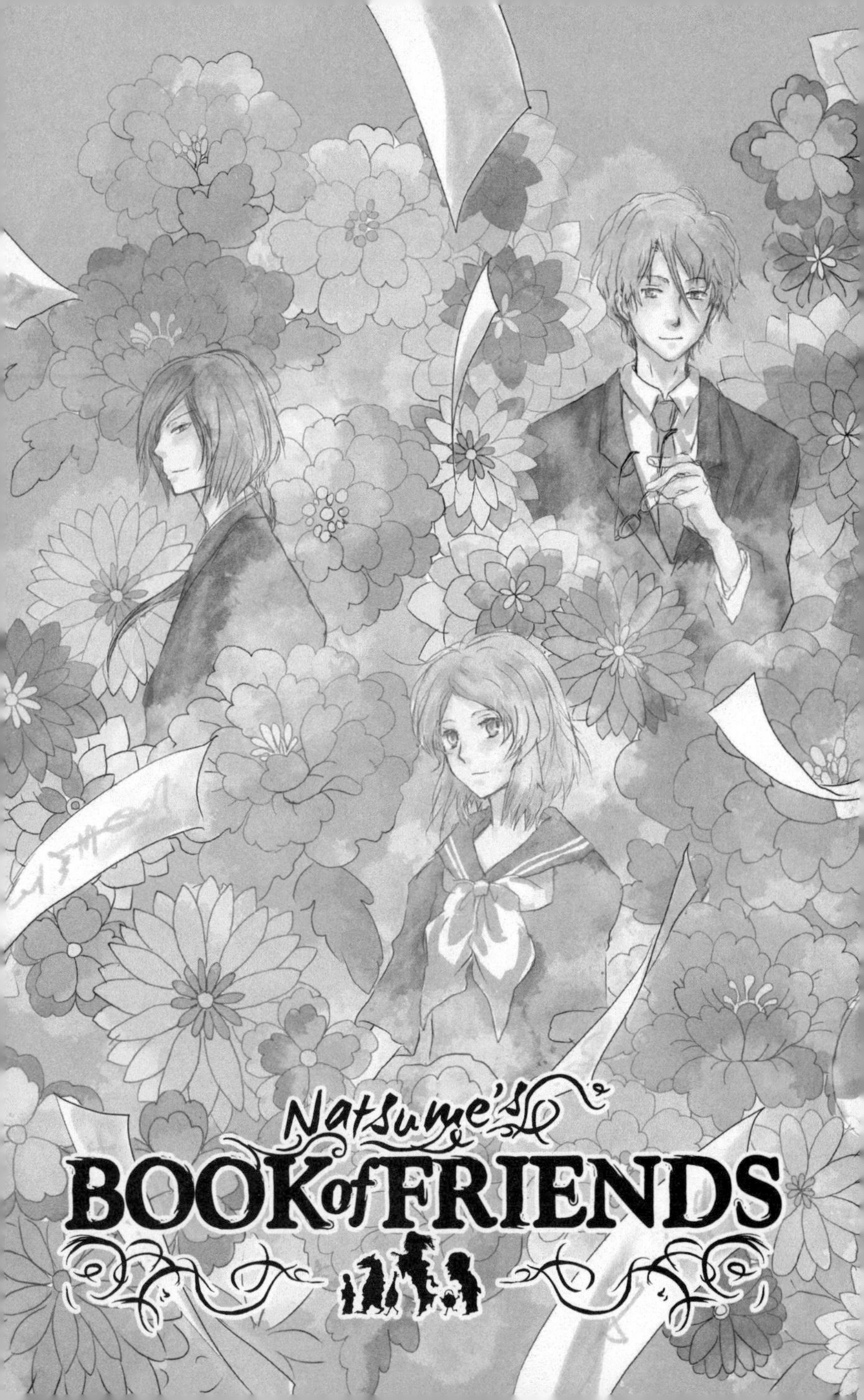
Natsume's
BOOK of FRIENDS

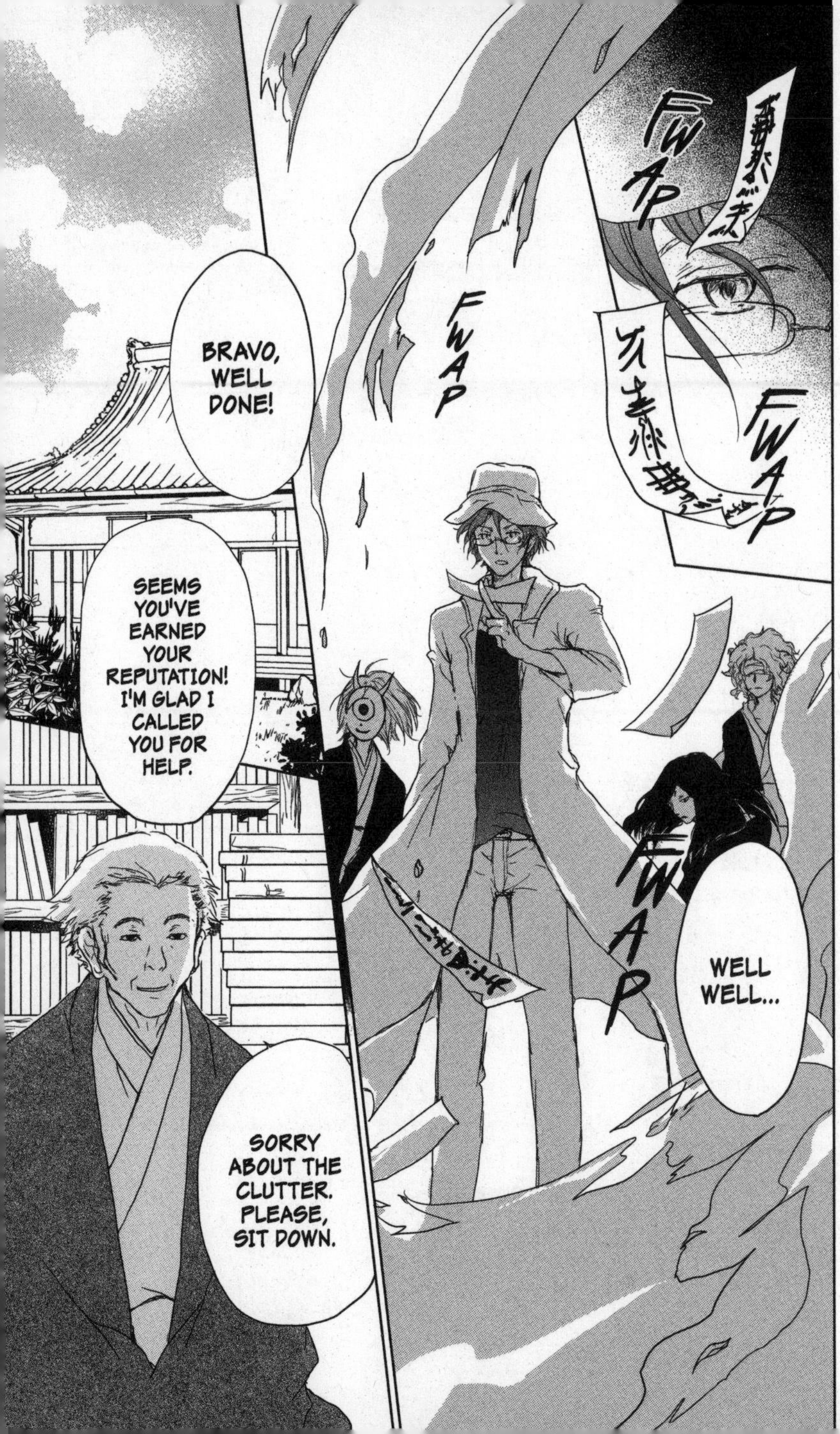
FWAP
FWAP
FWAP
FWAP
WELL WELL...
BRAVO, WELL DONE!
SEEMS YOU'VE EARNED YOUR REPUTATION! I'M GLAD I CALLED YOU FOR HELP.
SORRY ABOUT THE CLUTTER. PLEASE, SIT DOWN.

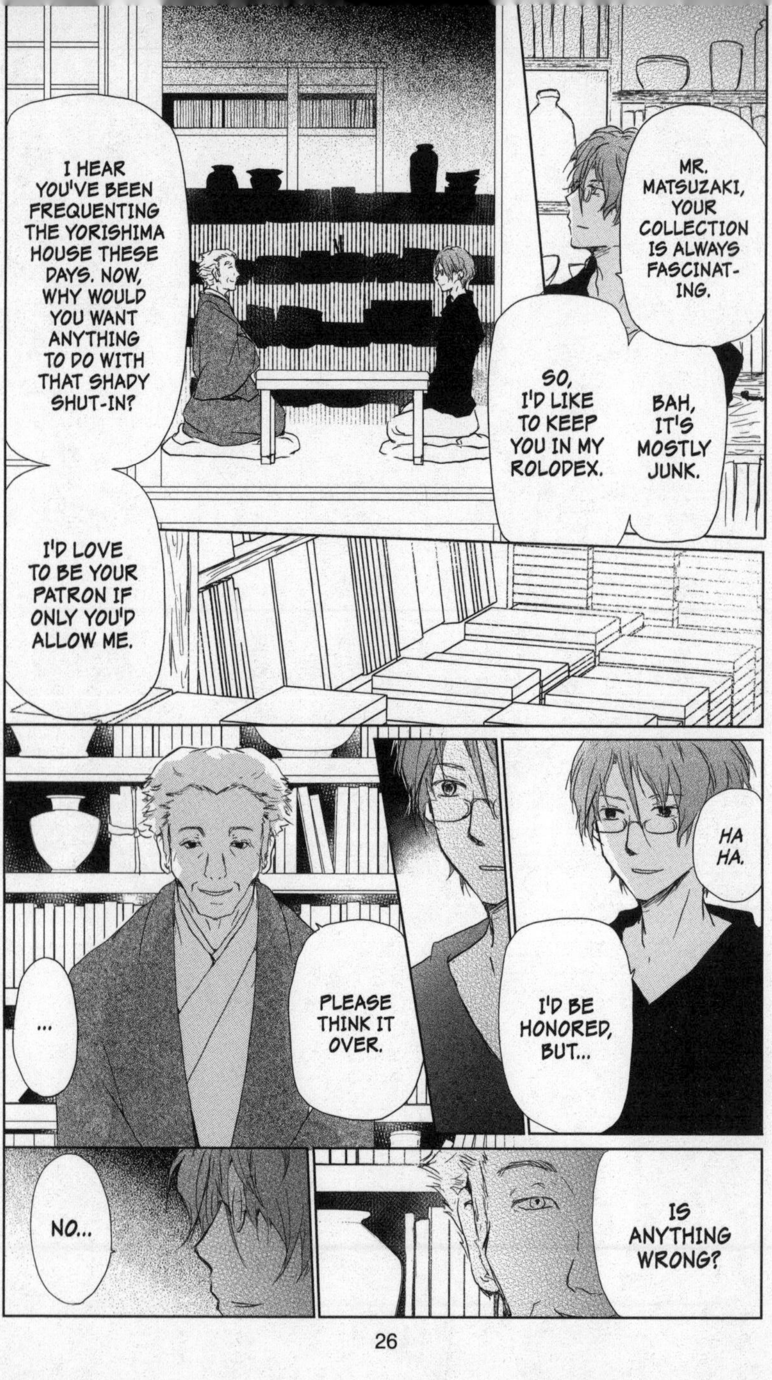
MR. MATSUZAKI, YOUR COLLECTION IS ALWAYS FASCINAT-ING.
BAH, IT'S MOSTLY JUNK.
SO, I'D LIKE TO KEEP YOU IN MY ROLODEX.
I HEAR YOU'VE BEEN FREQUENTING THE YORISHIMA HOUSE THESE DAYS. NOW, WHY WOULD YOU WANT ANYTHING TO DO WITH THAT SHADY SHUT-IN?
I'D LOVE TO BE YOUR PATRON IF ONLY YOU'D ALLOW ME.
HA HA.
I'D BE HONORED, BUT...
PLEASE THINK IT OVER.
...
IS ANYTHING WRONG?
NO...

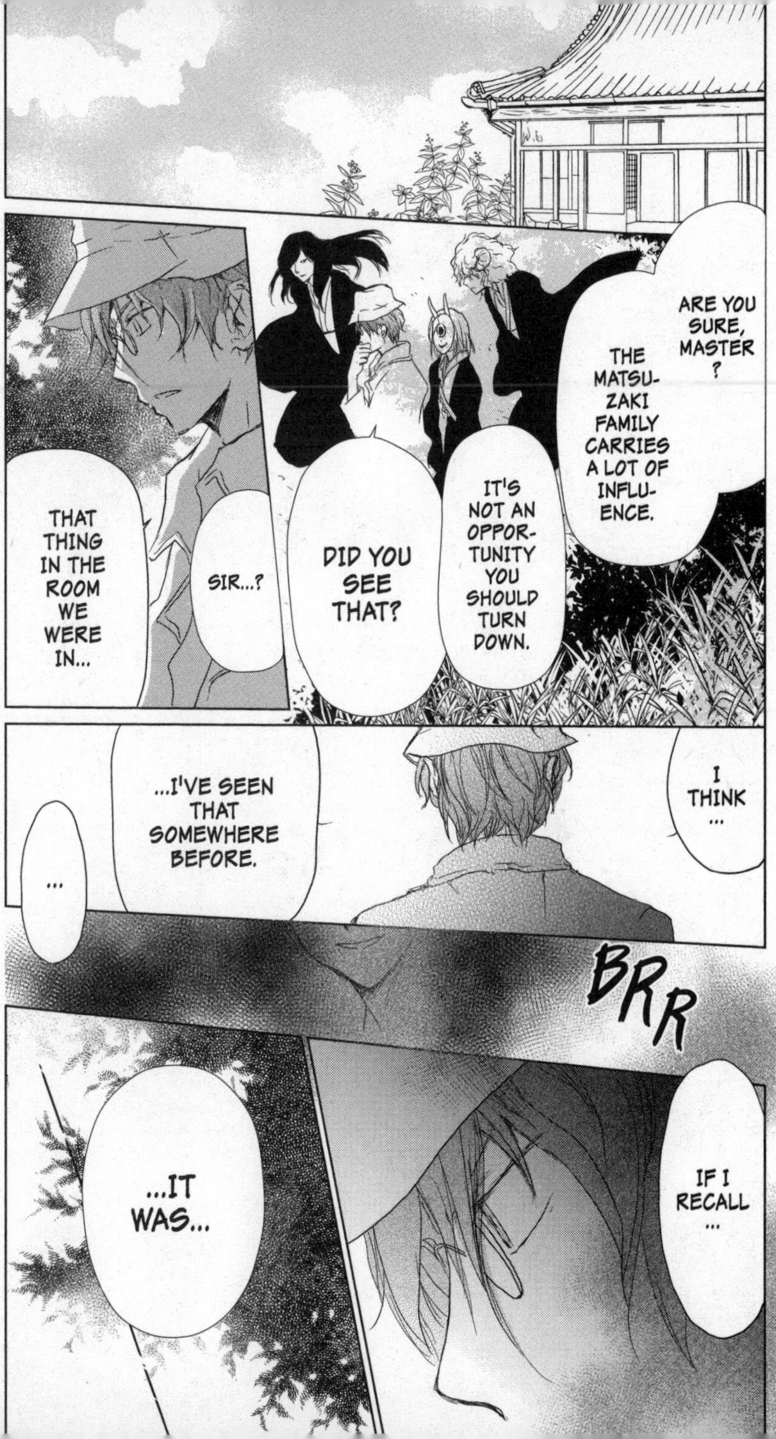
ARE YOU SURE, MASTER?
THE MATSU-ZAKI FAMILY CARRIES A LOT OF INFLU-ENCE.
IT'S NOT AN OPPOR-TUNITY YOU SHOULD TURN DOWN.
DID YOU SEE THAT?
SIR...?
THAT THING IN THE ROOM WE WERE IN...
I THINK...
...I'VE SEEN THAT SOMEWHERE BEFORE.
...
BRR
IF I RECALL...
...IT WAS...

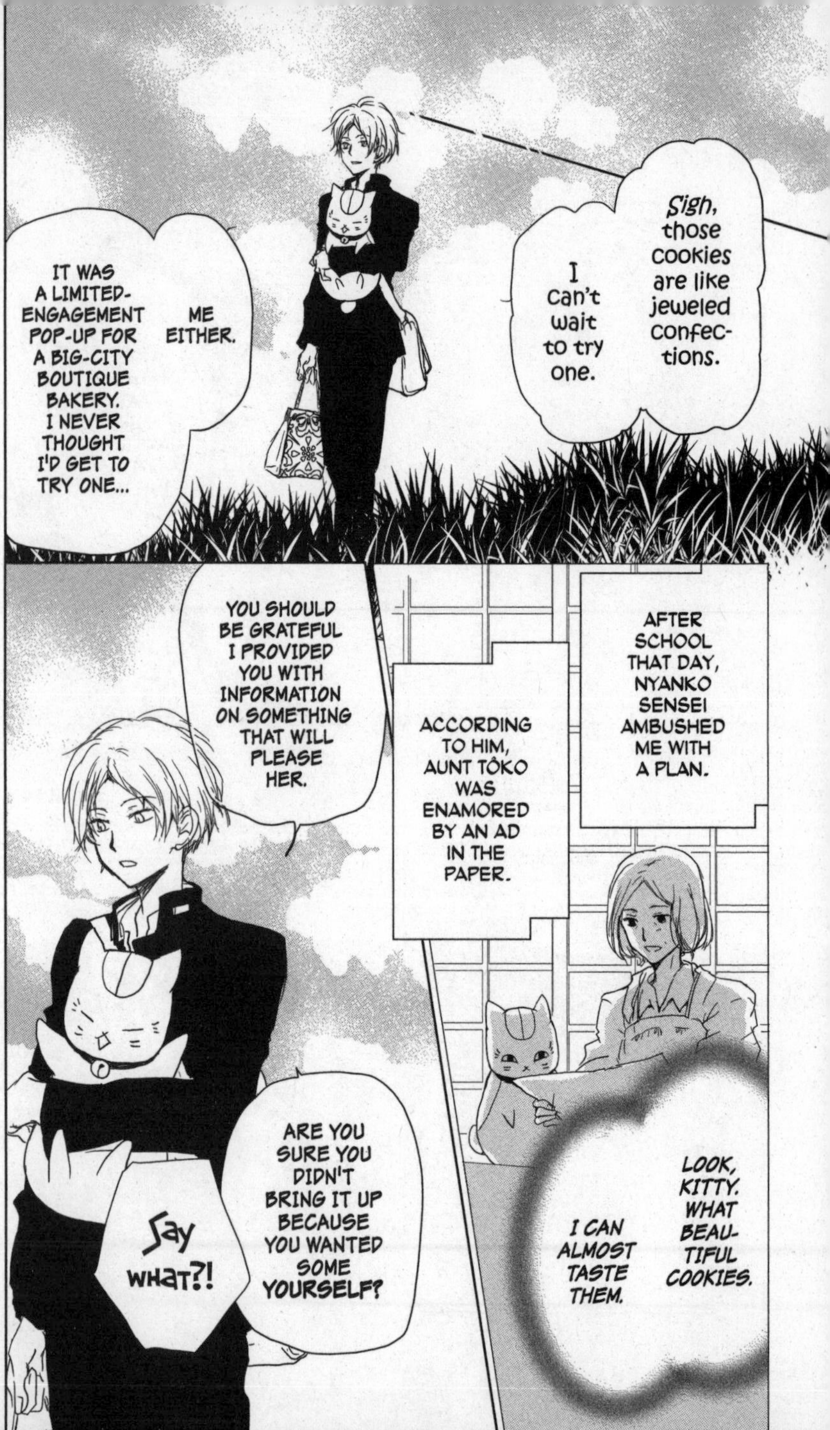

Sigh, those cookies are like jeweled confections.
I can't wait to try one.
ME EITHER.
IT WAS A LIMITED-ENGAGEMENT POP-UP FOR A BIG-CITY BOUTIQUE BAKERY. I NEVER THOUGHT I'D GET TO TRY ONE...
AFTER SCHOOL THAT DAY, NYANKO SENSEI AMBUSHED ME WITH A PLAN.
ACCORDING TO HIM, AUNT TÔKO WAS ENAMORED BY AN AD IN THE PAPER.
LOOK, KITTY. WHAT BEAUTIFUL COOKIES.
I CAN ALMOST TASTE THEM.
YOU SHOULD BE GRATEFUL I PROVIDED YOU WITH INFORMATION ON SOMETHING THAT WILL PLEASE HER.
ARE YOU SURE YOU DIDN'T BRING IT UP BECAUSE YOU WANTED SOME YOURSELF?
Say WHAT?!

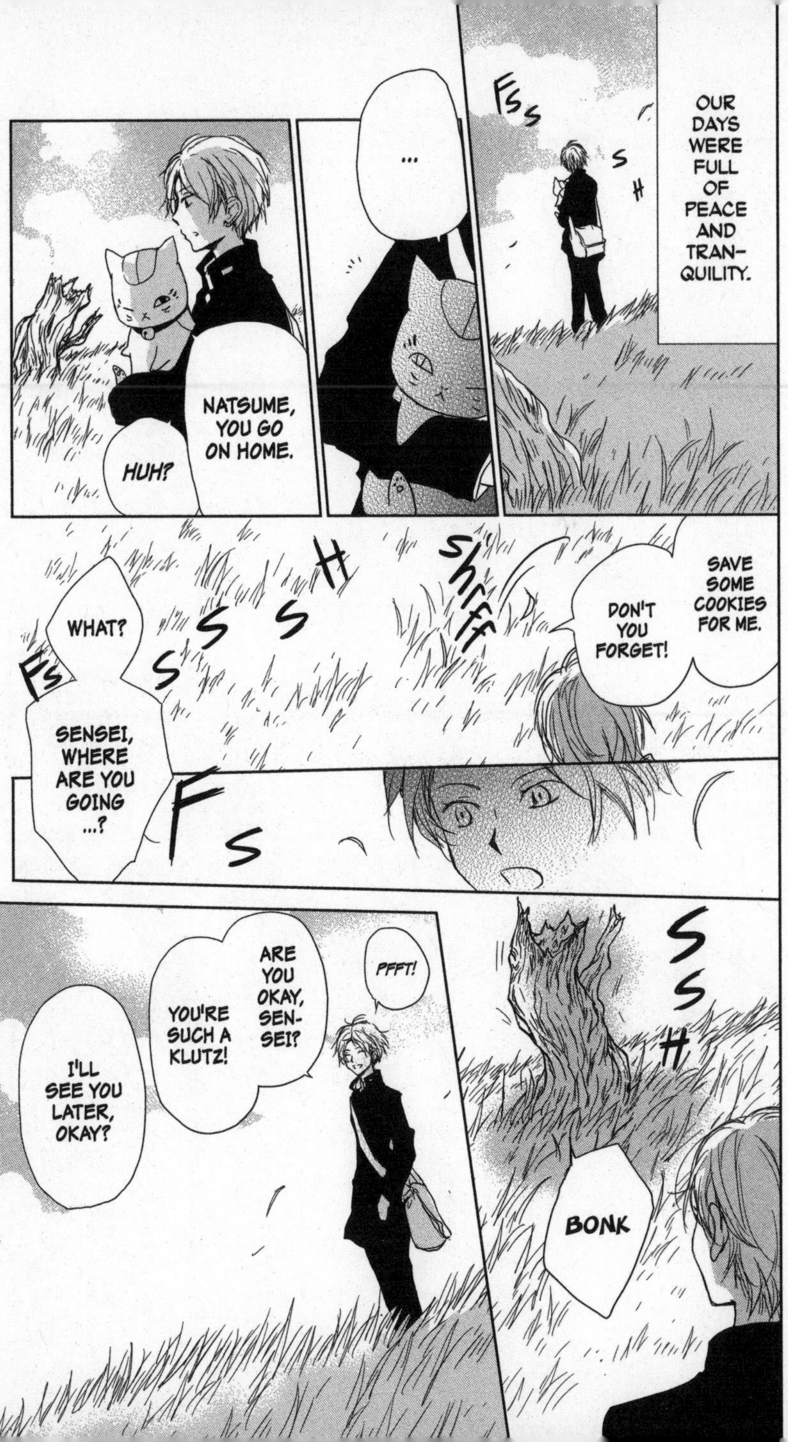
OUR DAYS WERE FULL OF PEACE AND TRAN-QUILITY.
FSS
SH
...
NATSUME, YOU GO ON HOME.
HUH?
SAVE SOME COOKIES FOR ME.
DON'T YOU FORGET!
shfff
H
S
S
WHAT?
S
Fs
SENSEI, WHERE ARE YOU GOING ...?
FS
SSH
BONK
PFFT!
ARE YOU OKAY, SEN-SEI?
YOU'RE SUCH A KLUTZ!
I'LL SEE YOU LATER, OKAY?

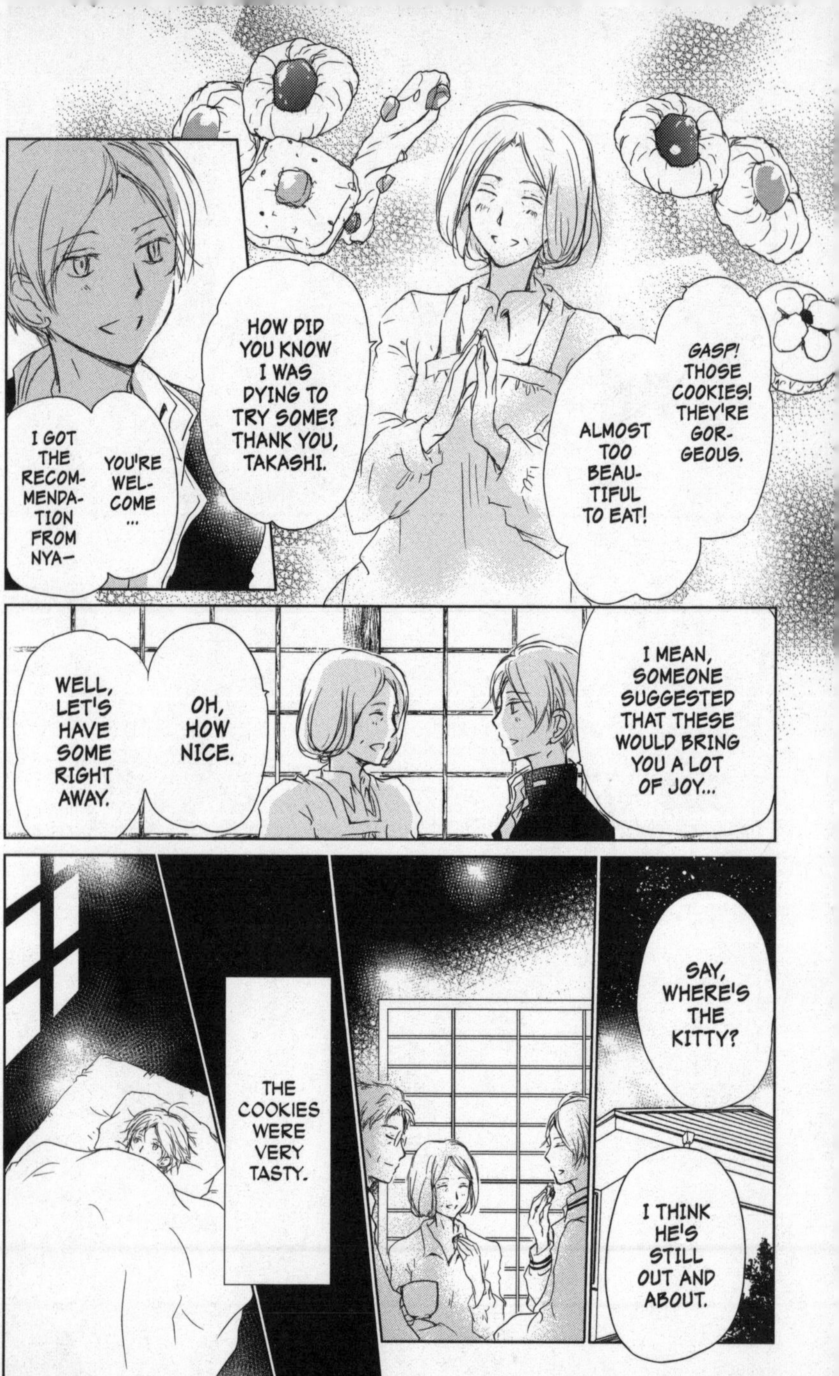
GASP! THOSE COOKIES! THEY'RE GORGEOUS.
ALMOST TOO BEAUTIFUL TO EAT!
HOW DID YOU KNOW I WAS DYING TO TRY SOME? THANK YOU, TAKASHI.
YOU'RE WELCOME...
I GOT THE RECOMMENDATION FROM NYA—
I MEAN, SOMEONE SUGGESTED THAT THESE WOULD BRING YOU A LOT OF JOY...
OH, HOW NICE.
WELL, LET'S HAVE SOME RIGHT AWAY.
SAY, WHERE'S THE KITTY?
I THINK HE'S STILL OUT AND ABOUT.
THE COOKIES WERE VERY TASTY.

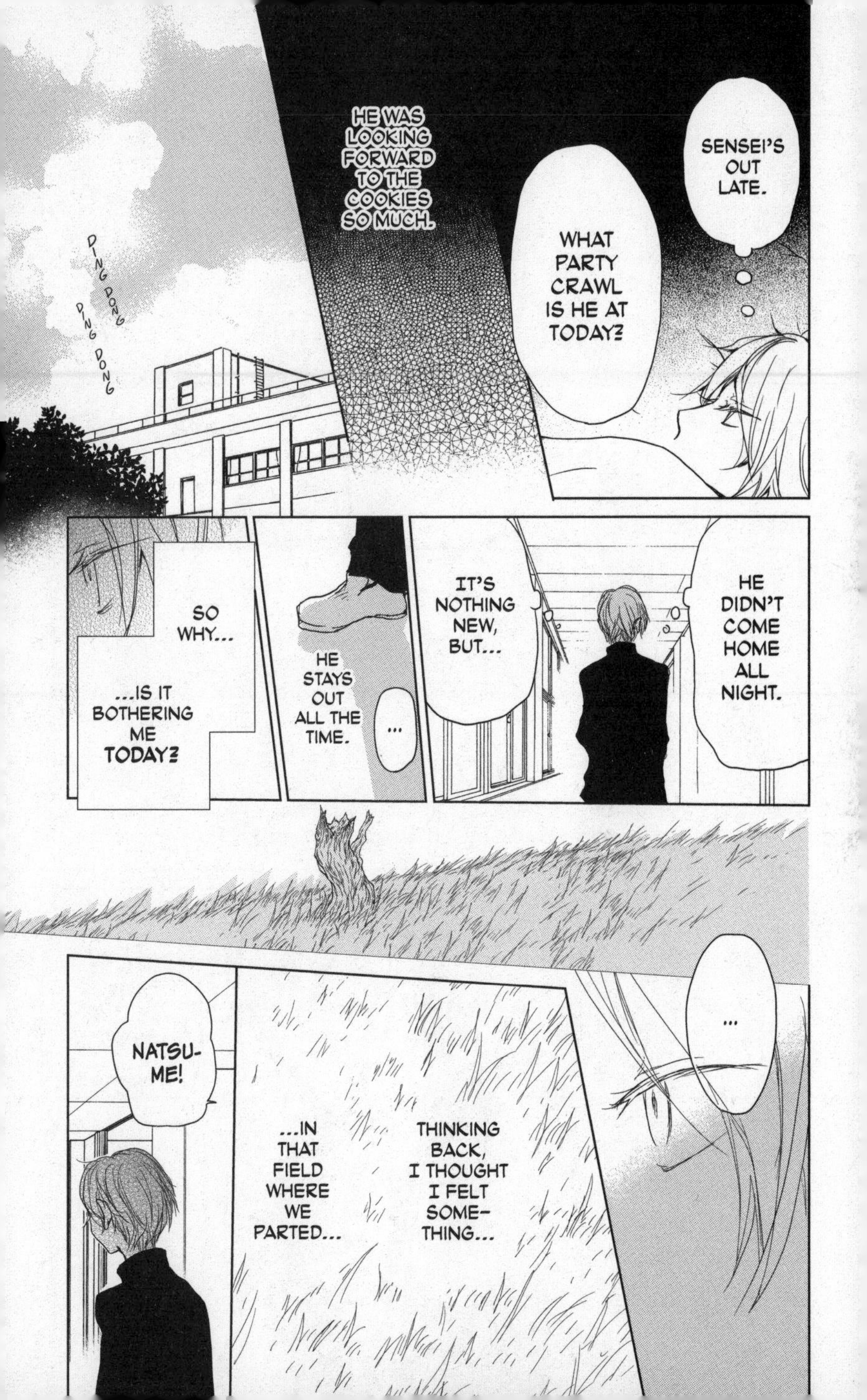
SENSEI'S OUT LATE.
WHAT PARTY CRAWL IS HE AT TODAY?
HE WAS LOOKING FORWARD TO THE COOKIES SO MUCH.
DING DONG
DING DONG
HE DIDN'T COME HOME ALL NIGHT.
IT'S NOTHING NEW, BUT...
...
HE STAYS OUT ALL THE TIME.
SO WHY...
...IS IT BOTHERING ME TODAY?
...
THINKING BACK, I THOUGHT I FELT SOME-THING...
...IN THAT FIELD WHERE WE PARTED...
NATSU-ME!

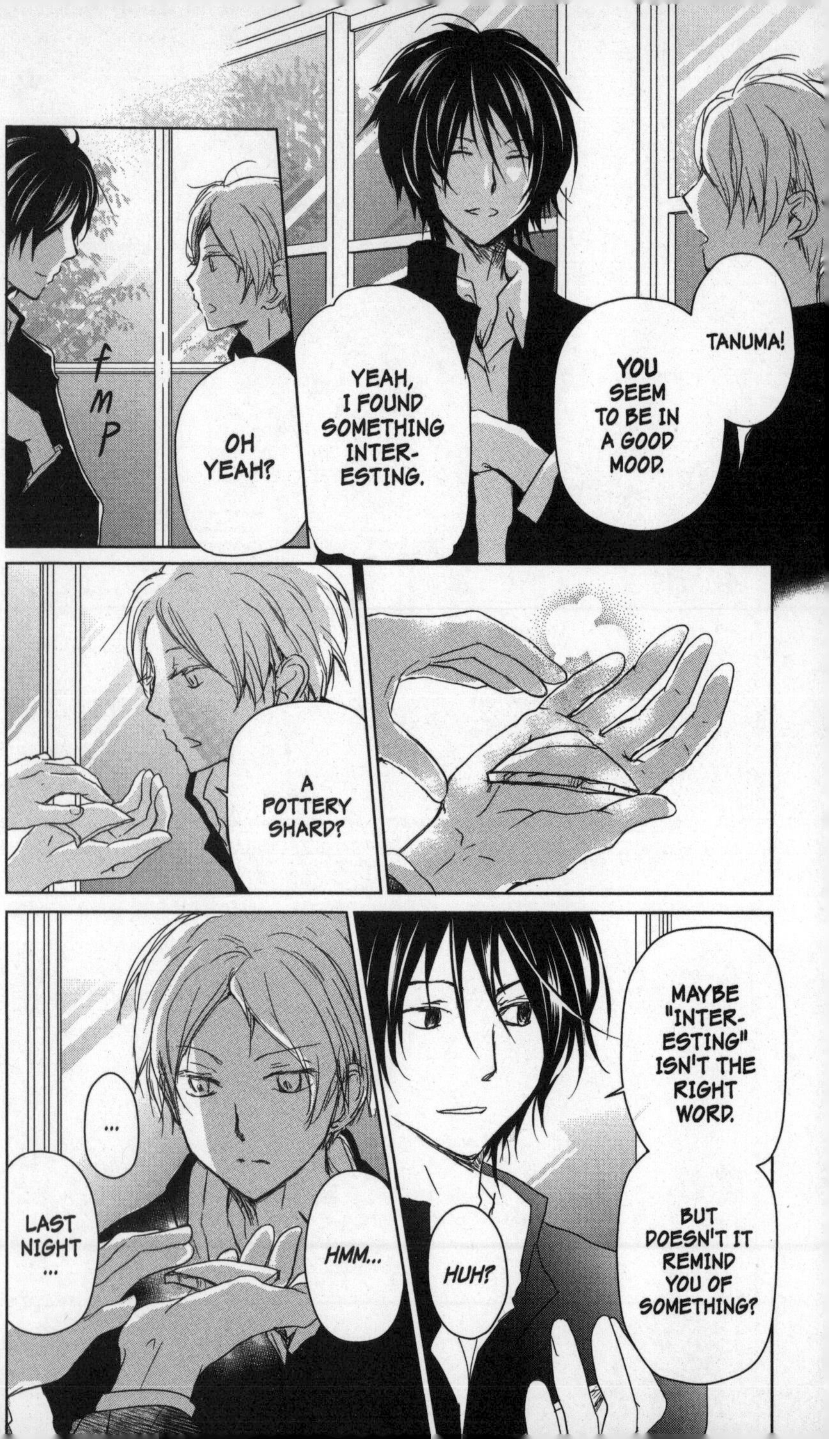
TANUMA!
YOU SEEM TO BE IN A GOOD MOOD.
YEAH, I FOUND SOMETHING INTER-ESTING.
OH YEAH?
fmp
A POTTERY SHARD?
MAYBE "INTER-ESTING" ISN'T THE RIGHT WORD.
BUT DOESN'T IT REMIND YOU OF SOMETHING?
HUH?
HMM...
...
LAST NIGHT ...

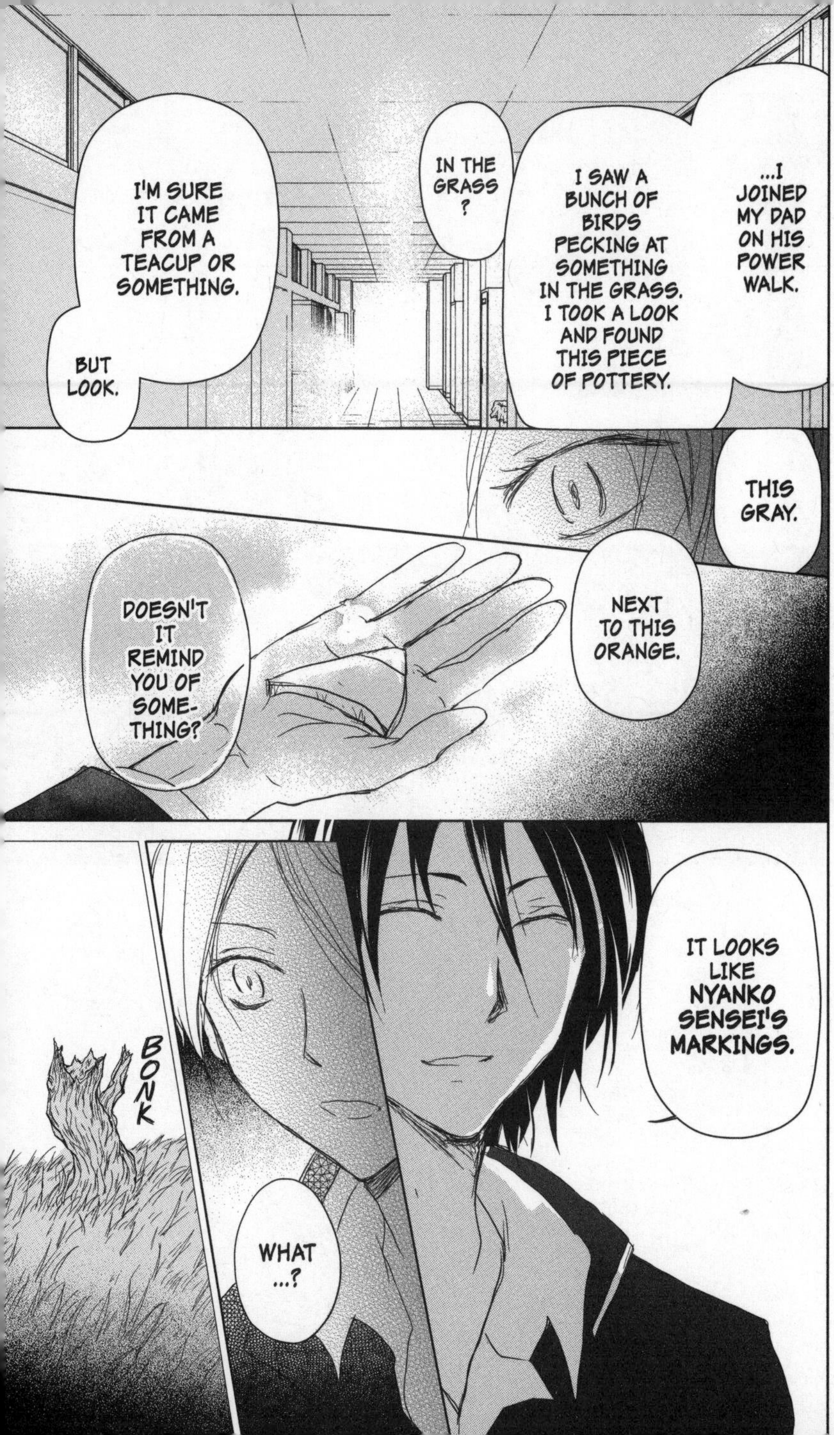
...I JOINED MY DAD ON HIS POWER WALK.
I SAW A BUNCH OF BIRDS PECKING AT SOMETHING IN THE GRASS. I TOOK A LOOK AND FOUND THIS PIECE OF POTTERY.
IN THE GRASS?
I'M SURE IT CAME FROM A TEACUP OR SOMETHING.
BUT LOOK.
THIS GRAY.
NEXT TO THIS ORANGE.
DOESN'T IT REMIND YOU OF SOME-THING?
IT LOOKS LIKE NYANKO SENSEI'S MARKINGS.
BONK
WHAT...?

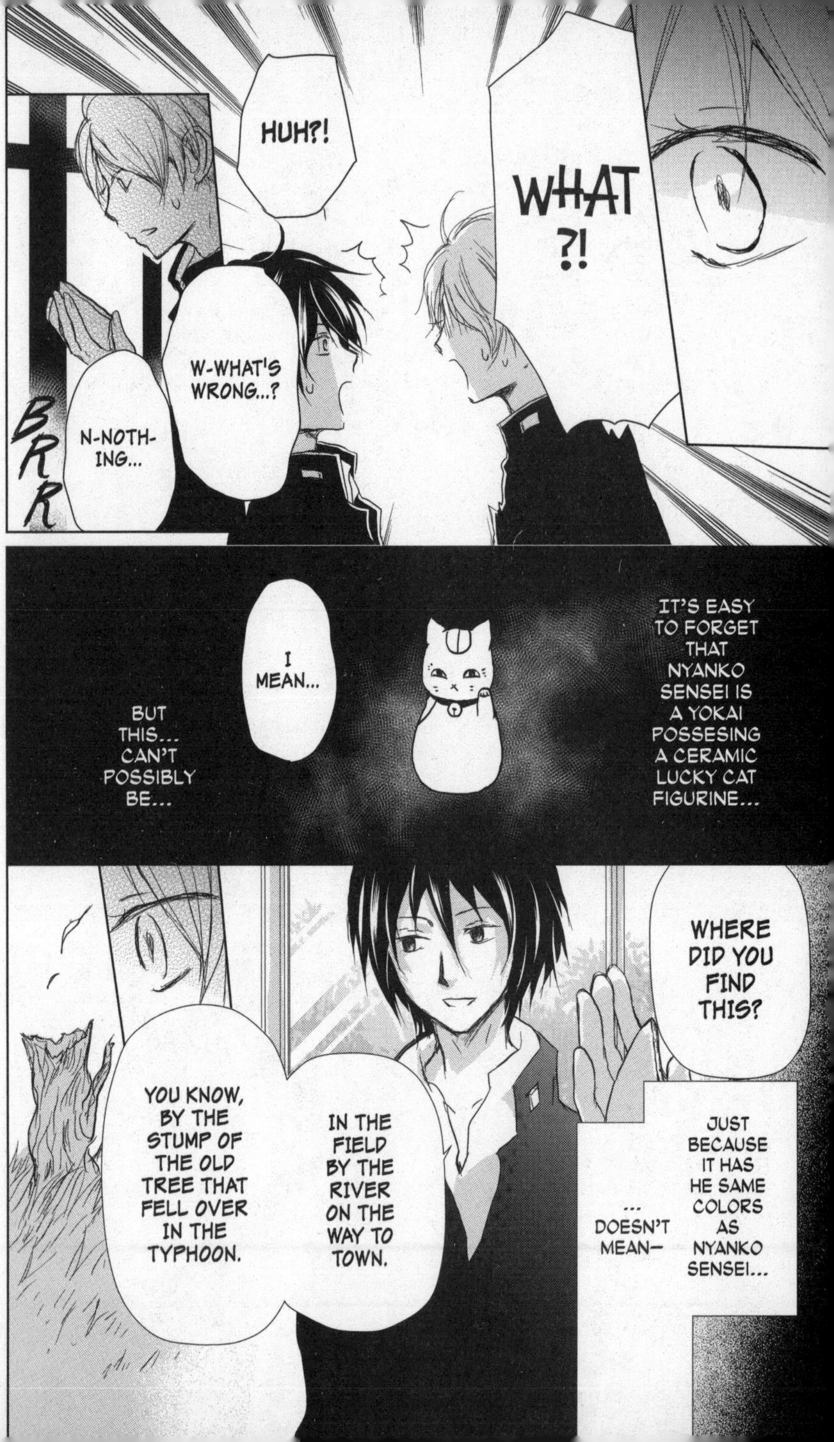
WHAT ?!
HUH?!
W-WHAT'S WRONG...?
N-NOTH-ING...
BRR
IT'S EASY TO FORGET THAT NYANKO SENSEI IS A YOKAI POSSESING A CERAMIC LUCKY CAT FIGURINE...
I MEAN...
BUT THIS... CAN'T POSSIBLY BE...
WHERE DID YOU FIND THIS?
JUST BECAUSE IT HAS HE SAME COLORS AS NYANKO SENSEI...
... DOESN'T MEAN—
IN THE FIELD BY THE RIVER ON THE WAY TO TOWN.
YOU KNOW, BY THE STUMP OF THE OLD TREE THAT FELL OVER IN THE TYPHOON.

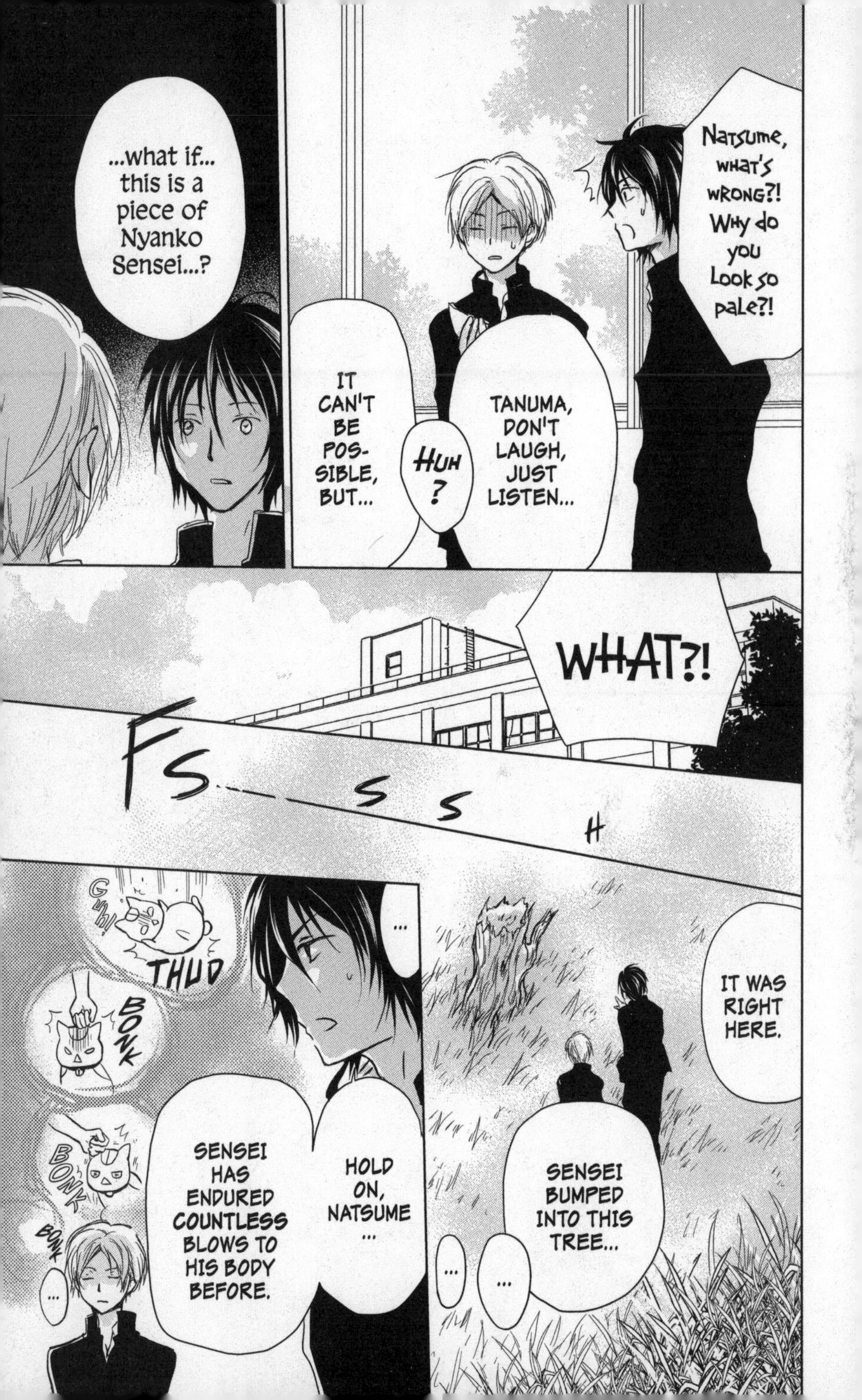

Natsume, what's wrong?! Why do you look so pale?!
TANUMA, DON'T LAUGH, JUST LISTEN...
HUH?
IT CAN'T BE POS-SIBLE, BUT...
...what if... this is a piece of Nyanko Sensei...?
WHAT?!
FSSSSH
IT WAS RIGHT HERE.
SENSEI BUMPED INTO THIS TREE...
...
...
...
HOLD ON, NATSUME...
SENSEI HAS ENDURED COUNTLESS BLOWS TO HIS BODY BEFORE.
Guh!
THUD
BONK
BONK
BONK
...

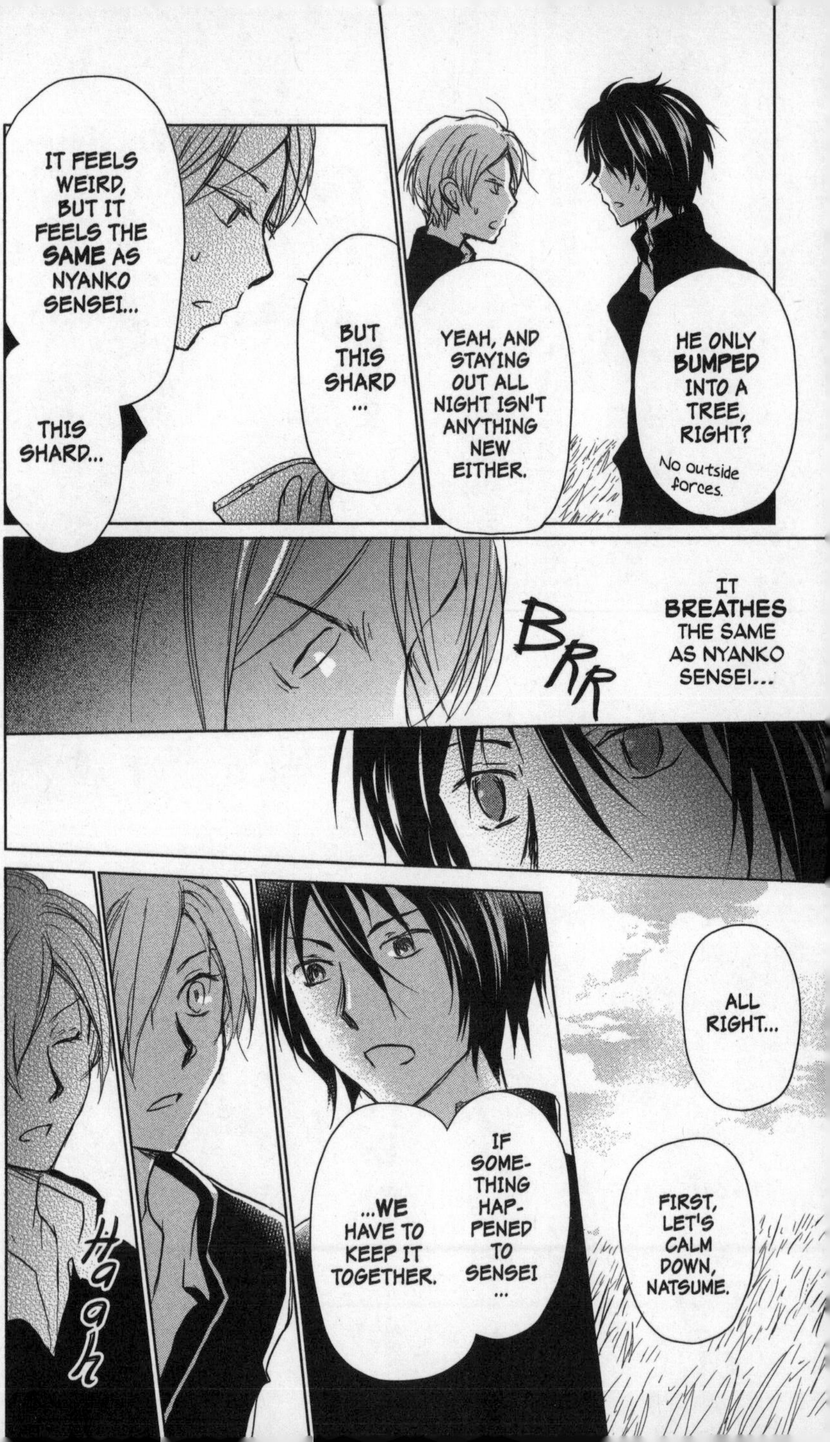
HE ONLY BUMPED INTO A TREE, RIGHT?
No outside forces.
YEAH, AND STAYING OUT ALL NIGHT ISN'T ANYTHING NEW EITHER.
BUT THIS SHARD ...
IT FEELS WEIRD, BUT IT FEELS THE SAME AS NYANKO SENSEI...
THIS SHARD...
IT BREATHES THE SAME AS NYANKO SENSEI...
BRR
ALL RIGHT...
FIRST, LET'S CALM DOWN, NATSUME.
IF SOME-THING HAP-PENED TO SENSEI ...
...WE HAVE TO KEEP IT TOGETHER.
Haah

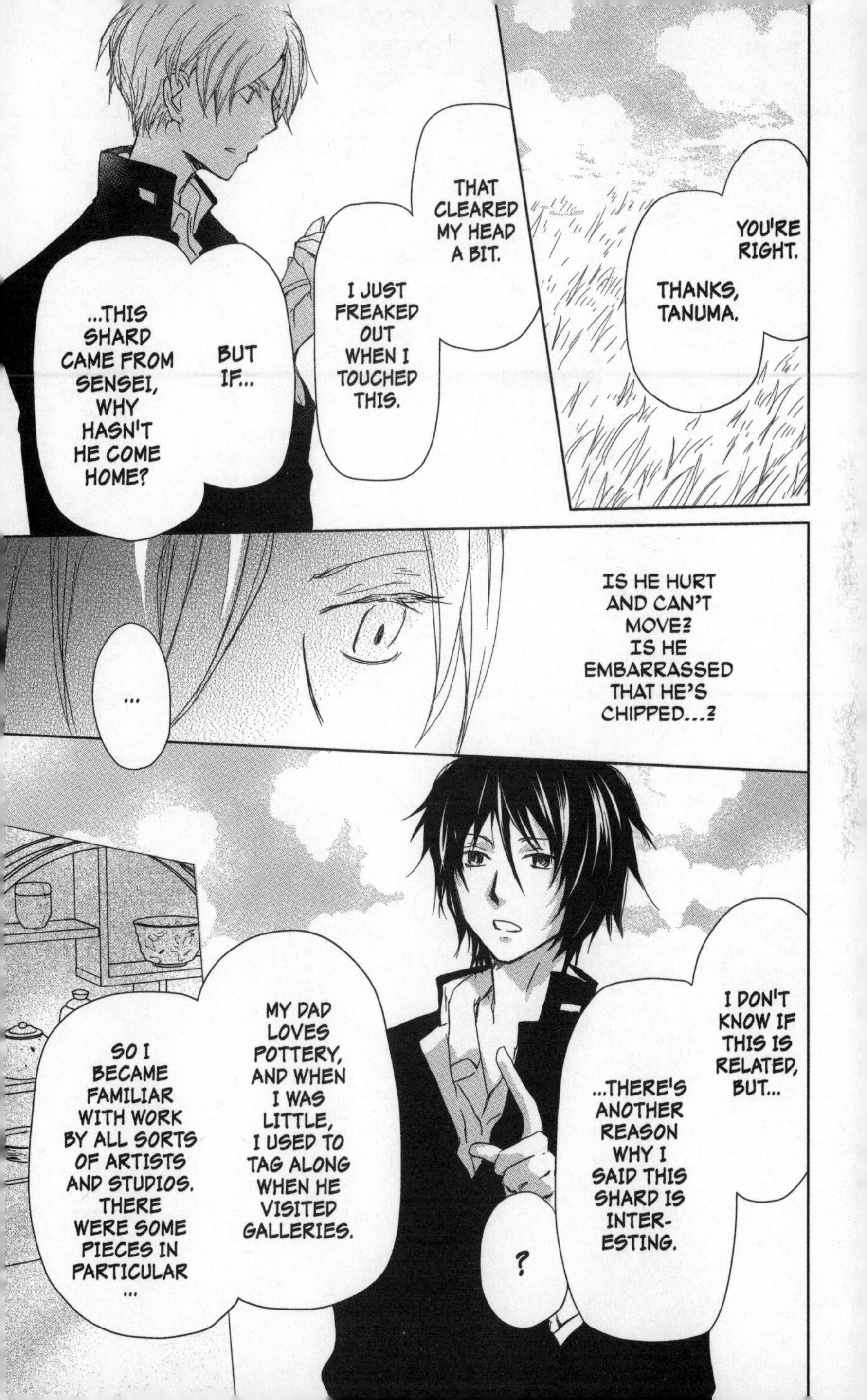
YOU'RE RIGHT.
THANKS, TANUMA.
THAT CLEARED MY HEAD A BIT.
I JUST FREAKED OUT WHEN I TOUCHED THIS.
BUT IF...
...THIS SHARD CAME FROM SENSEI, WHY HASN'T HE COME HOME?
IS HE HURT AND CAN'T MOVE? IS HE EMBARRASSED THAT HE'S CHIPPED...?
...
I DON'T KNOW IF THIS IS RELATED, BUT...
...THERE'S ANOTHER REASON WHY I SAID THIS SHARD IS INTER-ESTING.
?
MY DAD LOVES POTTERY, AND WHEN I WAS LITTLE, I USED TO TAG ALONG WHEN HE VISITED GALLERIES.
SO I BECAME FAMILIAR WITH WORK BY ALL SORTS OF ARTISTS AND STUDIOS. THERE WERE SOME PIECES IN PARTICULAR ...

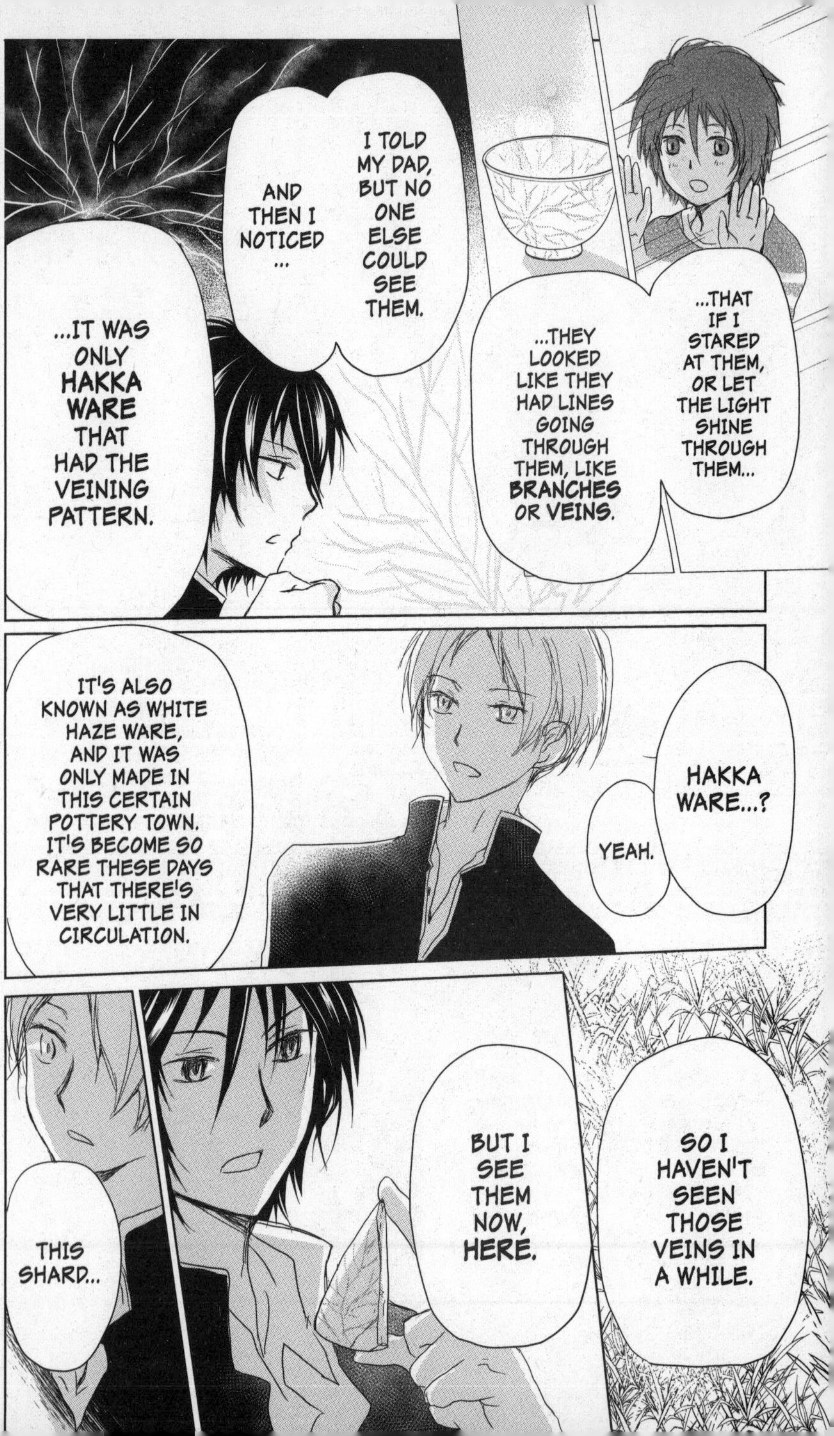
...THAT IF I STARED AT THEM, OR LET THE LIGHT SHINE THROUGH THEM...
...THEY LOOKED LIKE THEY HAD LINES GOING THROUGH THEM, LIKE **BRANCHES OR VEINS.**
I TOLD MY DAD, BUT NO ONE ELSE COULD SEE THEM.
AND THEN I NOTICED ...
...IT WAS ONLY **HAKKA WARE** THAT HAD THE VEINING PATTERN.
HAKKA WARE...?
YEAH.
IT'S ALSO KNOWN AS WHITE HAZE WARE, AND IT WAS ONLY MADE IN THIS CERTAIN POTTERY TOWN. IT'S BECOME SO RARE THESE DAYS THAT THERE'S VERY LITTLE IN CIRCULATION.
SO I HAVEN'T SEEN THOSE VEINS IN A WHILE.
BUT I SEE THEM NOW, **HERE.**
THIS SHARD...

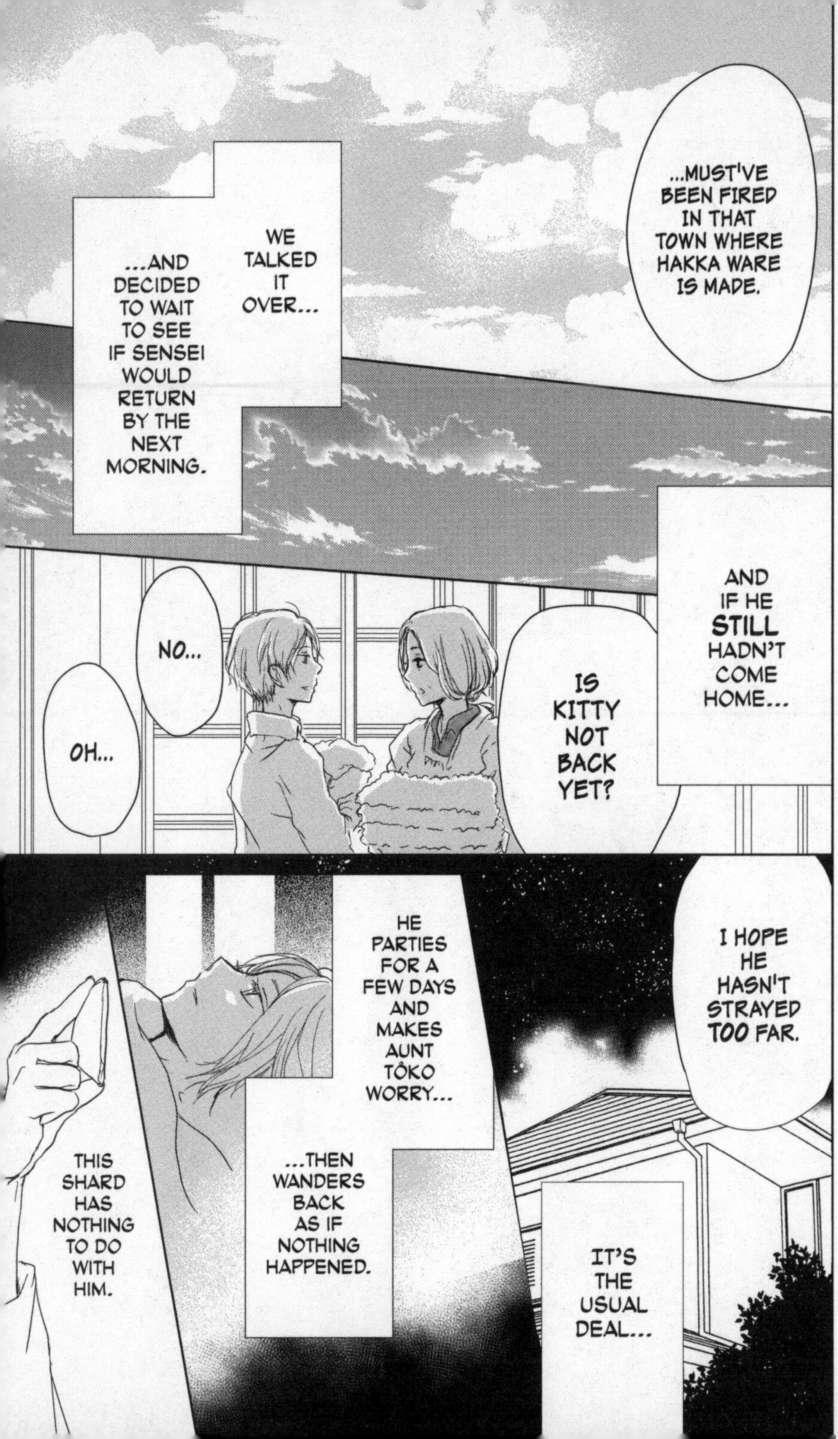
...MUST'VE BEEN FIRED IN THAT TOWN WHERE HAKKA WARE IS MADE.
WE TALKED IT OVER...
...AND DECIDED TO WAIT TO SEE IF SENSEI WOULD RETURN BY THE NEXT MORNING.
AND IF HE STILL HADN'T COME HOME...
IS KITTY NOT BACK YET?
NO...
OH...
I HOPE HE HASN'T STRAYED TOO FAR.
IT'S THE USUAL DEAL...
HE PARTIES FOR A FEW DAYS AND MAKES AUNT TÔKO WORRY...
...THEN WANDERS BACK AS IF NOTHING HAPPENED.
THIS SHARD HAS NOTHING TO DO WITH HIM.

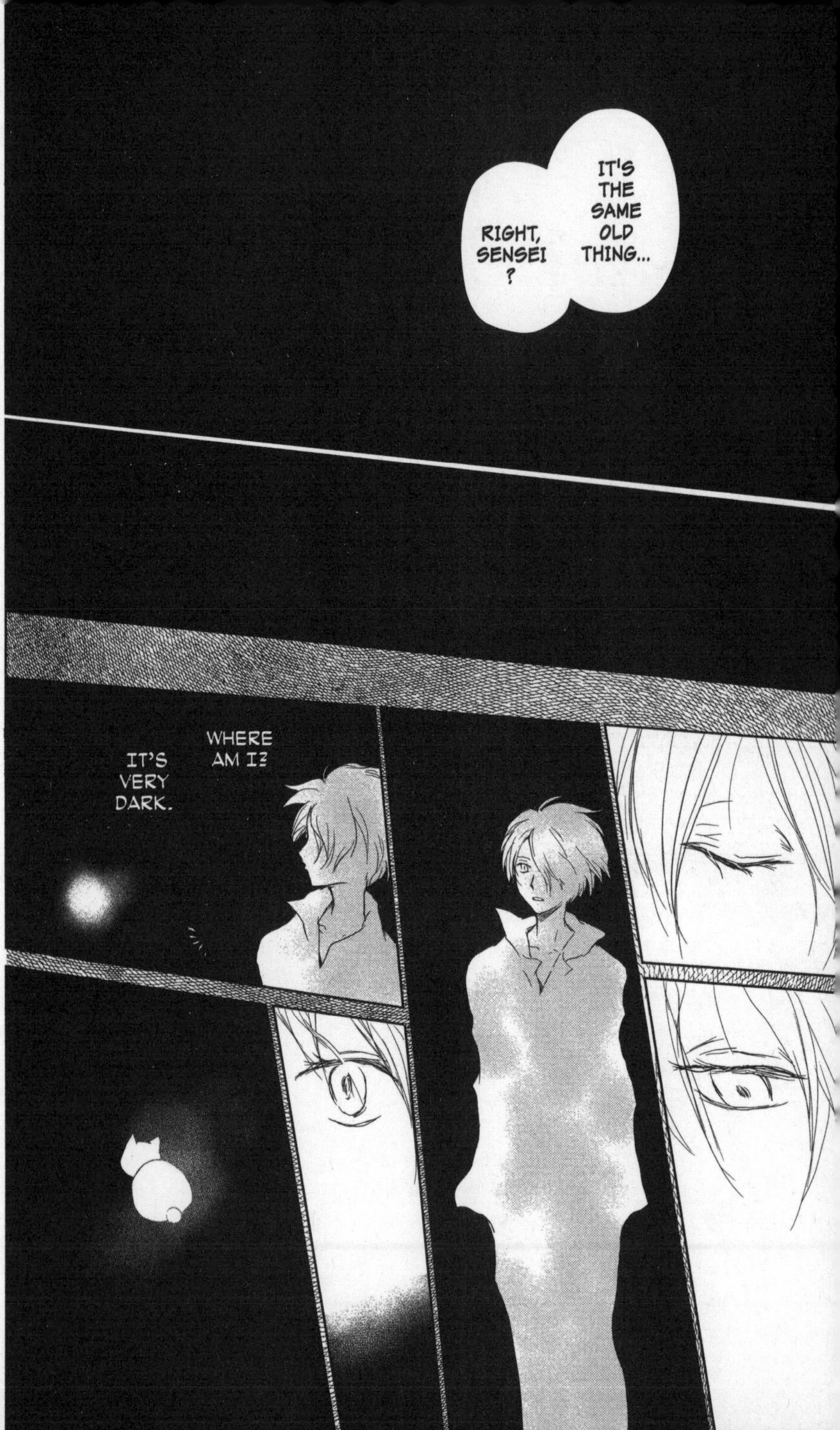
IT'S THE SAME OLD THING...
RIGHT, SENSEI?
WHERE AM I?
IT'S VERY DARK.

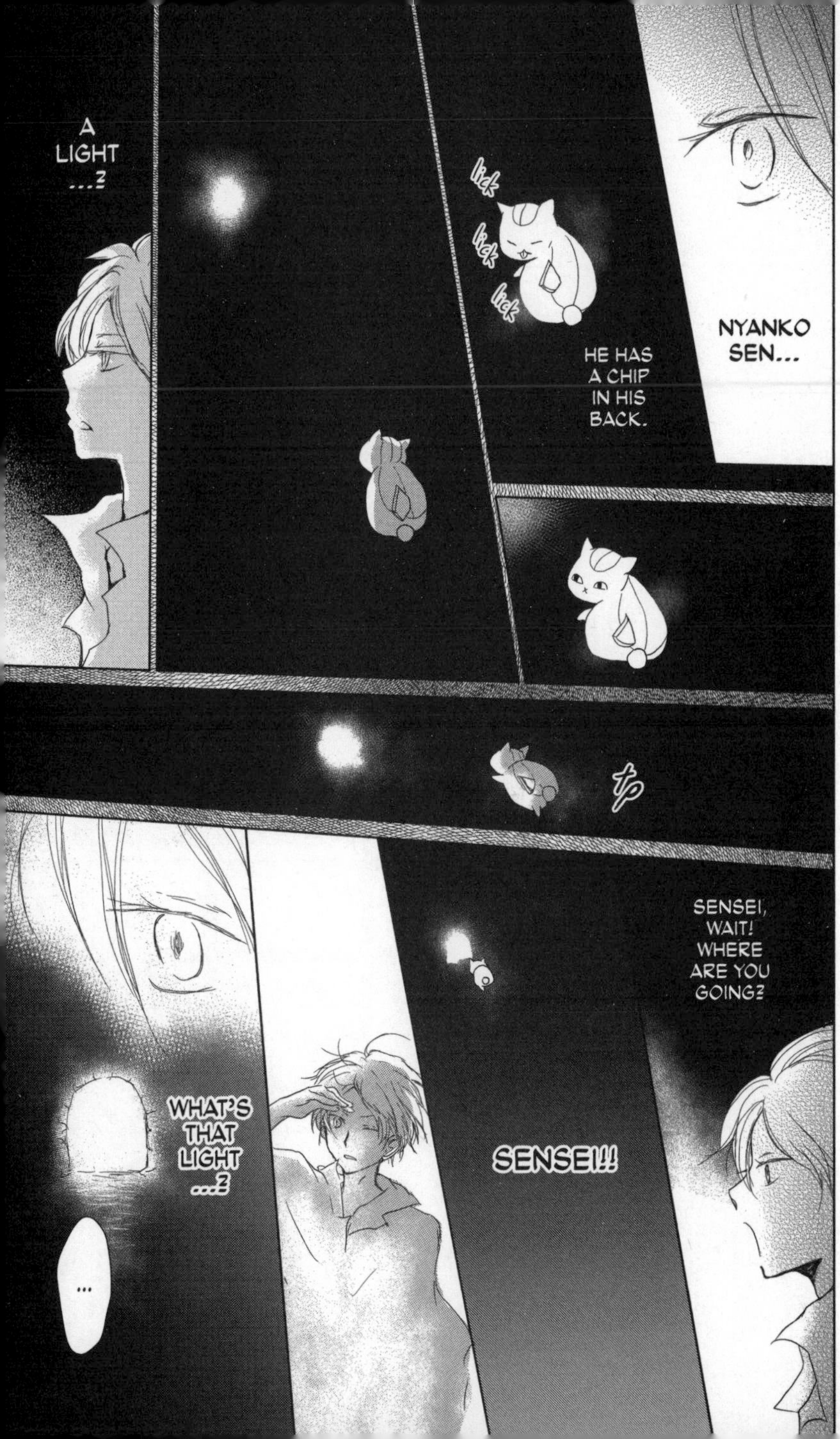
NYANKO SEN...
lick
lick
lick
HE HAS A CHIP IN HIS BACK.
A LIGHT ...?
tp
SENSEI, WAIT! WHERE ARE YOU GOING?
SENSEI!!!
WHAT'S THAT LIGHT ...?
...

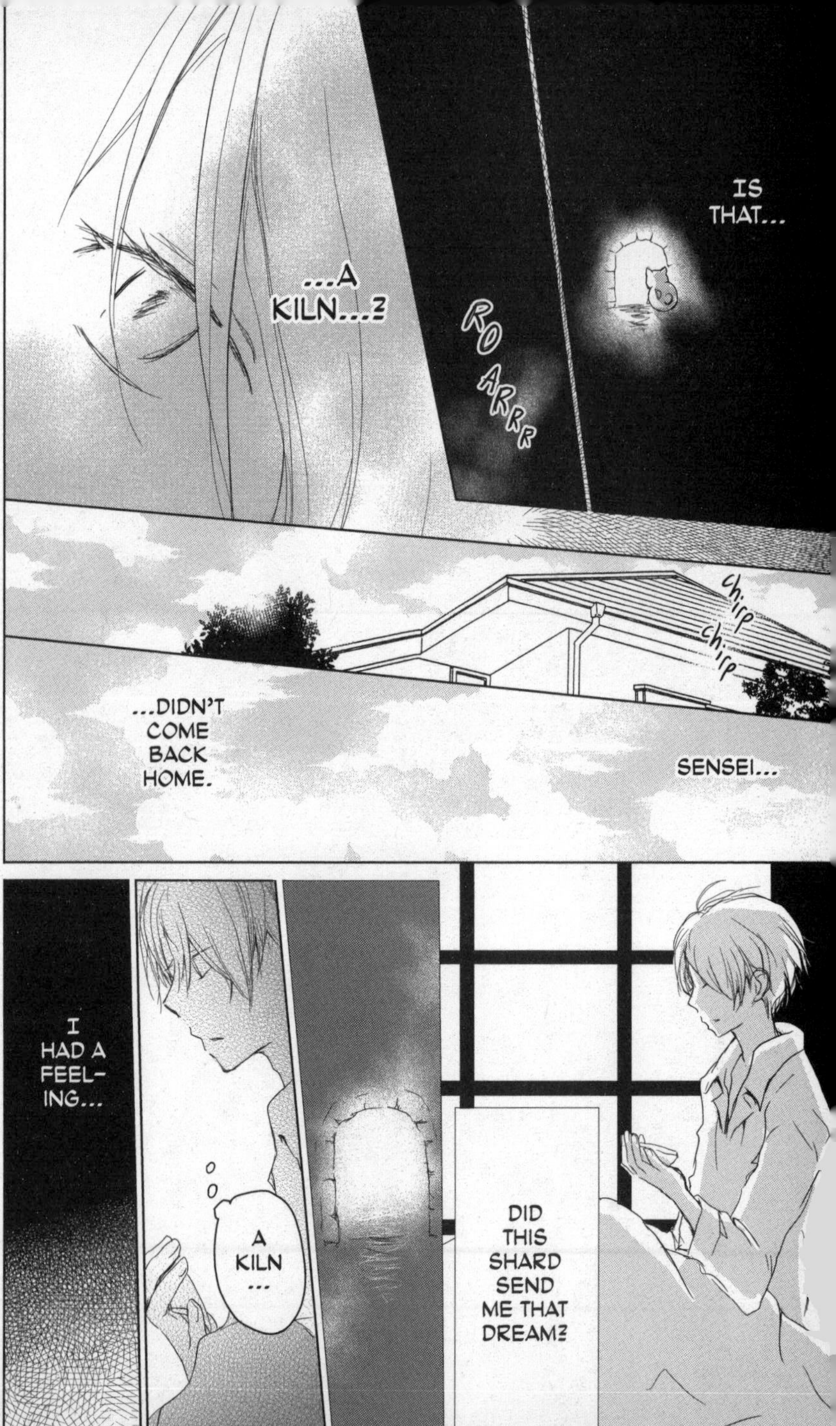
IS THAT...
ROARRR
...A KILN...?
chirp chirp
SENSEI...
...DIDN'T COME BACK HOME.
DID THIS SHARD SEND ME THAT DREAM?
A KILN ...
I HAD A FEEL-ING...

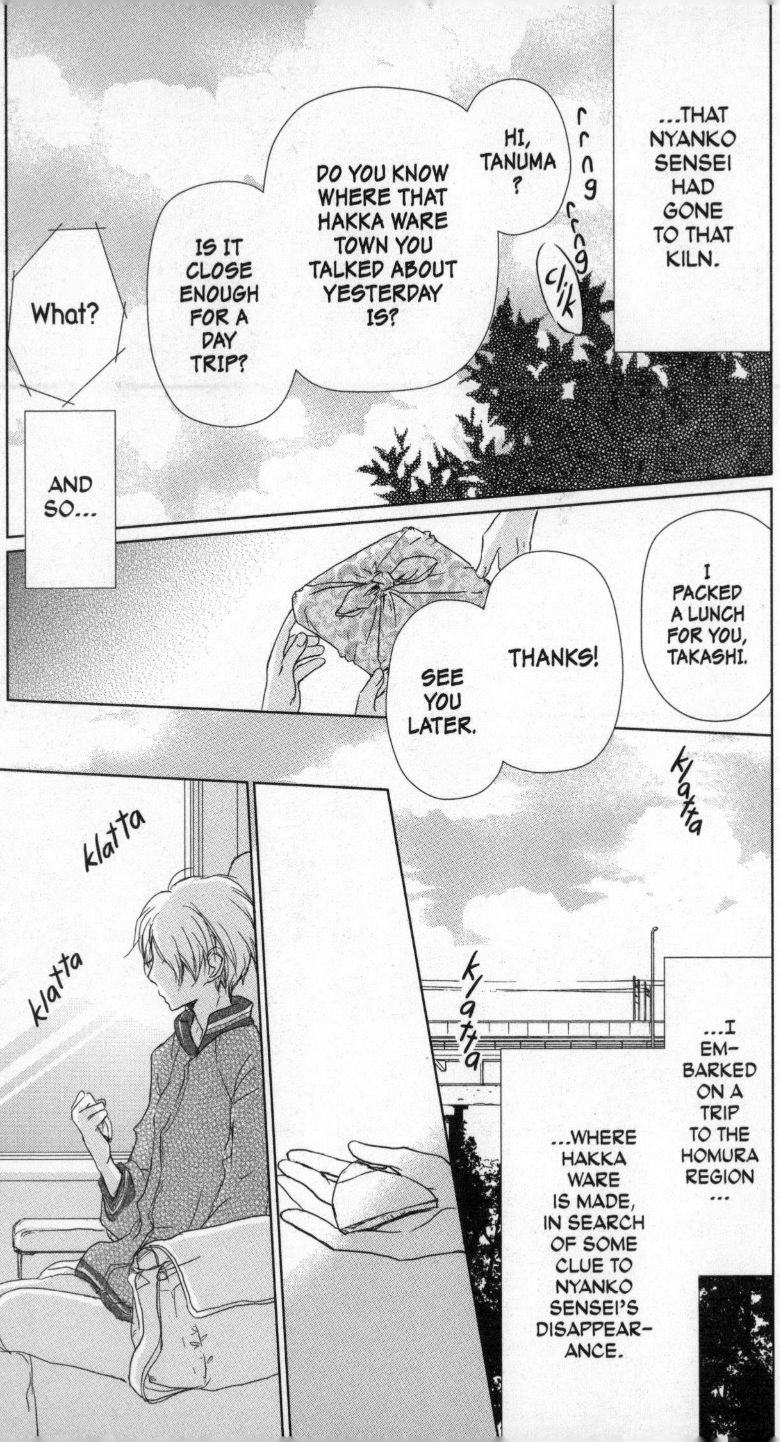
...THAT NYANKO SENSEI HAD GONE TO THAT KILN.
rrng
rrng
clik
HI, TANUMA?
DO YOU KNOW WHERE THAT HAKKA WARE TOWN YOU TALKED ABOUT YESTERDAY IS?
IS IT CLOSE ENOUGH FOR A DAY TRIP?
What?
AND SO...
I PACKED A LUNCH FOR YOU, TAKASHI.
THANKS!
SEE YOU LATER.
klatta
klatta
klatta
klatta
...I EM-BARKED ON A TRIP TO THE HOMURA REGION...
...WHERE HAKKA WARE IS MADE, IN SEARCH OF SOME CLUE TO NYANKO SENSEI'S DISAPPEAR-ANCE.

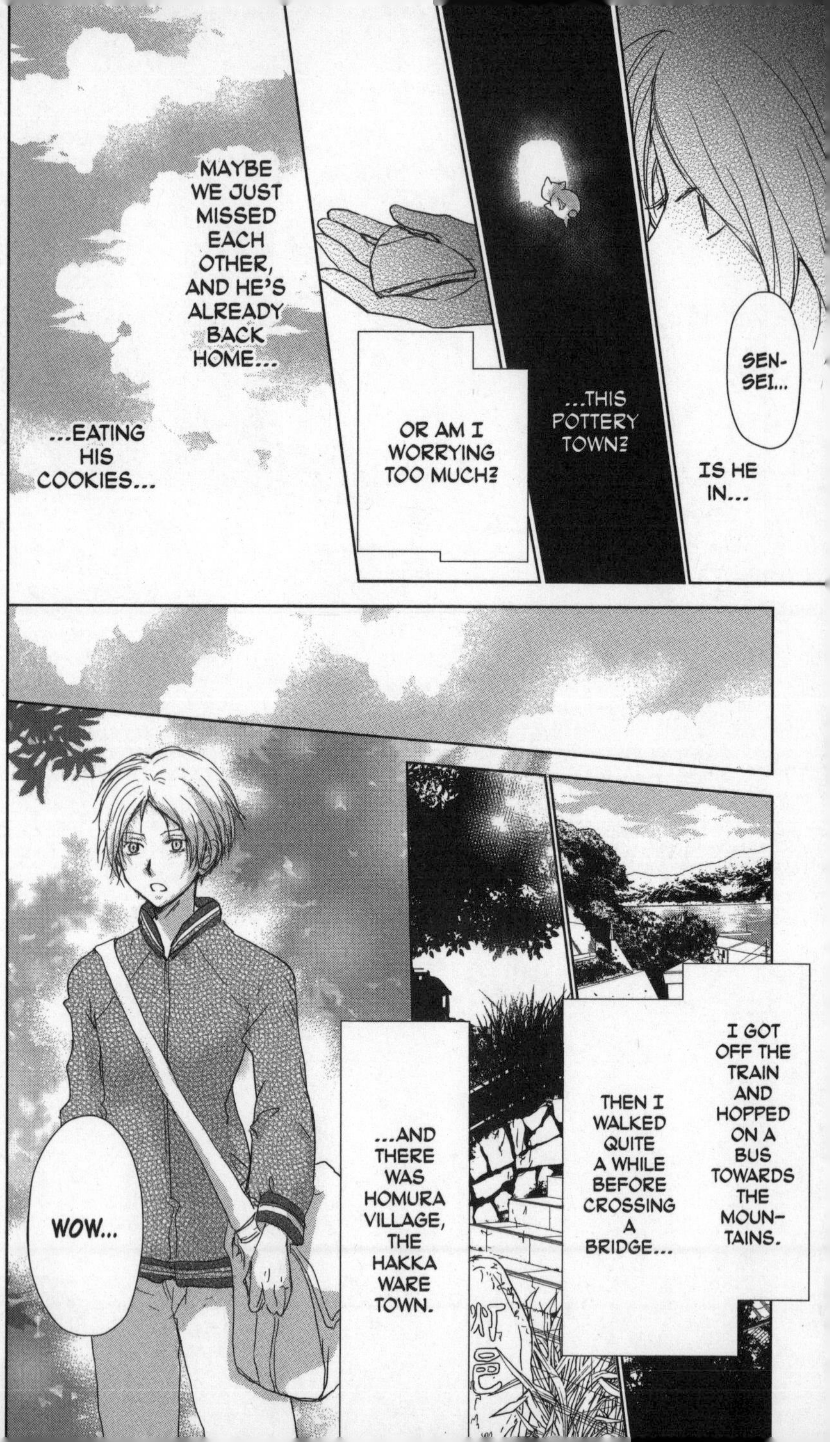
SEN-SEI...
IS HE IN...
...THIS POTTERY TOWN?
OR AM I WORRYING TOO MUCH?
MAYBE WE JUST MISSED EACH OTHER, AND HE'S ALREADY BACK HOME...
...EATING HIS COOKIES...
I GOT OFF THE TRAIN AND HOPPED ON A BUS TOWARDS THE MOUN-TAINS.
THEN I WALKED QUITE A WHILE BEFORE CROSSING A BRIDGE...
...AND THERE WAS HOMURA VILLAGE, THE HAKKA WARE TOWN.
WOW...

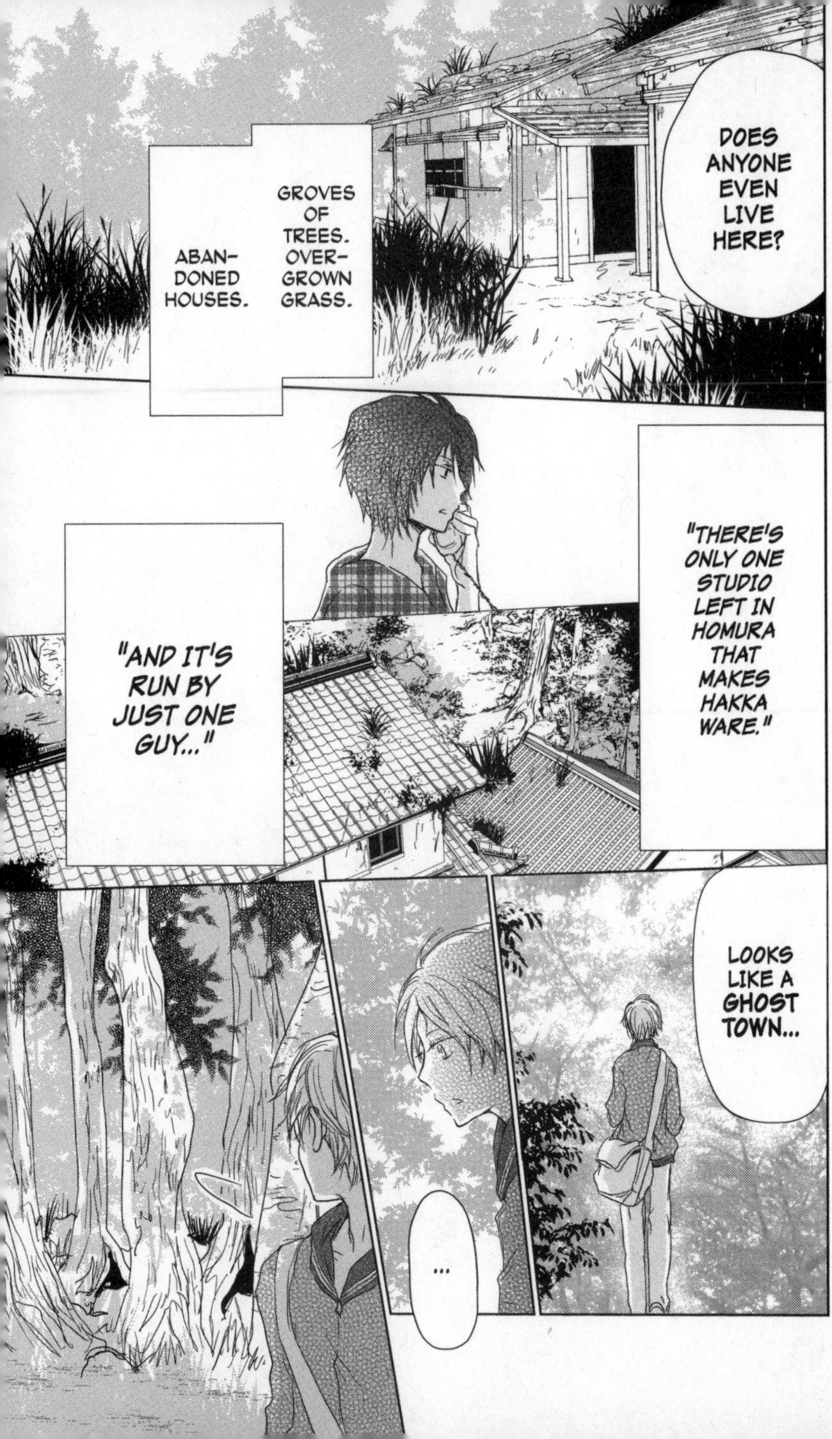
DOES ANYONE EVEN LIVE HERE?
GROVES OF TREES. OVER-GROWN GRASS.
ABAN-DONED HOUSES.
"THERE'S ONLY ONE STUDIO LEFT IN HOMURA THAT MAKES HAKKA WARE."
"AND IT'S RUN BY JUST ONE GUY..."
LOOKS LIKE A GHOST TOWN...
...

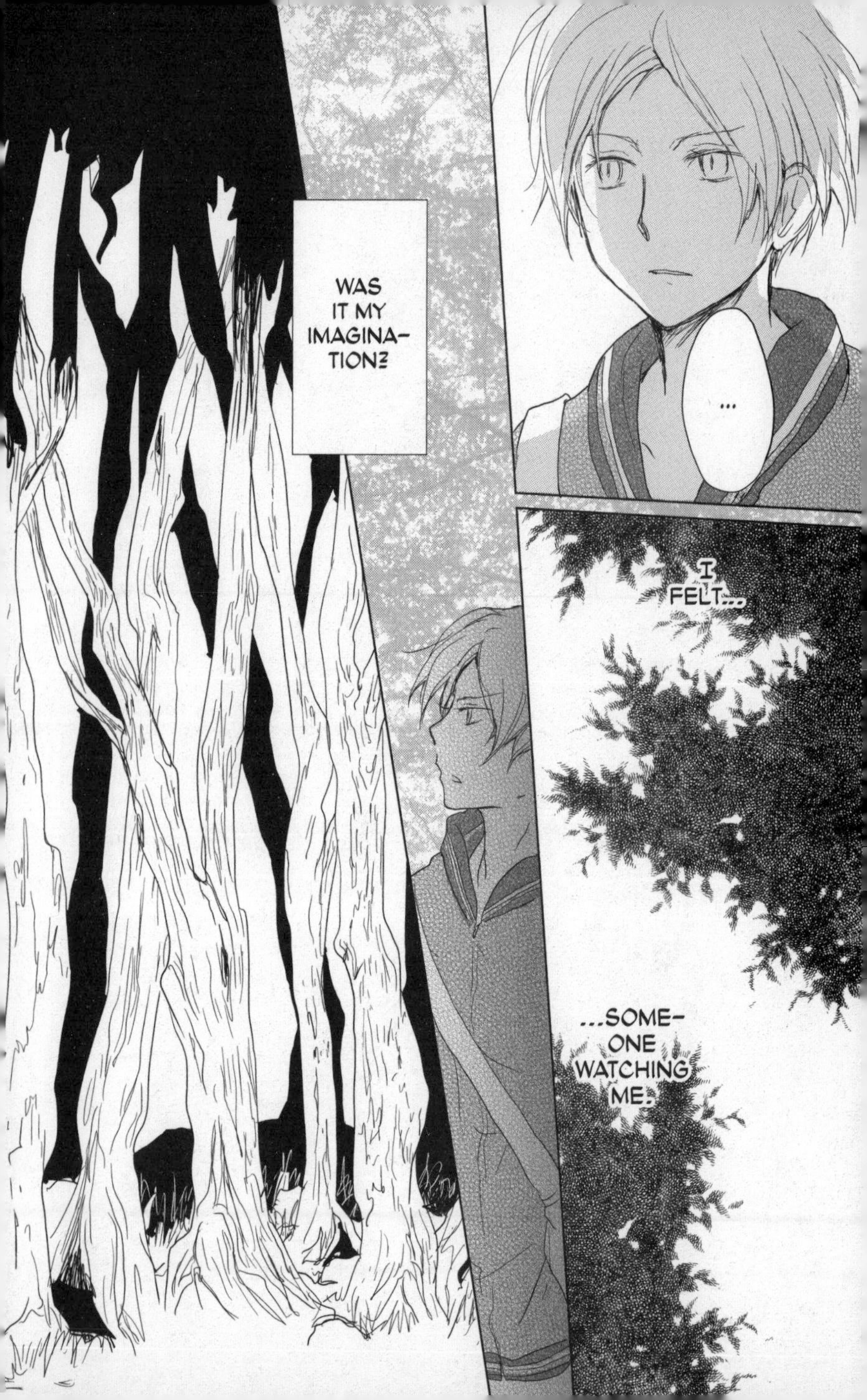
...
I FELT...
...SOMEONE WATCHING ME.
WAS IT MY IMAGINATION?

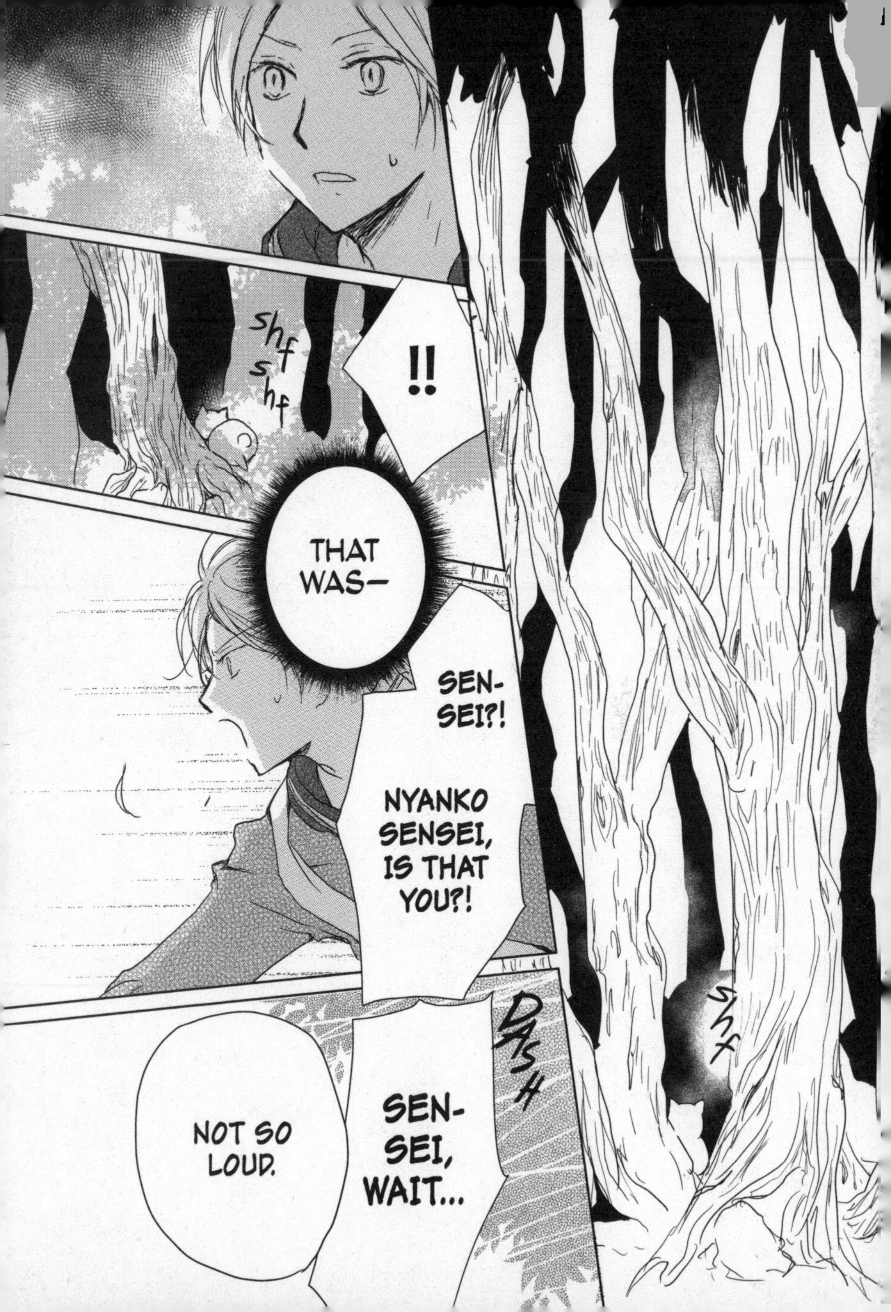
shf
shf shf
!!
THAT WAS—
SEN-SEI?!
NYANKO SENSEI, IS THAT YOU?!
DASH
SEN-SEI, WAIT...
NOT SO LOUD.

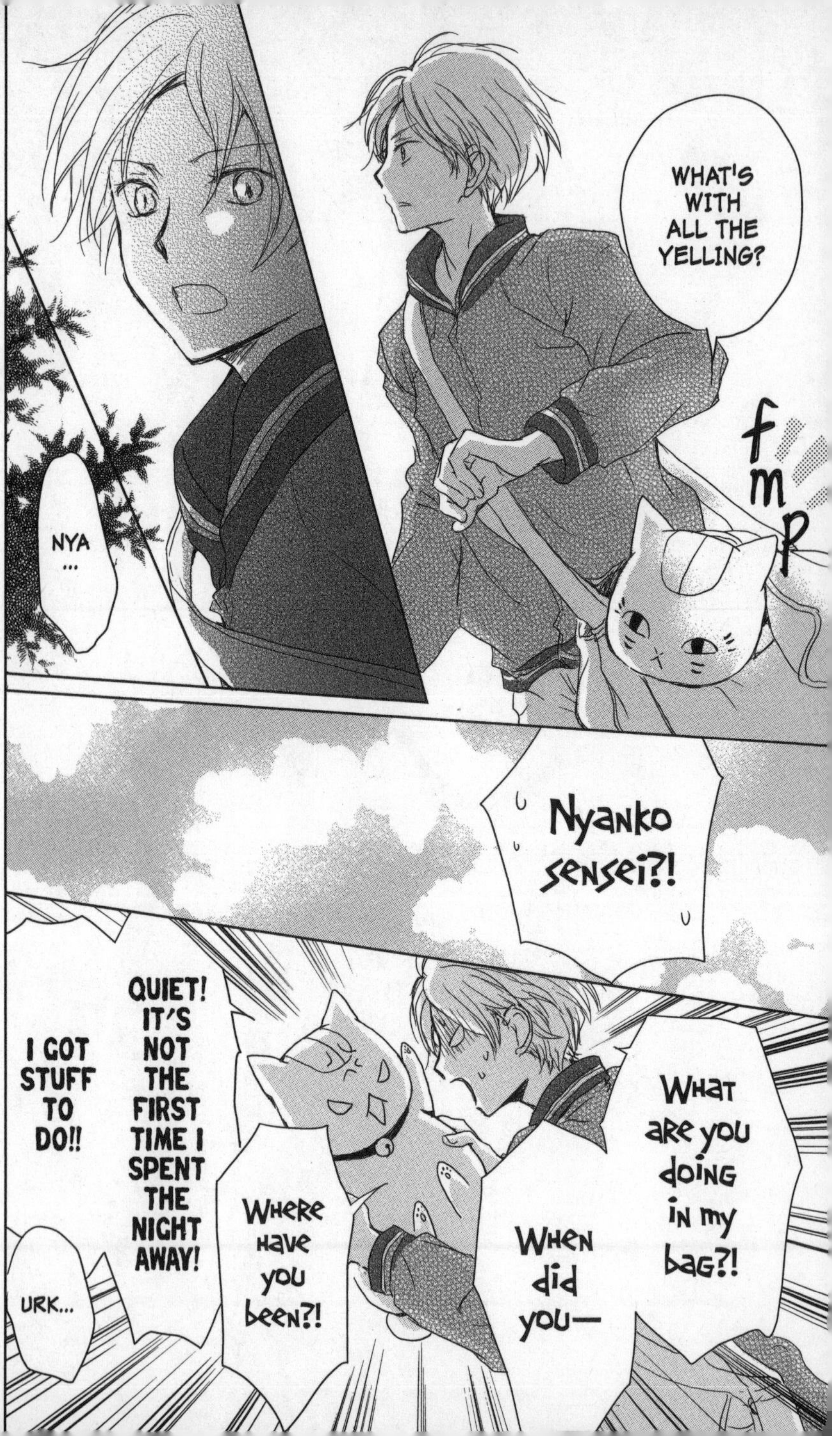
WHAT'S WITH ALL THE YELLING?
fmp
NYA ...
Nyanko sensei?!
What are you doing in my bag?!
When did you—
Where have you been?!
QUIET! IT'S NOT THE FIRST TIME I SPENT THE NIGHT AWAY!
I GOT STUFF TO DO!!
URK...

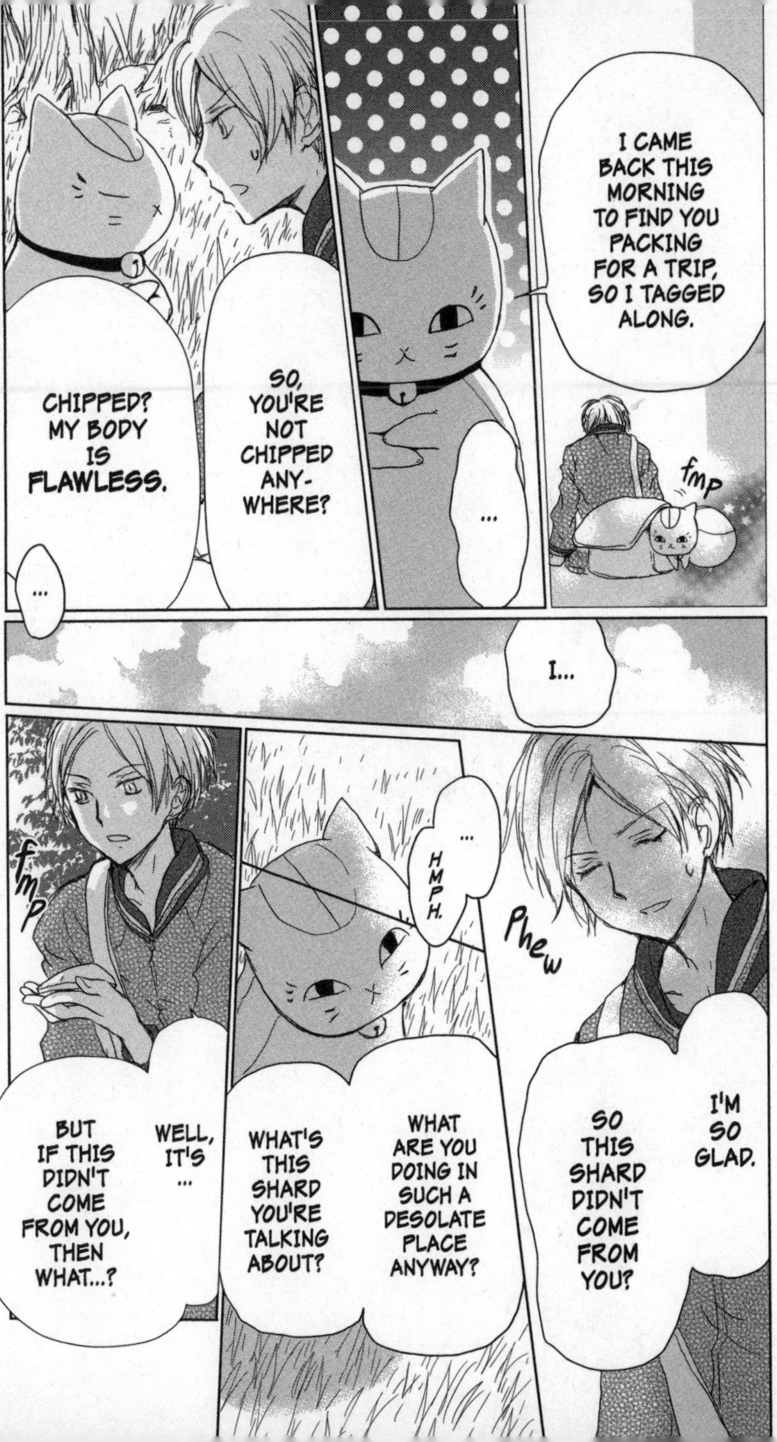
I CAME BACK THIS MORNING TO FIND YOU PACKING FOR A TRIP, SO I TAGGED ALONG.
fmp
...
SO, YOU'RE NOT CHIPPED ANYWHERE?
CHIPPED? MY BODY IS FLAWLESS.
...
I...
I'M SO GLAD.
SO THIS SHARD DIDN'T COME FROM YOU?
Phew
... HMPH.
WHAT ARE YOU DOING IN SUCH A DESOLATE PLACE ANYWAY?
WHAT'S THIS SHARD YOU'RE TALKING ABOUT?
fmp
WELL, IT'S ...
BUT IF THIS DIDN'T COME FROM YOU, THEN WHAT...?

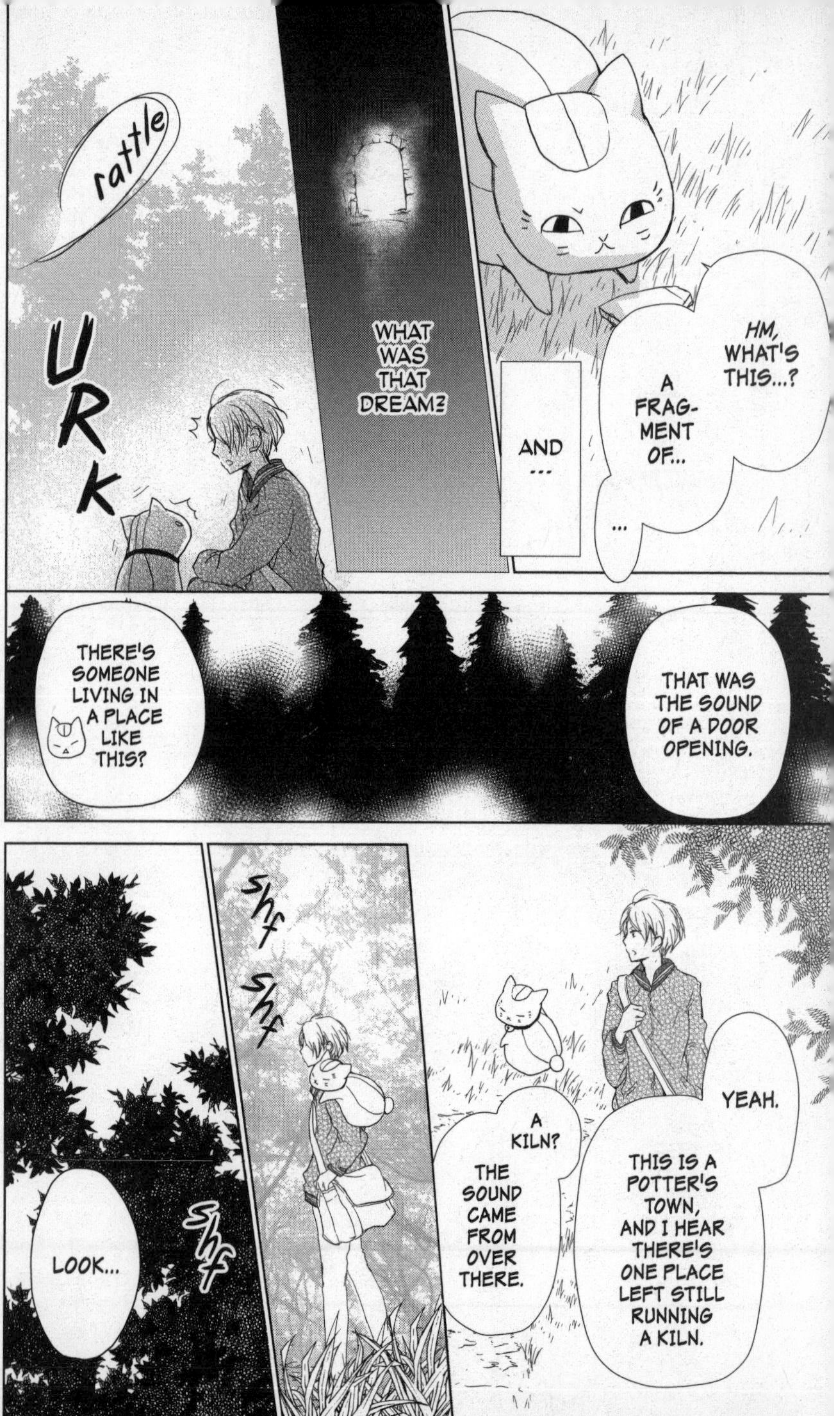
HM, WHAT'S THIS...?
A FRAG-MENT OF...
...
AND ...
WHAT WAS THAT DREAM?
rattle
URK
THAT WAS THE SOUND OF A DOOR OPENING.
THERE'S SOMEONE LIVING IN A PLACE LIKE THIS?
YEAH.
THIS IS A POTTER'S TOWN, AND I HEAR THERE'S ONE PLACE LEFT STILL RUNNING A KILN.
A KILN?
THE SOUND CAME FROM OVER THERE.
shf
shf
shf
LOOK...

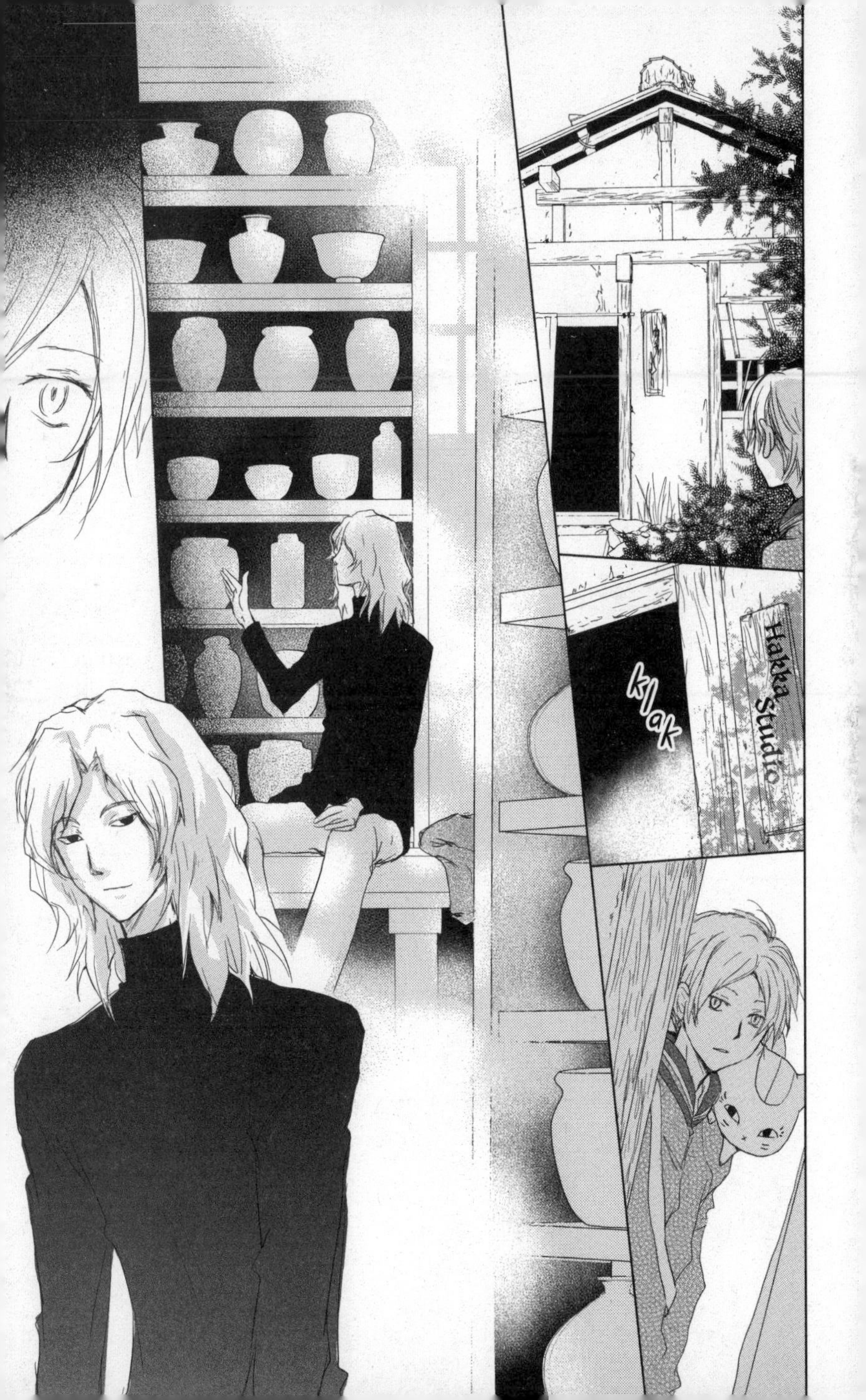
Hakka Studio
klak

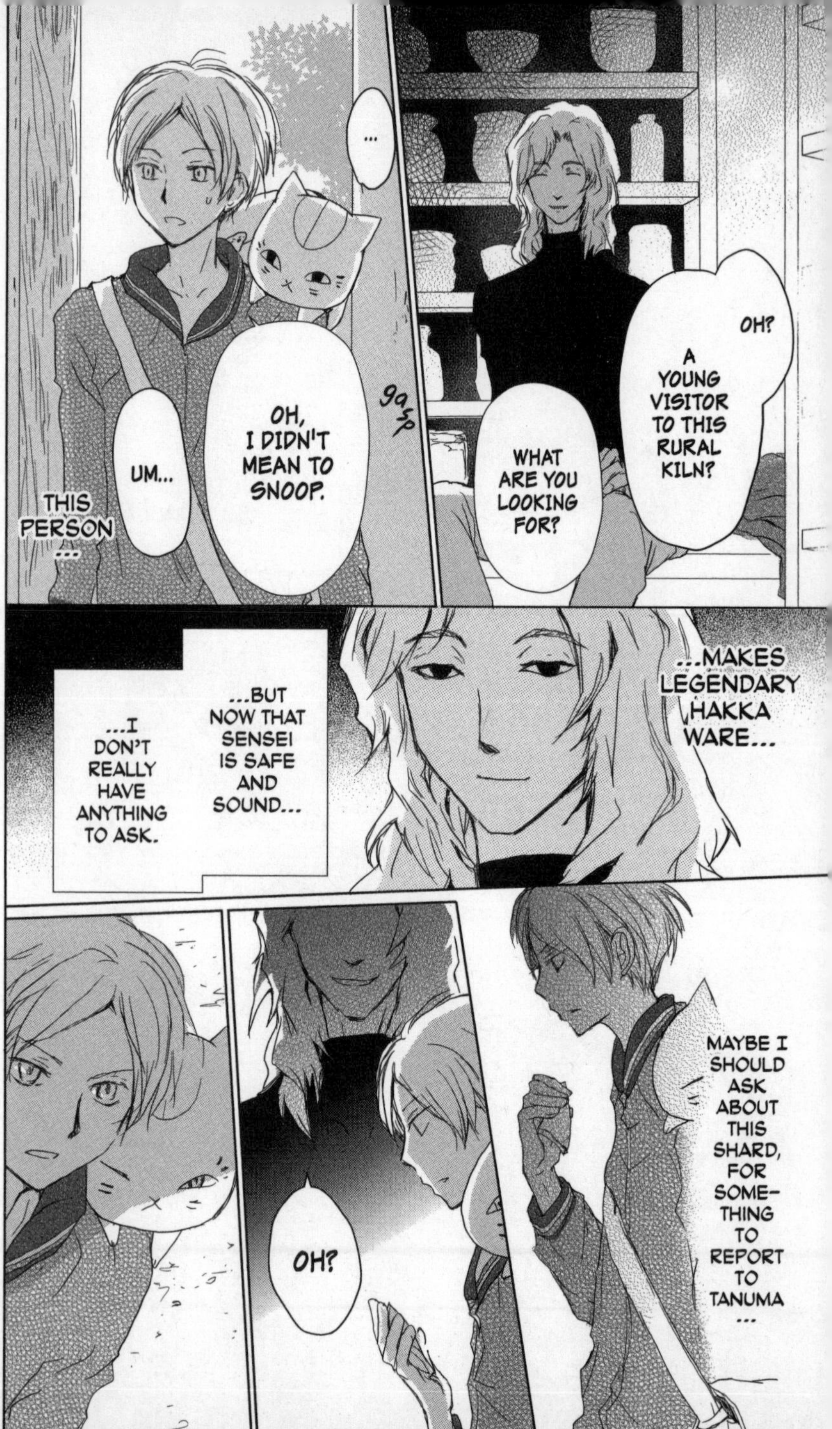
OH?
A YOUNG VISITOR TO THIS RURAL KILN?
WHAT ARE YOU LOOKING FOR?
...
gasp
OH, I DIDN'T MEAN TO SNOOP.
UM...
THIS PERSON...
...MAKES LEGENDARY HAKKA WARE...
...BUT NOW THAT SENSEI IS SAFE AND SOUND...
...I DON'T REALLY HAVE ANYTHING TO ASK.
MAYBE I SHOULD ASK ABOUT THIS SHARD, FOR SOMETHING TO REPORT TO TANUMA...
OH?

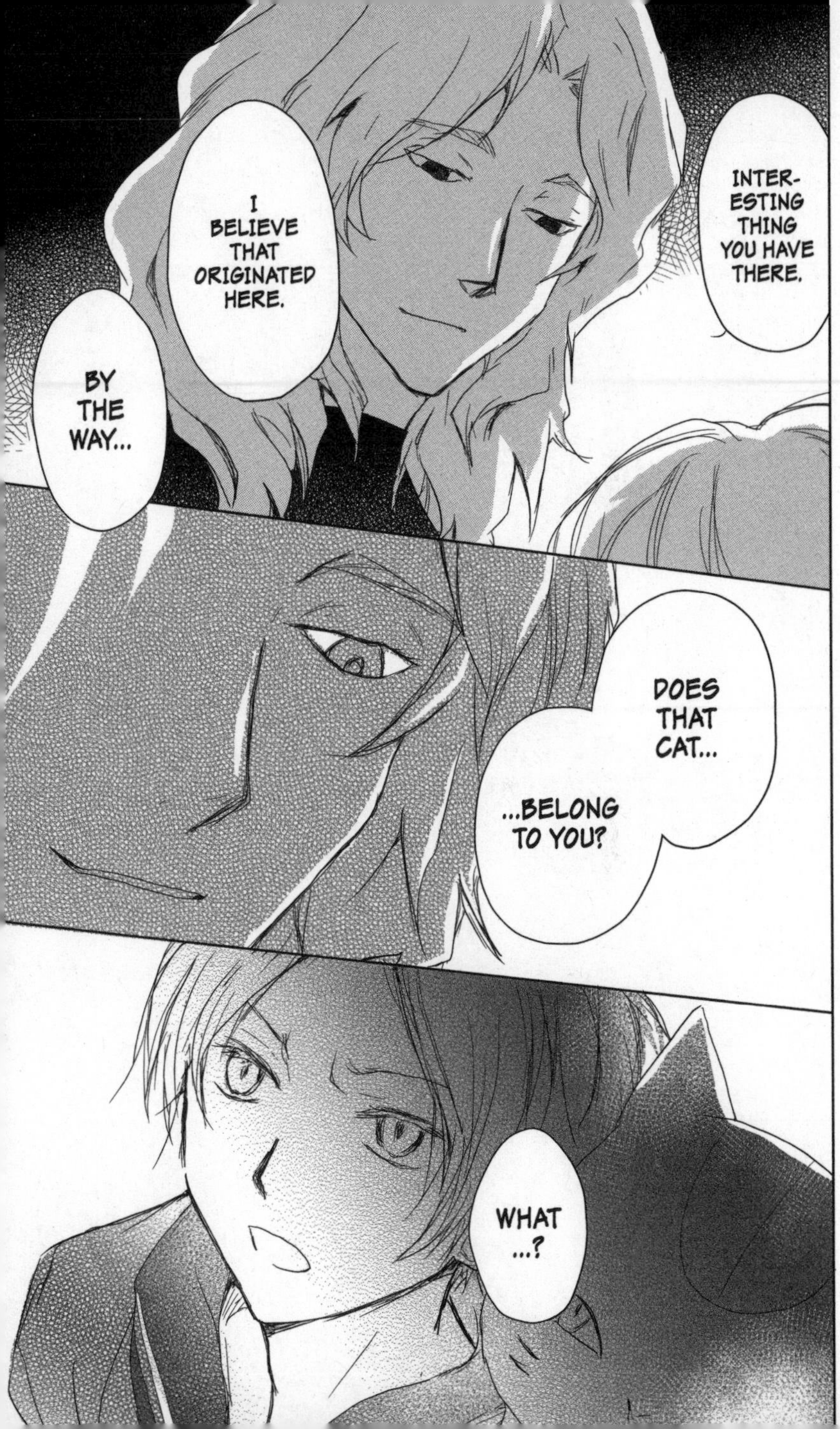
INTER-ESTING THING YOU HAVE THERE.
I BELIEVE THAT ORIGINATED HERE.
BY THE WAY...
DOES THAT CAT...
...BELONG TO YOU?
WHAT ...?

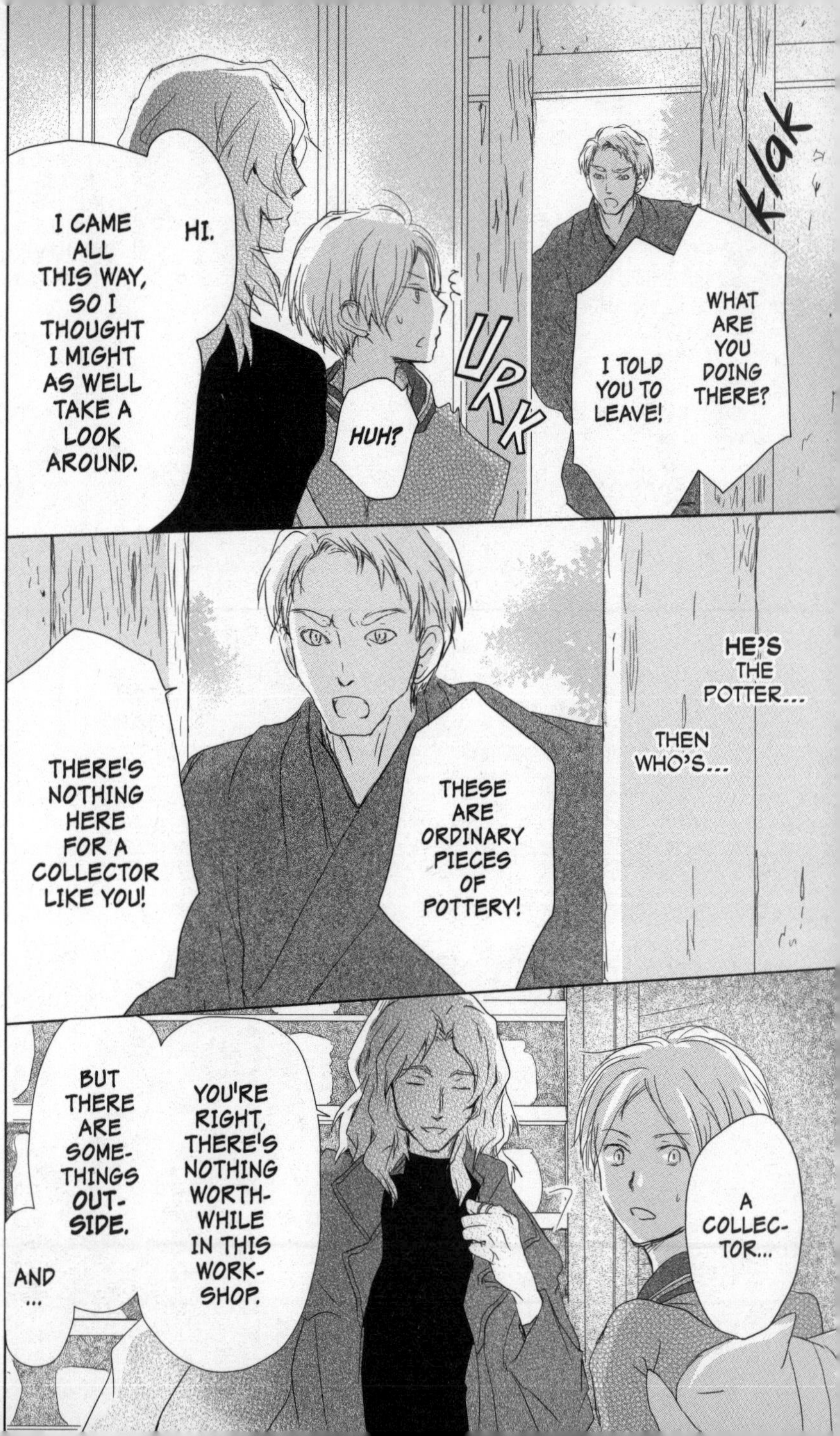
klak
WHAT ARE YOU DOING THERE?
I TOLD YOU TO LEAVE!
URK
HUH?
HI.
I CAME ALL THIS WAY, SO I THOUGHT I MIGHT AS WELL TAKE A LOOK AROUND.
HE'S THE POTTER...
THEN WHO'S...
THESE ARE ORDINARY PIECES OF POTTERY!
THERE'S NOTHING HERE FOR A COLLECTOR LIKE YOU!
A COLLEC-TOR...
YOU'RE RIGHT, THERE'S NOTHING WORTH-WHILE IN THIS WORK-SHOP.
BUT THERE ARE SOME-THINGS OUT-SIDE.
AND ...

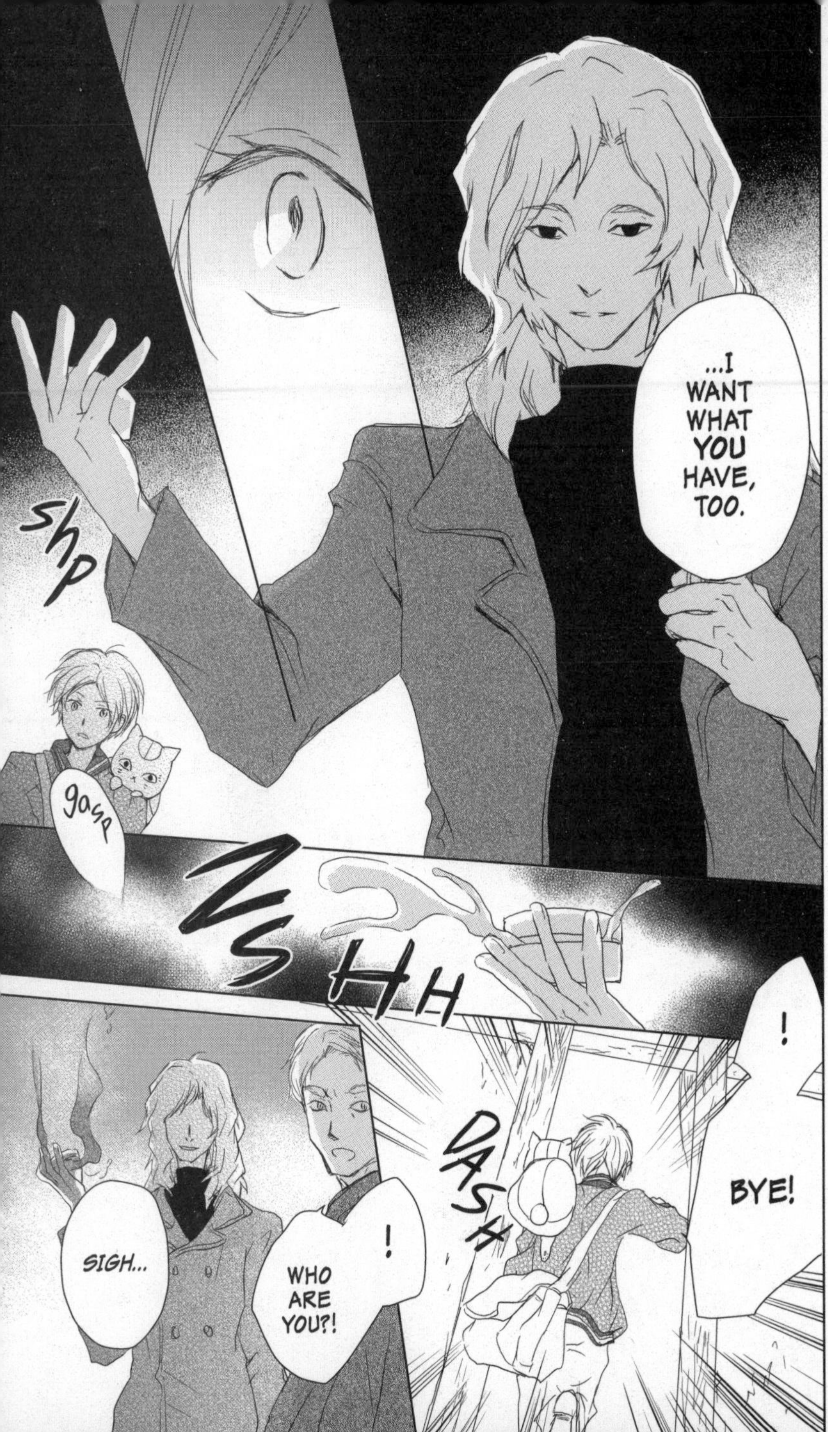
...I WANT WHAT YOU HAVE, TOO.
SHP
gasp
ZSHH
!
BYE!
DASH
!
WHO ARE YOU?!
SIGH...

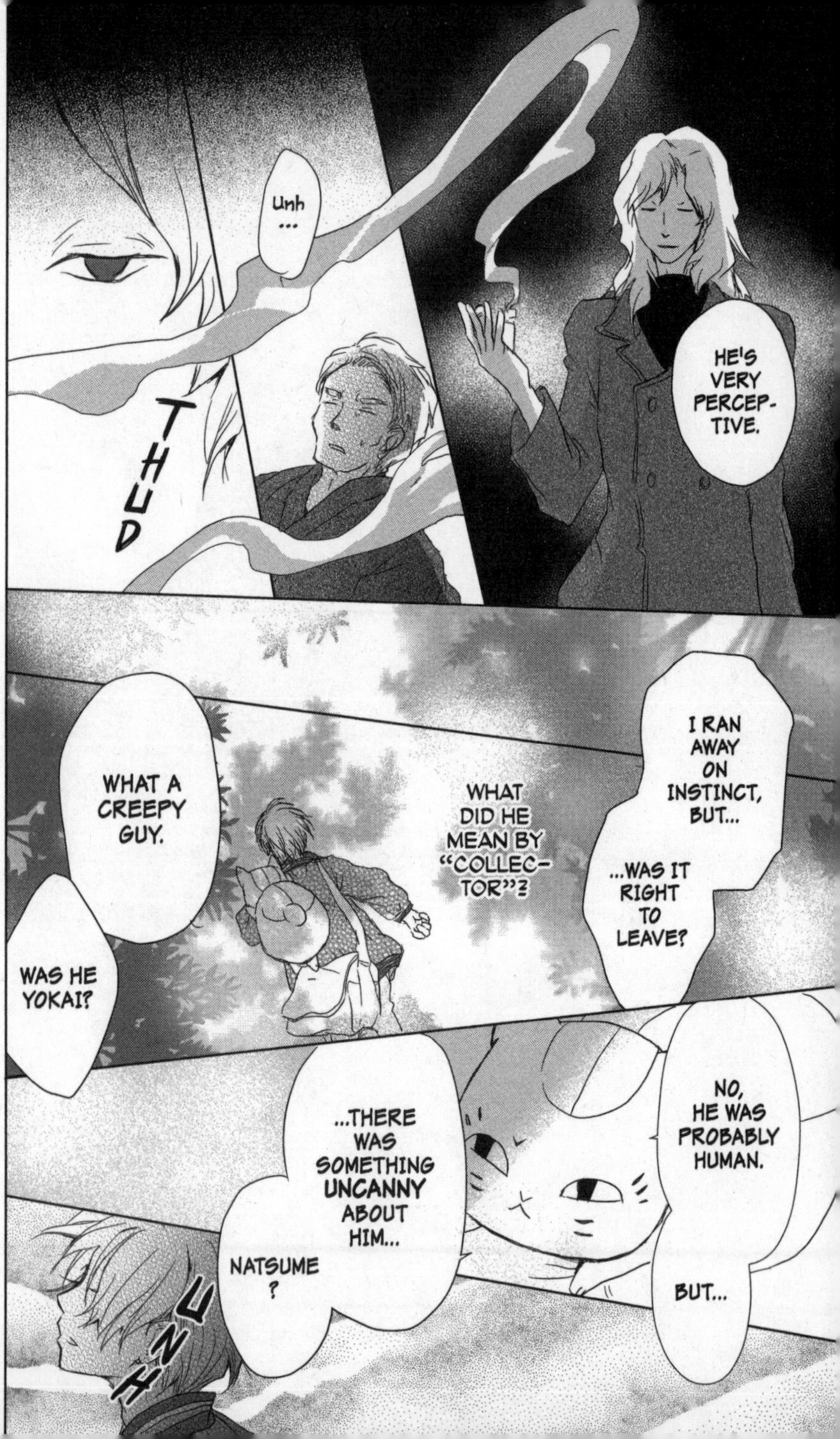
HE'S VERY PERCEPTIVE.
Unh ...
THUD
I RAN AWAY ON INSTINCT, BUT...
...WAS IT RIGHT TO LEAVE?
WHAT DID HE MEAN BY "COLLECTOR"?
WHAT A CREEPY GUY.
WAS HE YOKAI?
NO, HE WAS PROBABLY HUMAN.
BUT...
...THERE WAS SOMETHING UNCANNY ABOUT HIM...
NATSUME?
UNH

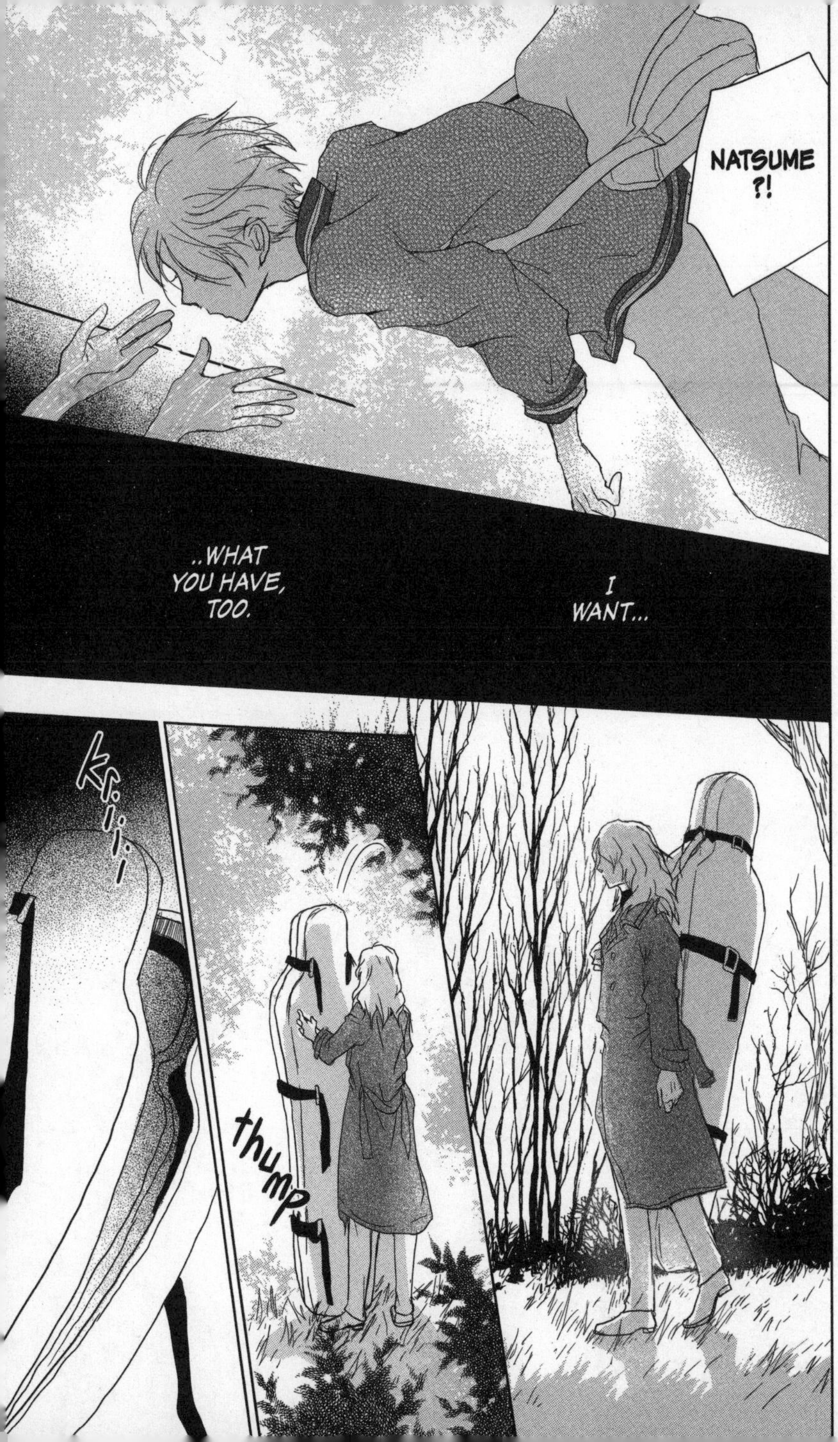
NATSUME ?!
I WANT...
..WHAT YOU HAVE, TOO.
thump
kriii

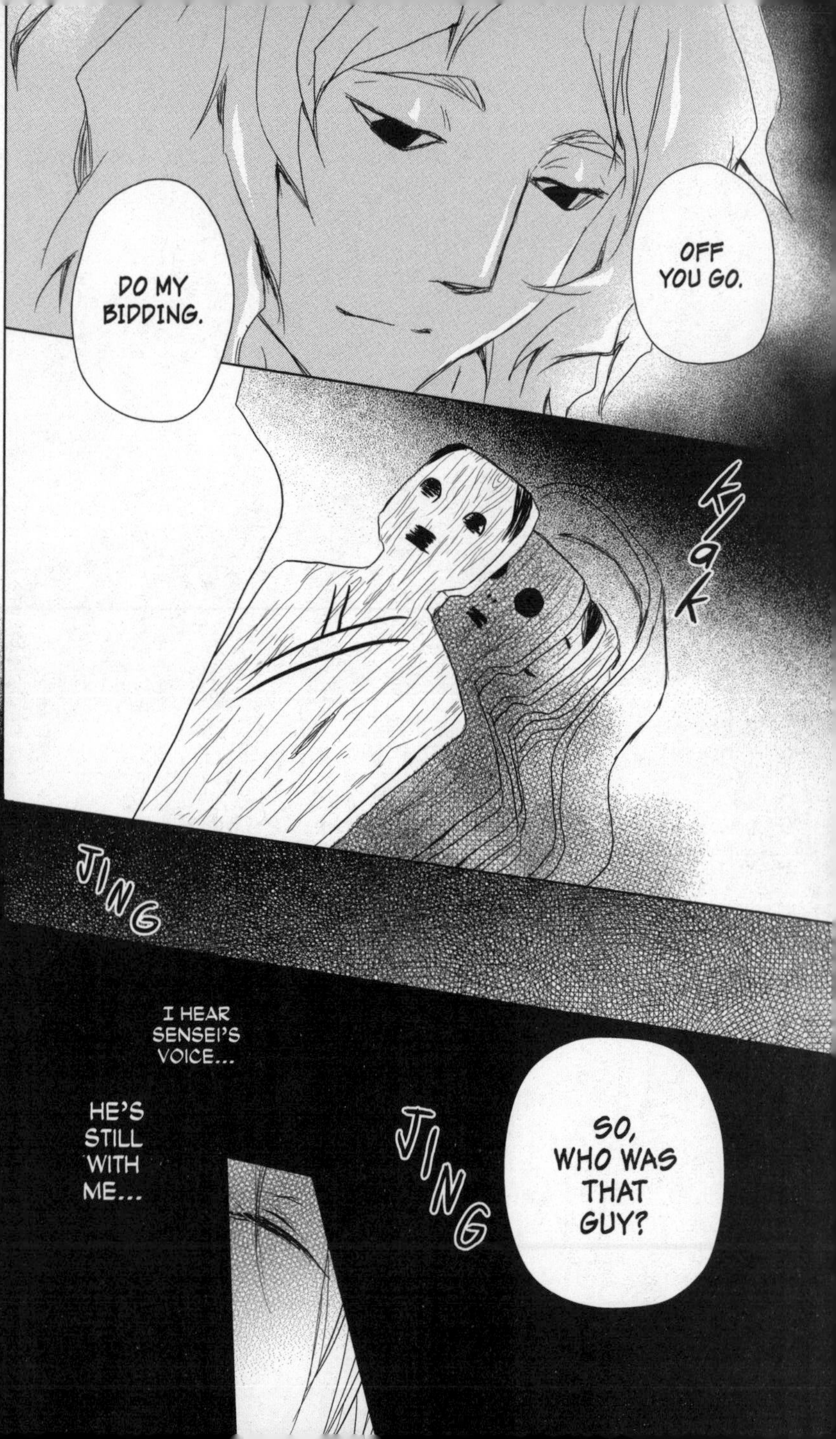
OFF YOU GO.
DO MY BIDDING.
KLAK
JING
SO, WHO WAS THAT GUY?
JING
I HEAR SENSEI'S VOICE...
HE'S STILL WITH ME...

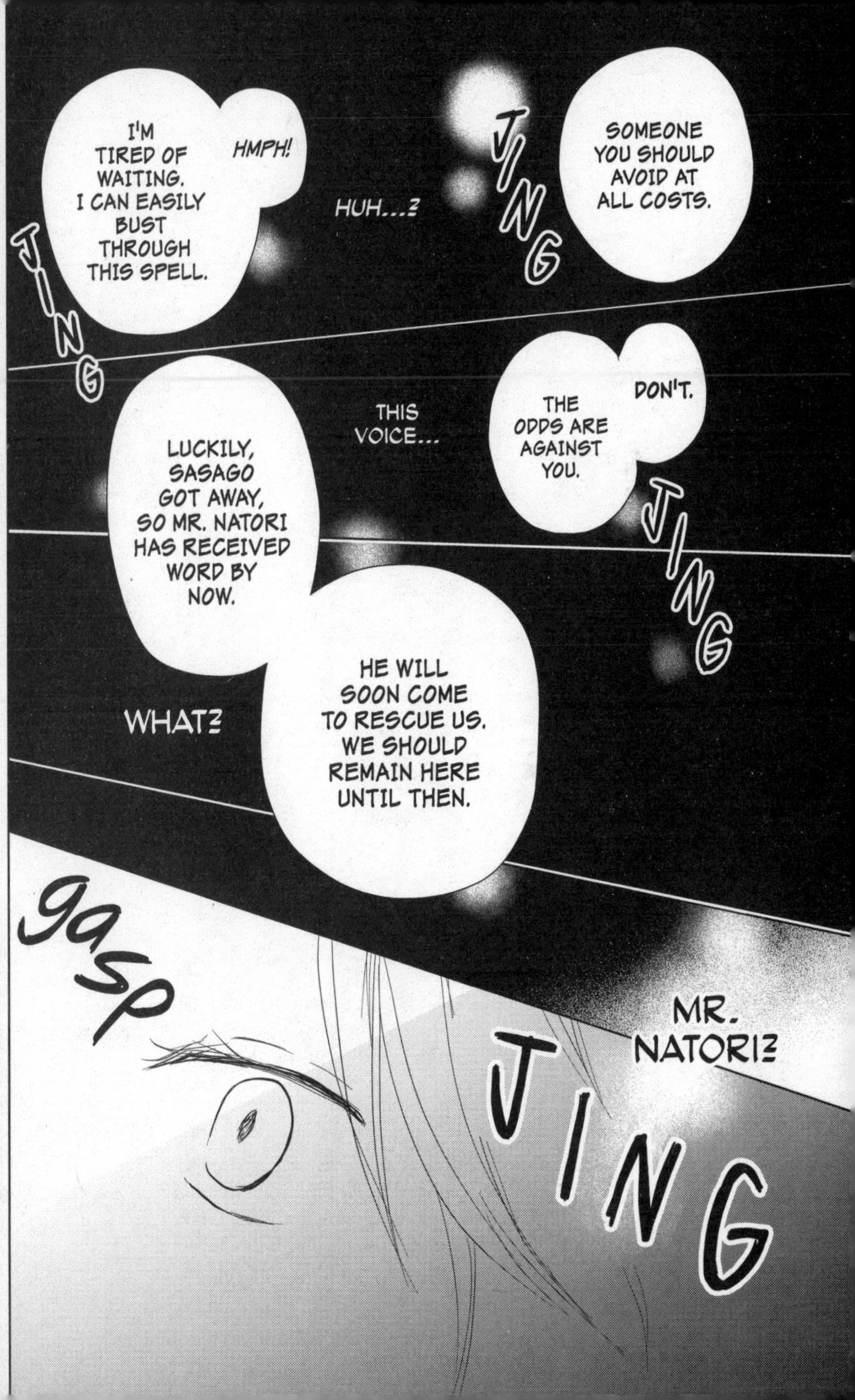
SOMEONE YOU SHOULD AVOID AT ALL COSTS.
JING
HUH...?
HMPH!
I'M TIRED OF WAITING. I CAN EASILY BUST THROUGH THIS SPELL.
JING
DON'T.
THE ODDS ARE AGAINST YOU.
JING
THIS VOICE...
LUCKILY, SASAGO GOT AWAY, SO MR. NATORI HAS RECEIVED WORD BY NOW.
HE WILL SOON COME TO RESCUE US. WE SHOULD REMAIN HERE UNTIL THEN.
WHAT?
MR. NATORI?
JING
gasp

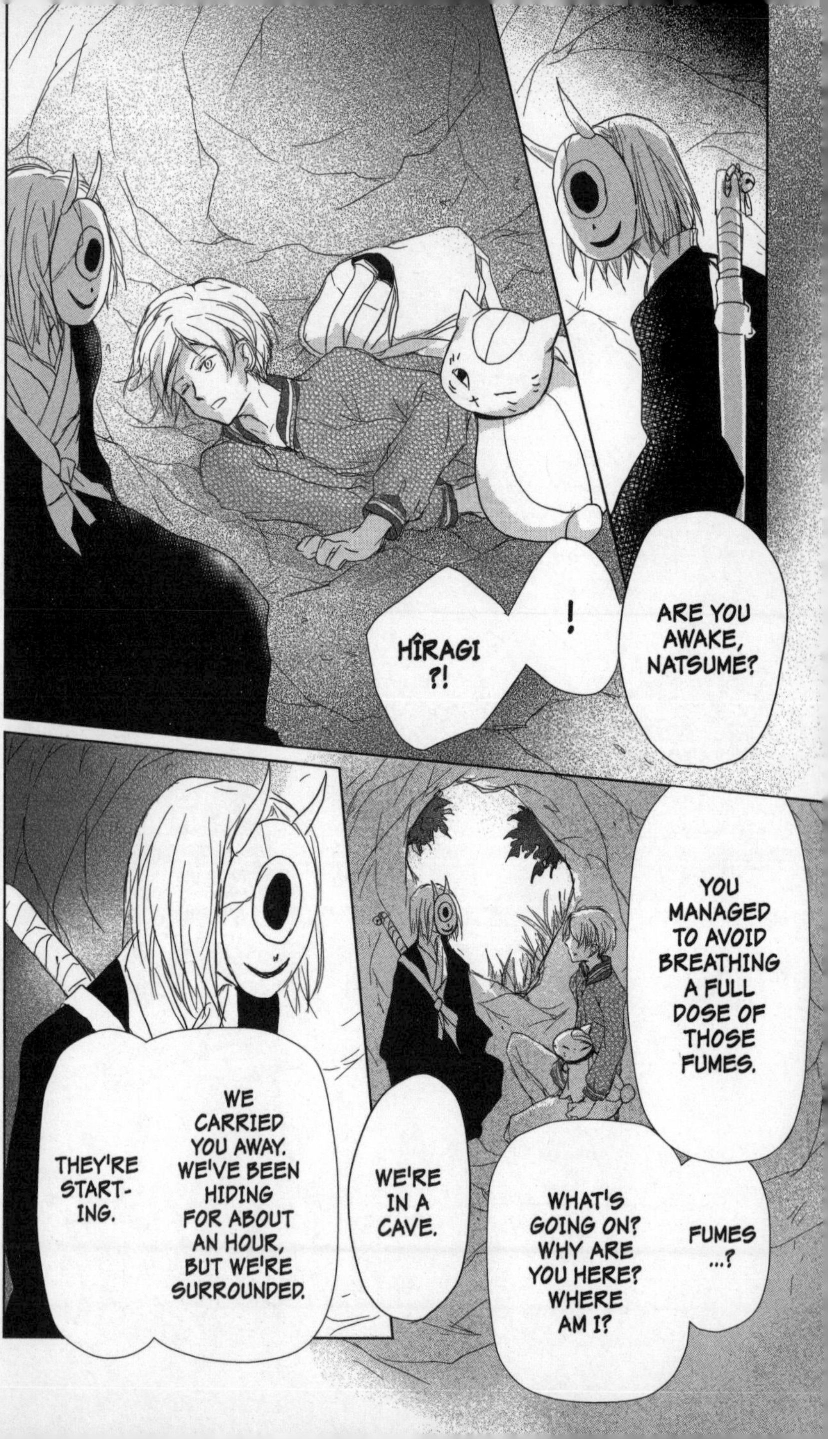
ARE YOU AWAKE, NATSUME?
!
HÎRAGI ?!
YOU MANAGED TO AVOID BREATHING A FULL DOSE OF THOSE FUMES.
FUMES ...?
WHAT'S GOING ON? WHY ARE YOU HERE? WHERE AM I?
WE'RE IN A CAVE.
WE CARRIED YOU AWAY. WE'VE BEEN HIDING FOR ABOUT AN HOUR, BUT WE'RE SURROUNDED.
THEY'RE START-ING.

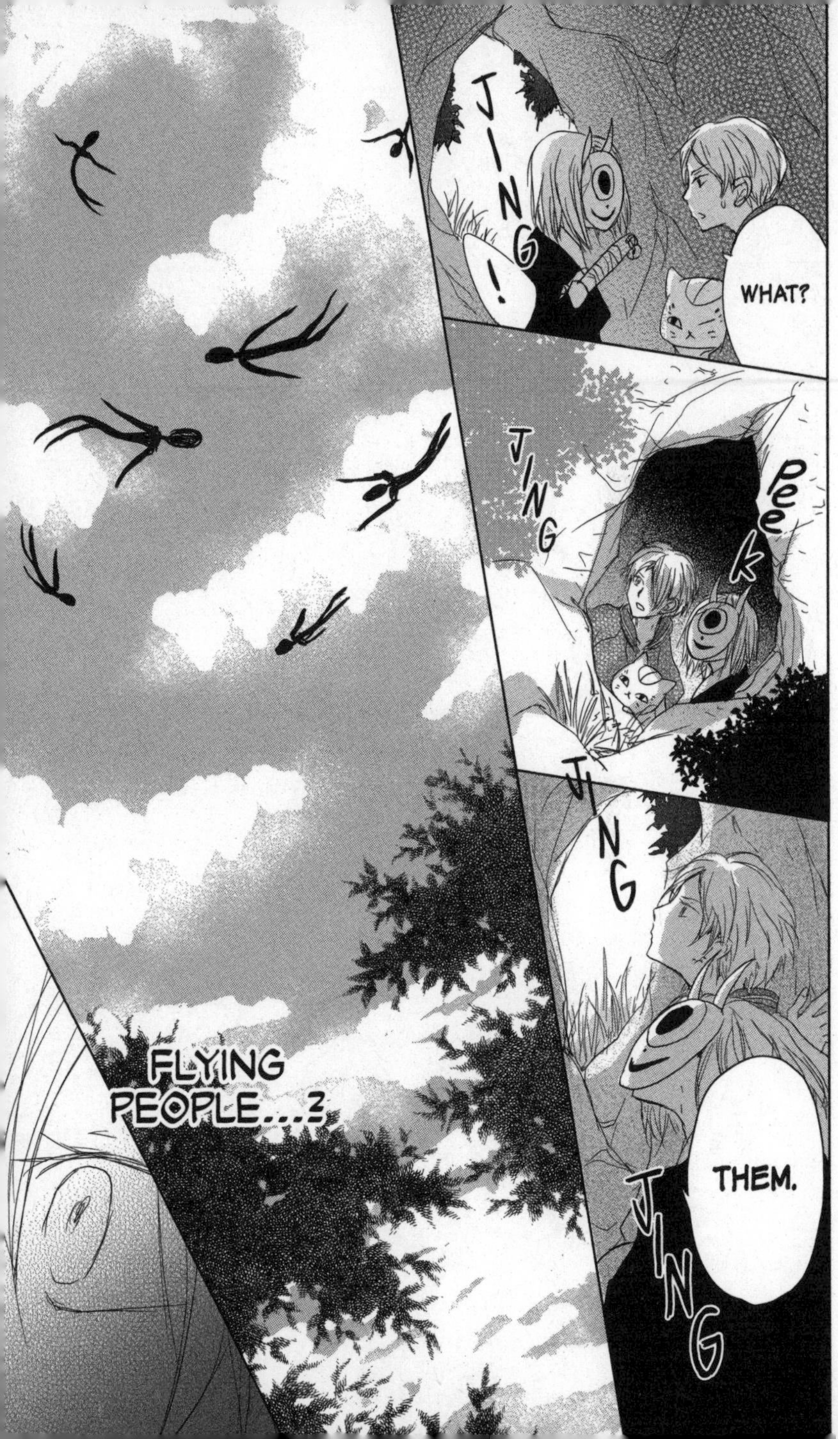

JING!
WHAT?
JING
Peek
JING
THEM.
JING
FLYING PEOPLE...?

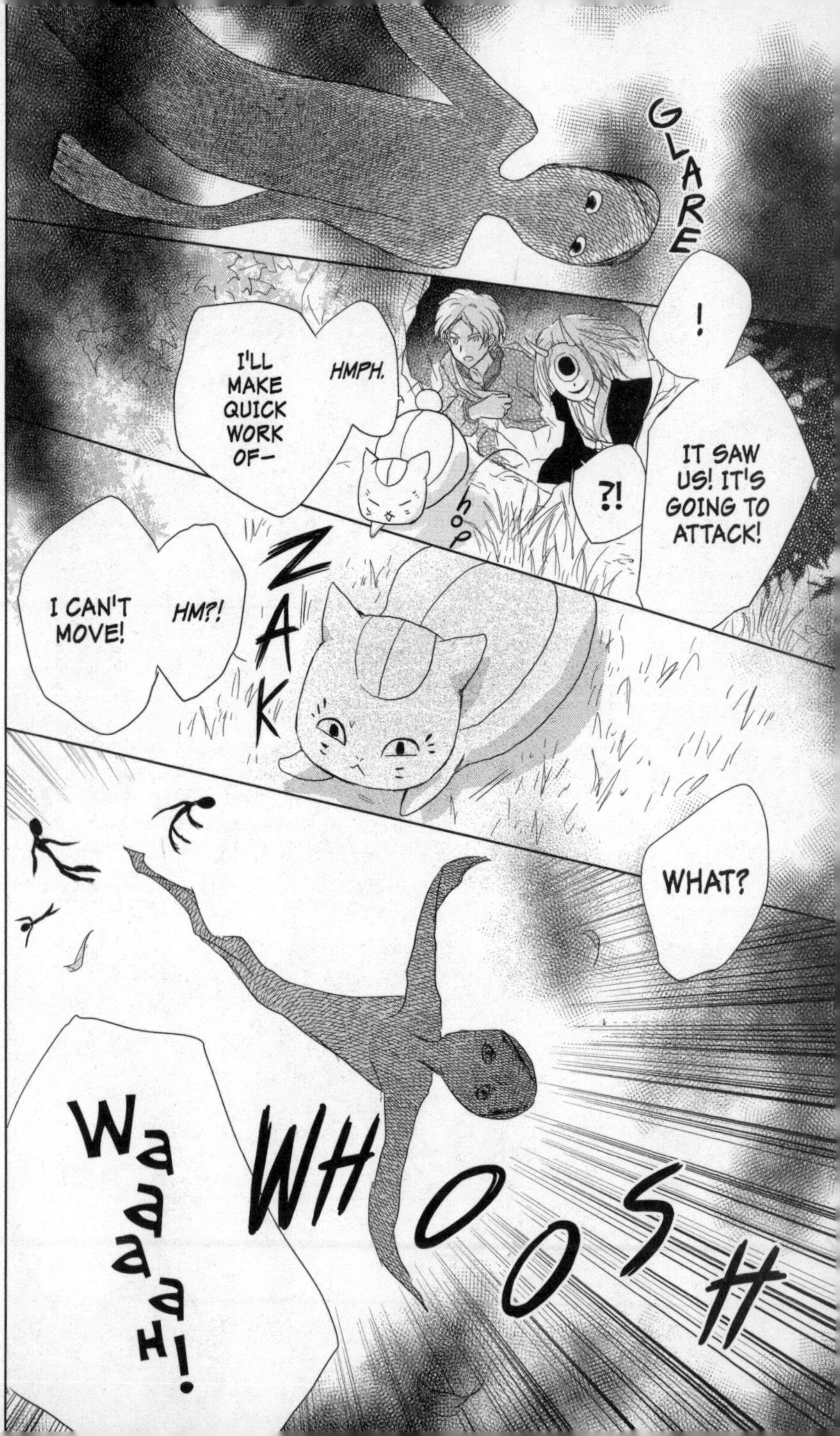
GLARE
!
IT SAW US! IT'S GOING TO ATTACK!
?!
HMPH.
I'LL MAKE QUICK WORK OF–
hop
ZAK
HM?!
I CAN'T MOVE!
WHAT?
WHOOSH
Waaaaah!

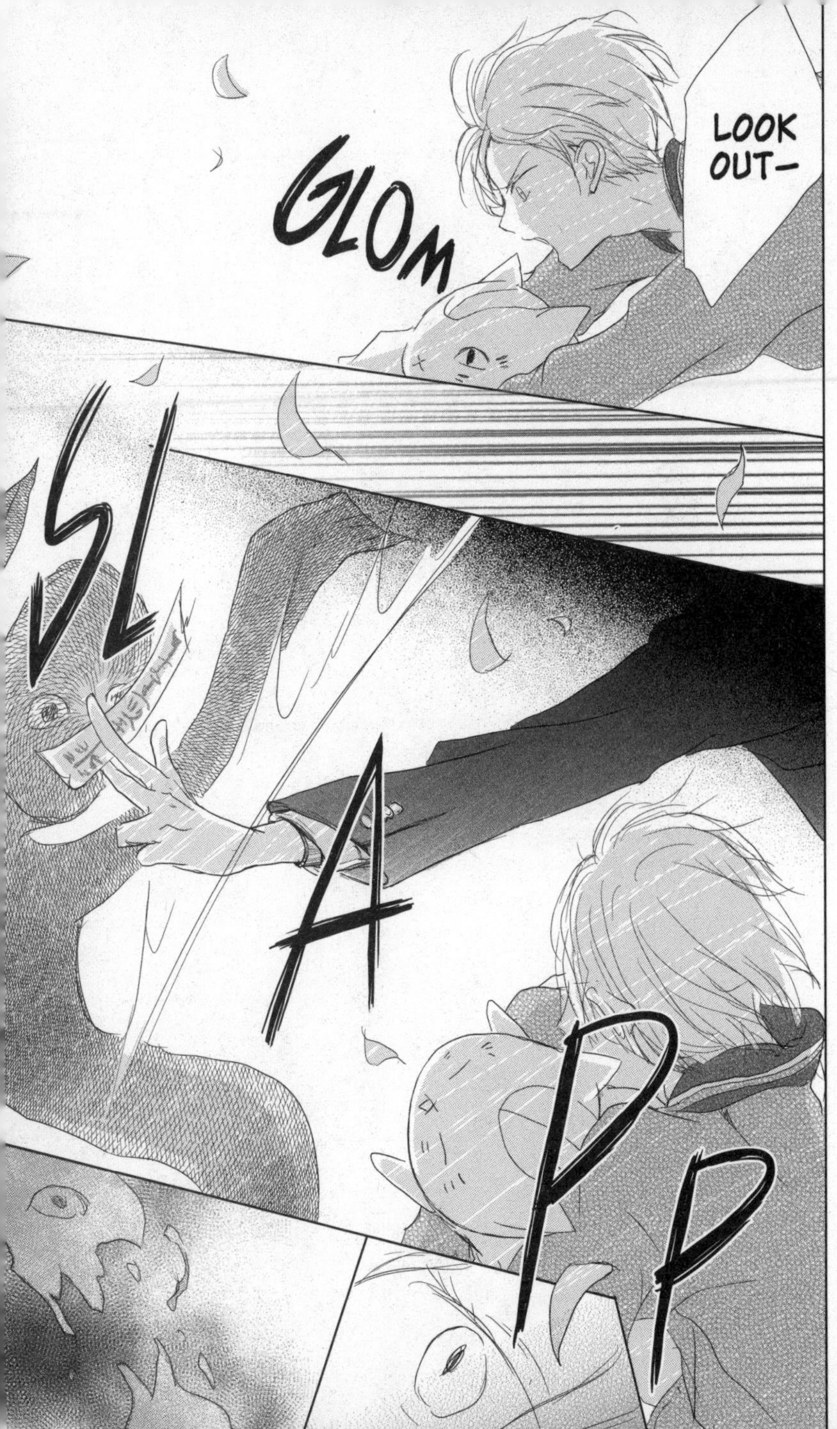
LOOK OUT—
GLOM
SLAPP

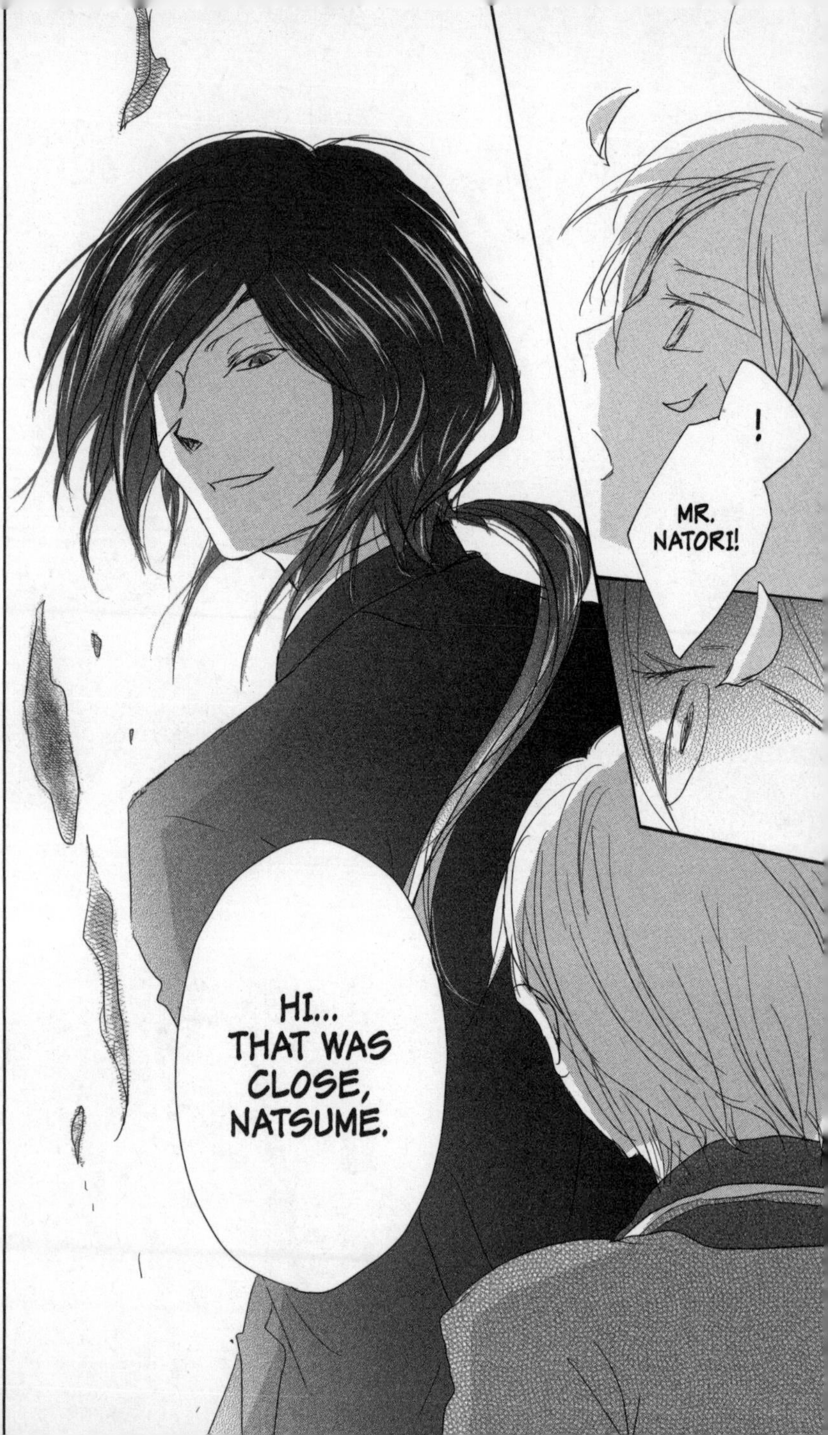
!
MR. NATORI!
HI... THAT WAS CLOSE, NATSUME.

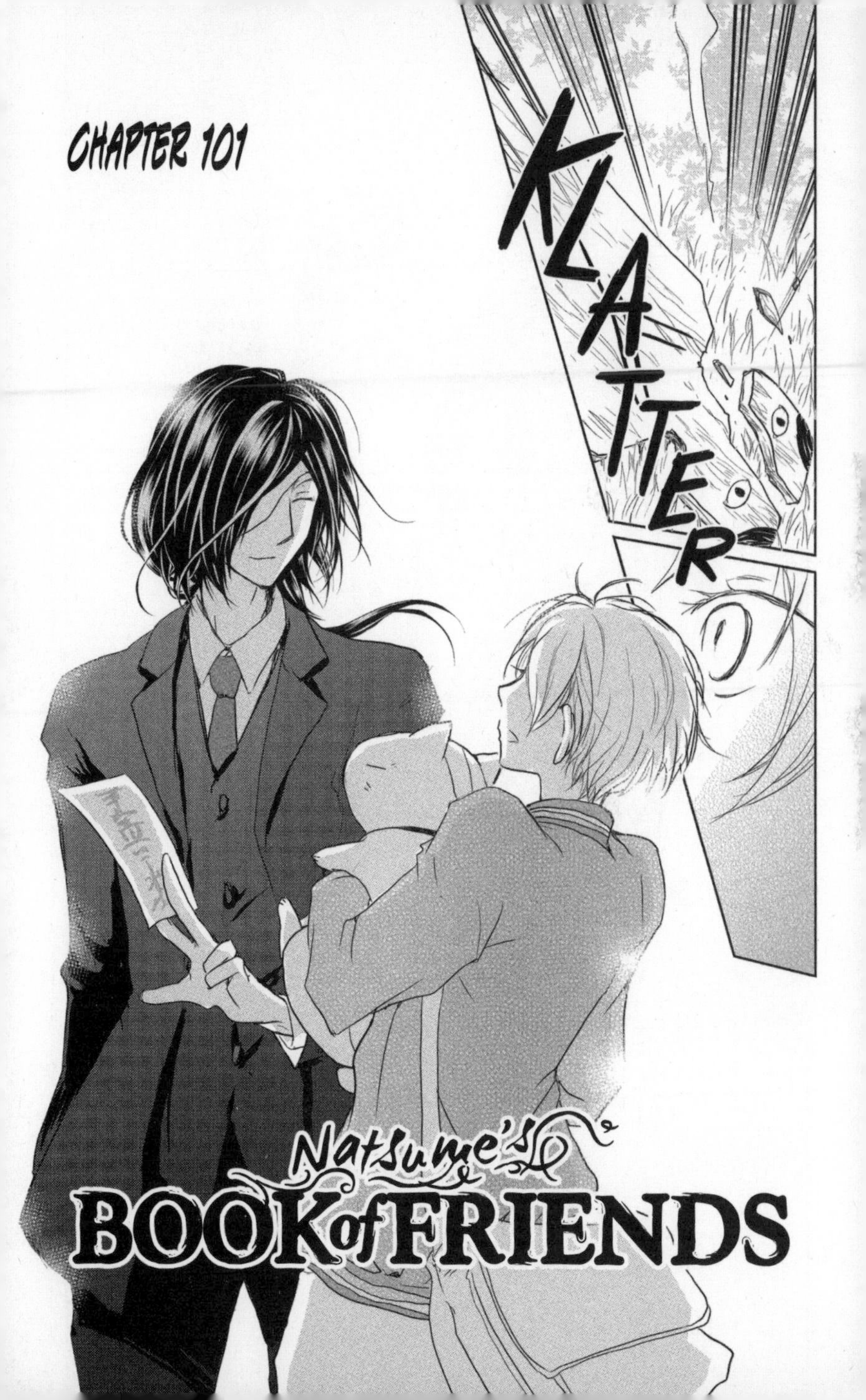
CHAPTER 101
KLATTER
Natsume's
BOOK of FRIENDS

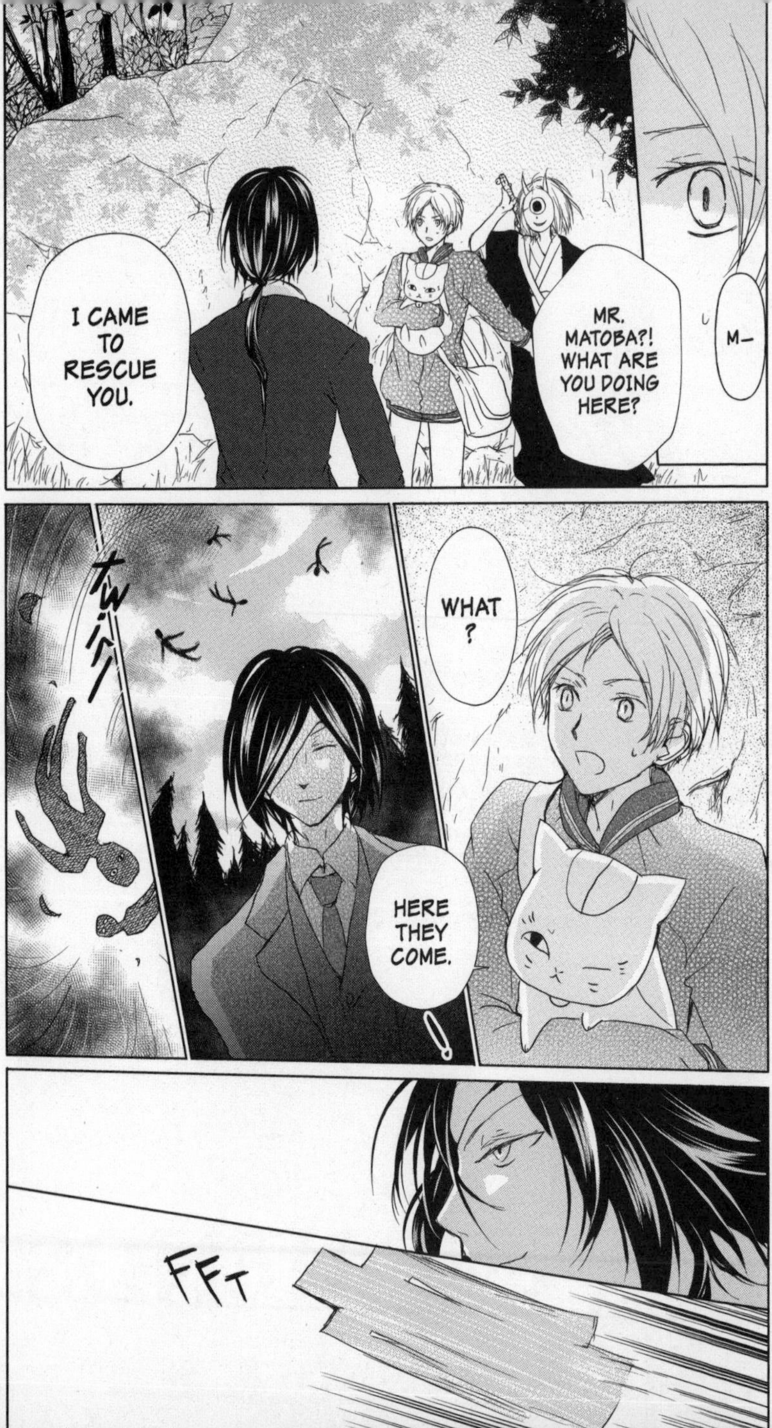
M—
MR. MATOBA?! WHAT ARE YOU DOING HERE?
I CAME TO RESCUE YOU.
WHAT?
HERE THEY COME.
FFT

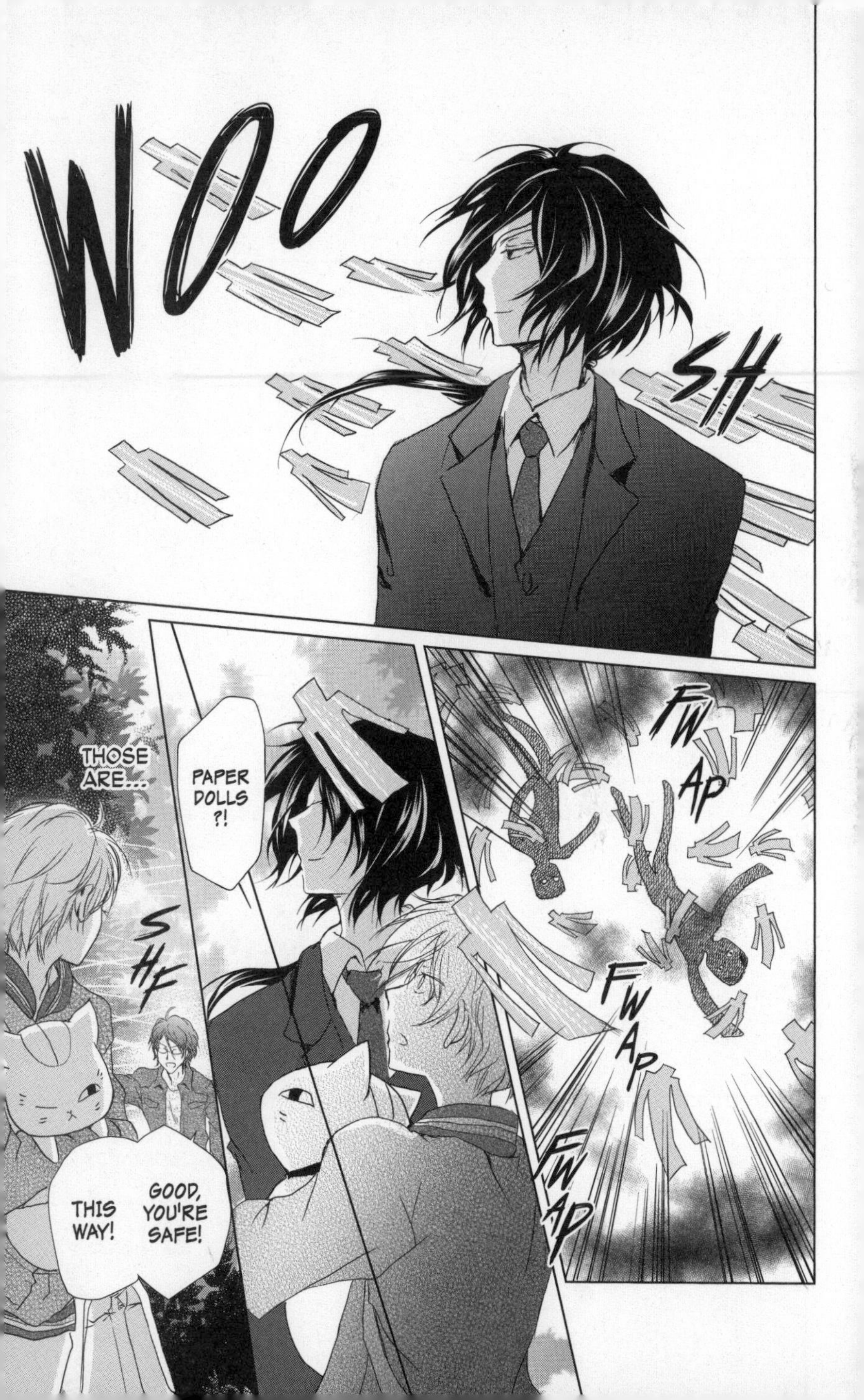
WOOOSH
FWAP
FWAP
FWAP
THOSE ARE...
PAPER DOLLS?!
SHF
GOOD, YOU'RE SAFE!
THIS WAY!

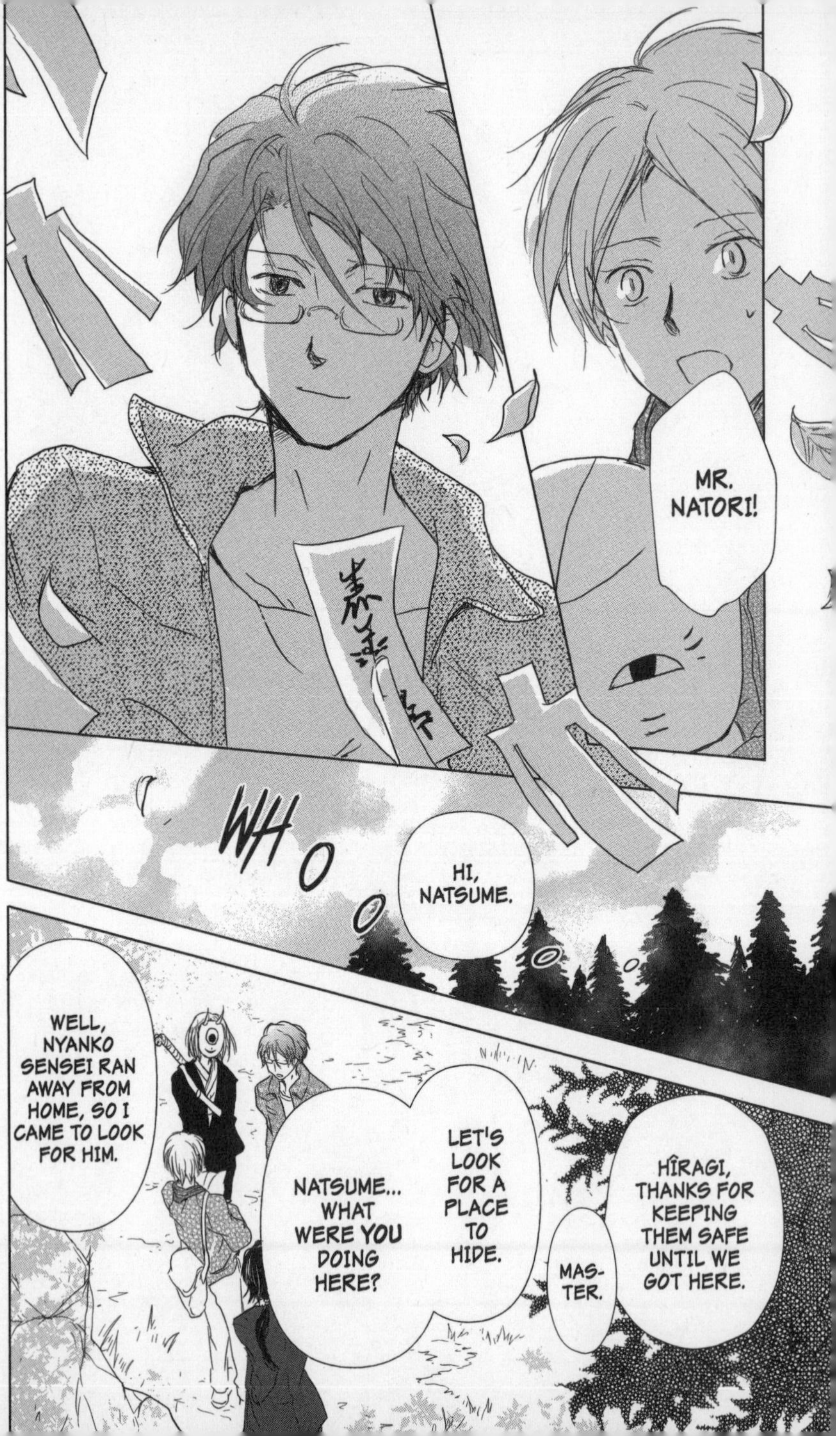
MR. NATORI!
WHOOOO
HI, NATSUME.
HÎRAGI, THANKS FOR KEEPING THEM SAFE UNTIL WE GOT HERE.
MAS-TER.
LET'S LOOK FOR A PLACE TO HIDE.
NATSUME... WHAT WERE YOU DOING HERE?
WELL, NYANKO SENSEI RAN AWAY FROM HOME, SO I CAME TO LOOK FOR HIM.

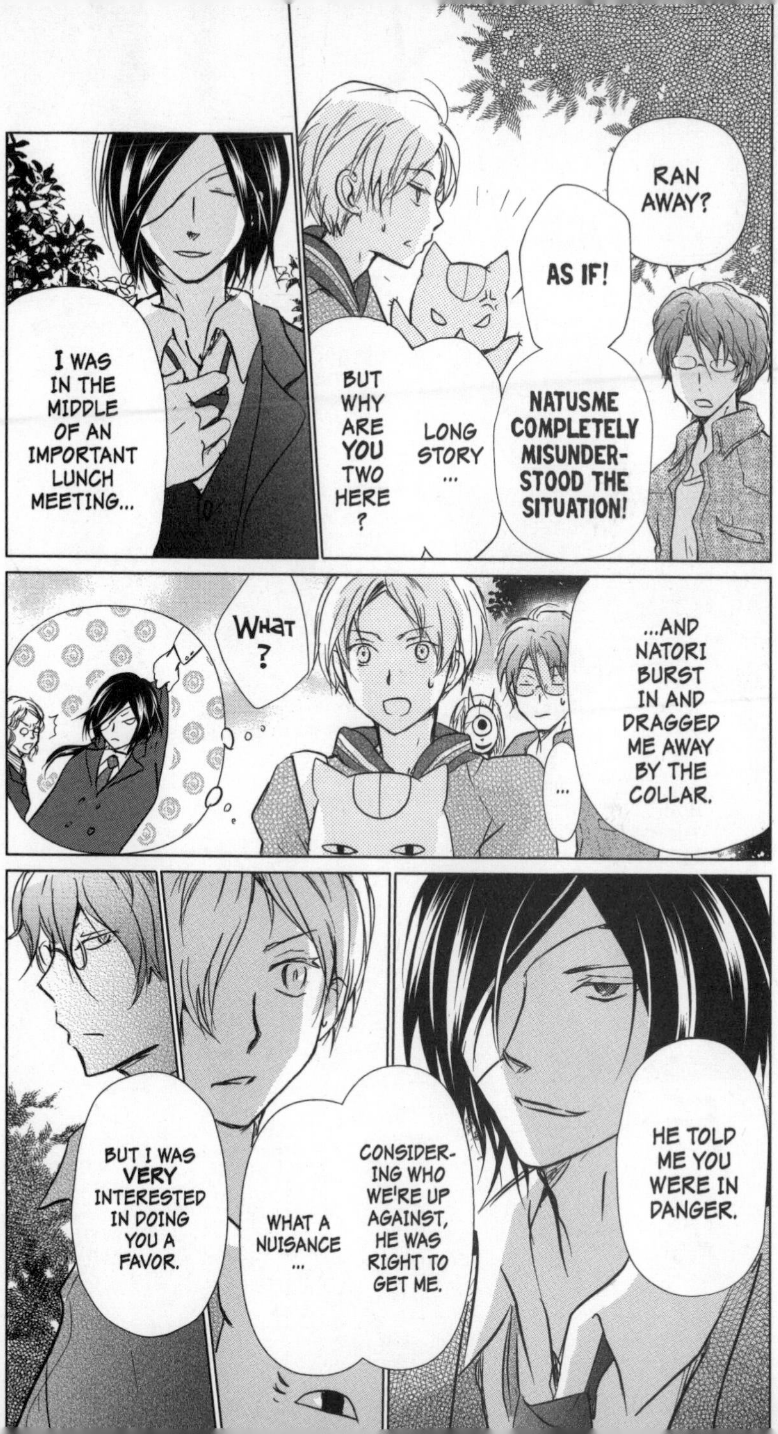
RAN AWAY?
AS IF!
NATUSME COMPLETELY MISUNDERSTOOD THE SITUATION!
LONG STORY ...
BUT WHY ARE YOU TWO HERE ?
I WAS IN THE MIDDLE OF AN IMPORTANT LUNCH MEETING...
...AND NATORI BURST IN AND DRAGGED ME AWAY BY THE COLLAR.
...
WHAT ?
HE TOLD ME YOU WERE IN DANGER.
CONSIDERING WHO WE'RE UP AGAINST, HE WAS RIGHT TO GET ME.
WHAT A NUISANCE ...
BUT I WAS VERY INTERESTED IN DOING YOU A FAVOR.

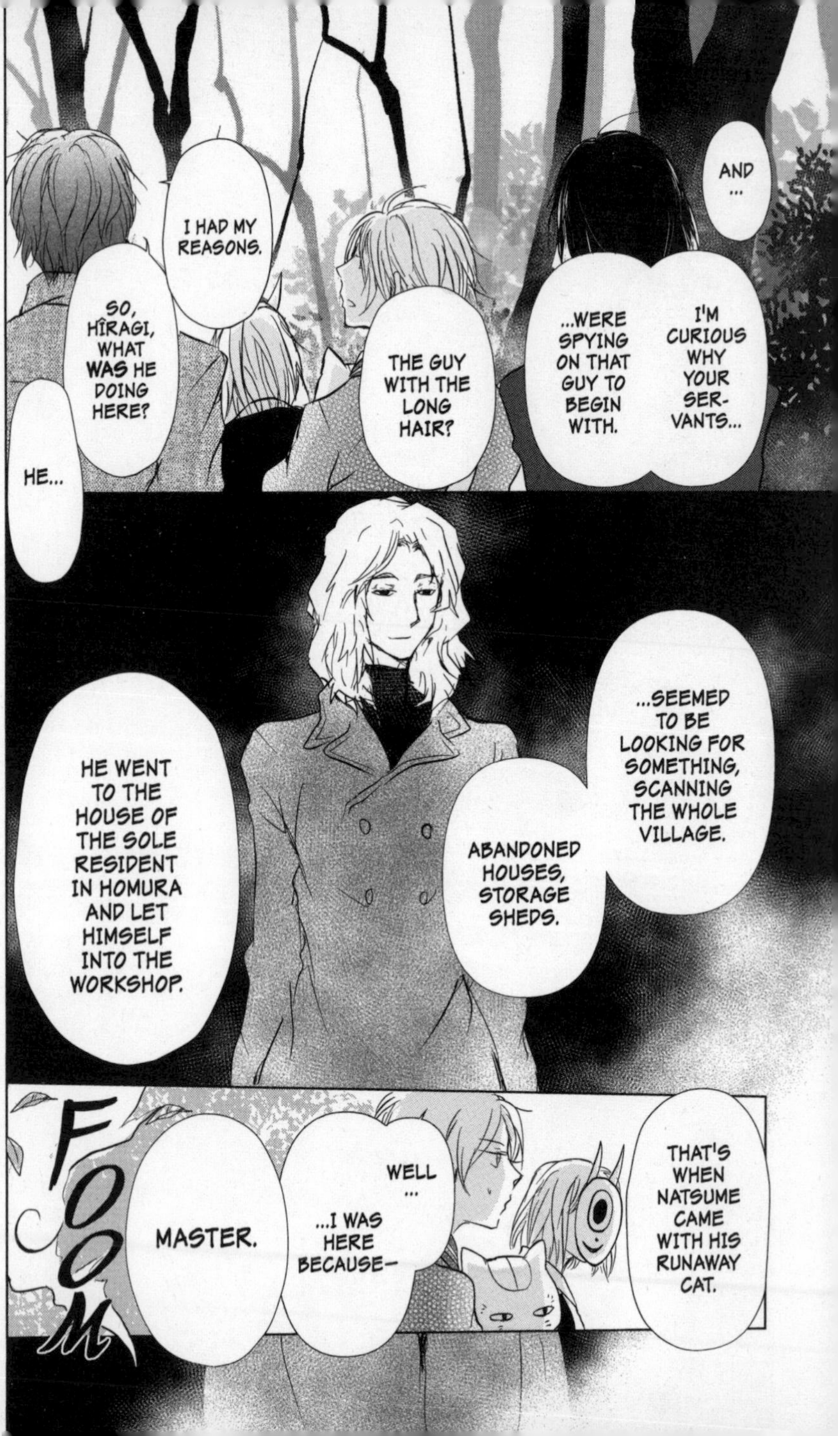
AND ...
I'M CURIOUS WHY YOUR SER-VANTS...
...WERE SPYING ON THAT GUY TO BEGIN WITH.
THE GUY WITH THE LONG HAIR?
I HAD MY REASONS.
SO, HÎRAGI, WHAT WAS HE DOING HERE?
HE...
...SEEMED TO BE LOOKING FOR SOMETHING, SCANNING THE WHOLE VILLAGE.
ABANDONED HOUSES, STORAGE SHEDS.
HE WENT TO THE HOUSE OF THE SOLE RESIDENT IN HOMURA AND LET HIMSELF INTO THE WORKSHOP.
THAT'S WHEN NATSUME CAME WITH HIS RUNAWAY CAT.
WELL ...
...I WAS HERE BECAUSE—
MASTER.
FOOM

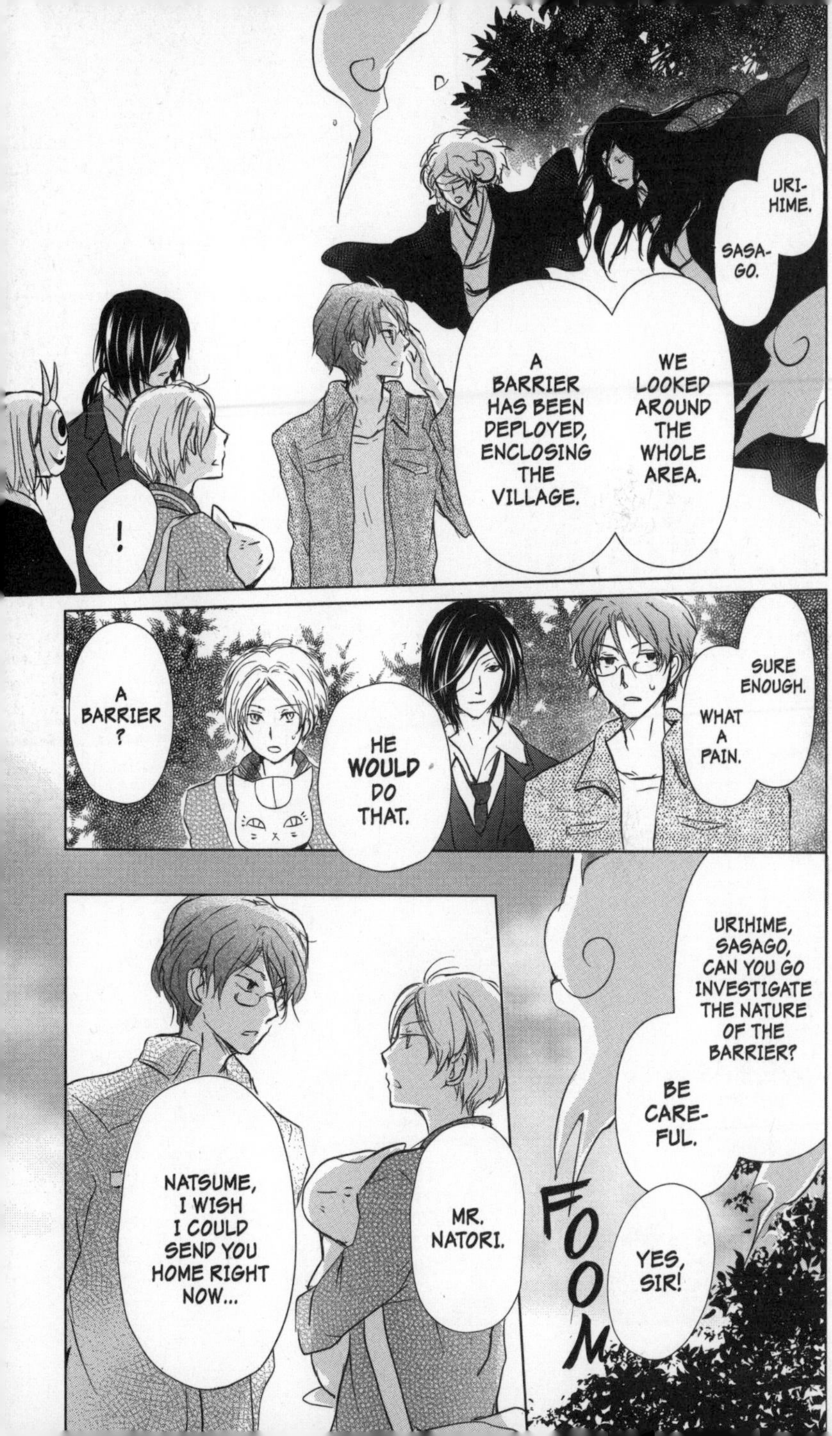
URI-HIME.
SASA-GO.
WE LOOKED AROUND THE WHOLE AREA.
A BARRIER HAS BEEN DEPLOYED, ENCLOSING THE VILLAGE.
!
SURE ENOUGH.
WHAT A PAIN.
HE WOULD DO THAT.
A BARRIER?
URIHIME, SASAGO, CAN YOU GO INVESTIGATE THE NATURE OF THE BARRIER?
BE CARE-FUL.
YES, SIR!
FOOM
MR. NATORI.
NATSUME, I WISH I COULD SEND YOU HOME RIGHT NOW...

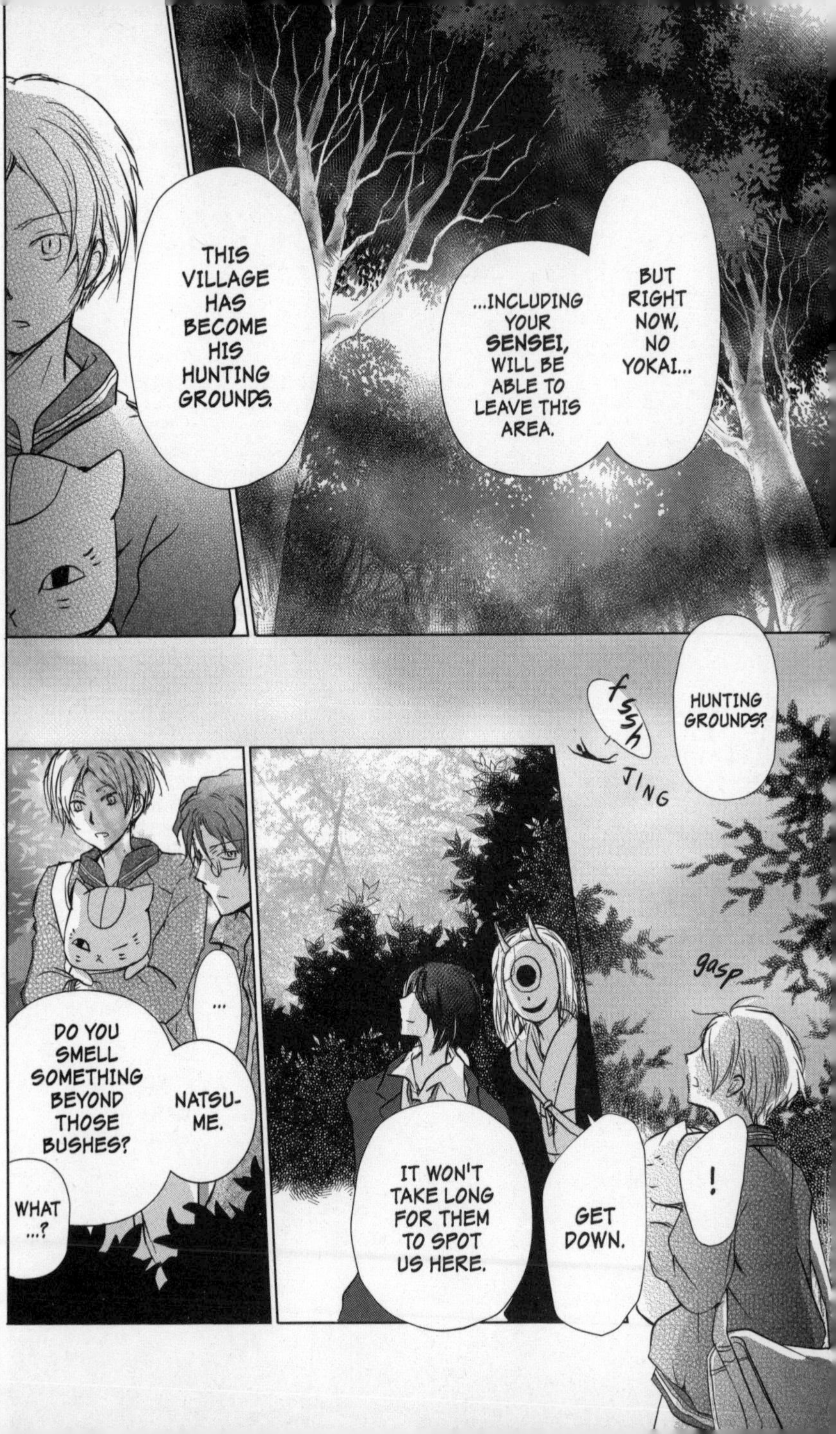
BUT RIGHT NOW, NO YOKAI...
...INCLUDING YOUR SENSEI, WILL BE ABLE TO LEAVE THIS AREA.
THIS VILLAGE HAS BECOME HIS HUNTING GROUNDS.
HUNTING GROUNDS?
fssh
JING
gasp
!
GET DOWN.
IT WON'T TAKE LONG FOR THEM TO SPOT US HERE.
...
NATSUME.
DO YOU SMELL SOMETHING BEYOND THOSE BUSHES?
WHAT ...?

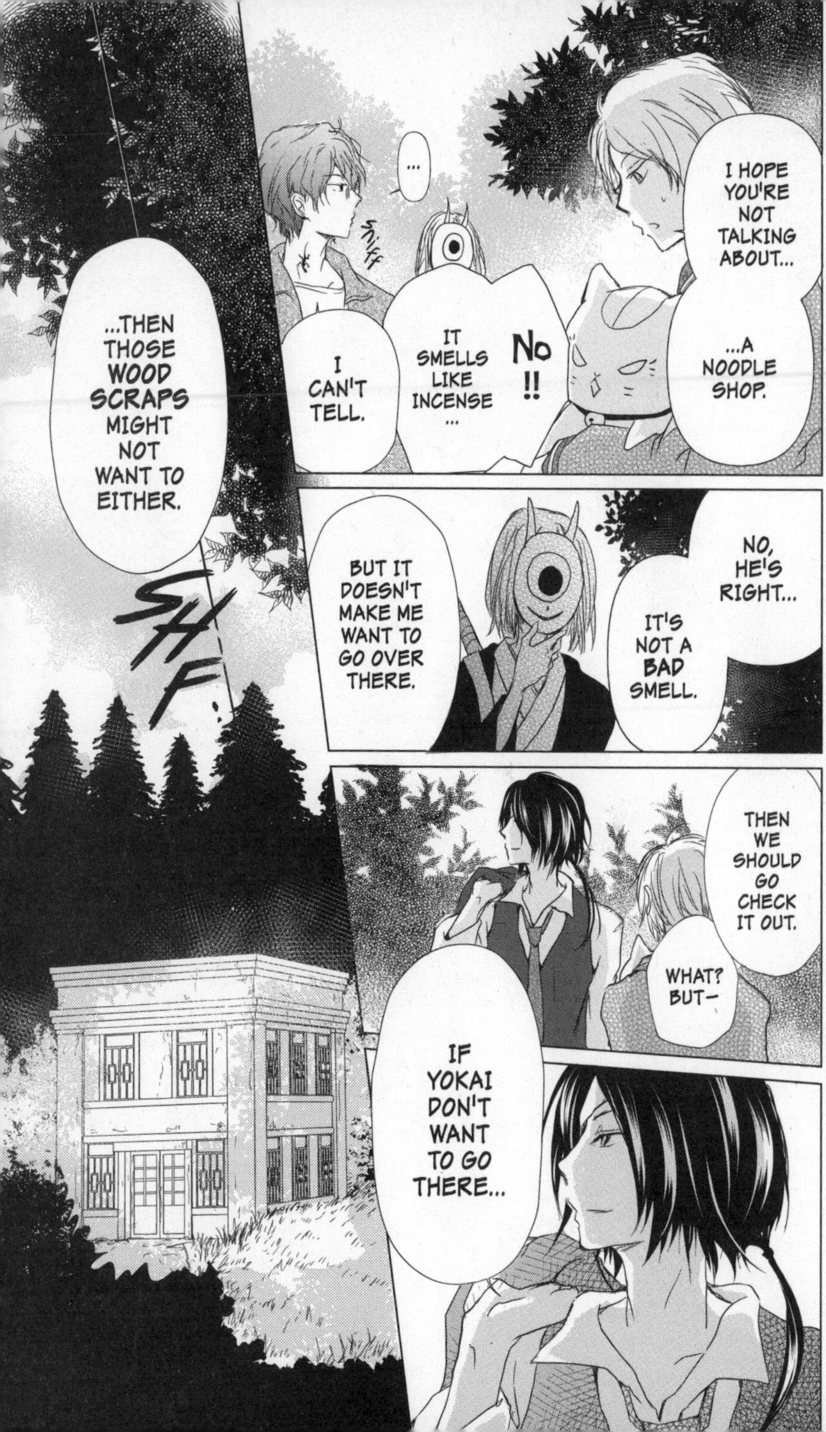
I HOPE YOU'RE NOT TALKING ABOUT...
...A NOODLE SHOP.
No!!
...
SNIFF
IT SMELLS LIKE INCENSE...
I CAN'T TELL.
NO, HE'S RIGHT...
IT'S NOT A BAD SMELL.
BUT IT DOESN'T MAKE ME WANT TO GO OVER THERE.
THEN WE SHOULD GO CHECK IT OUT.
WHAT? BUT—
IF YOKAI DON'T WANT TO GO THERE...
...THEN THOSE WOOD SCRAPS MIGHT NOT WANT TO EITHER.
SHF

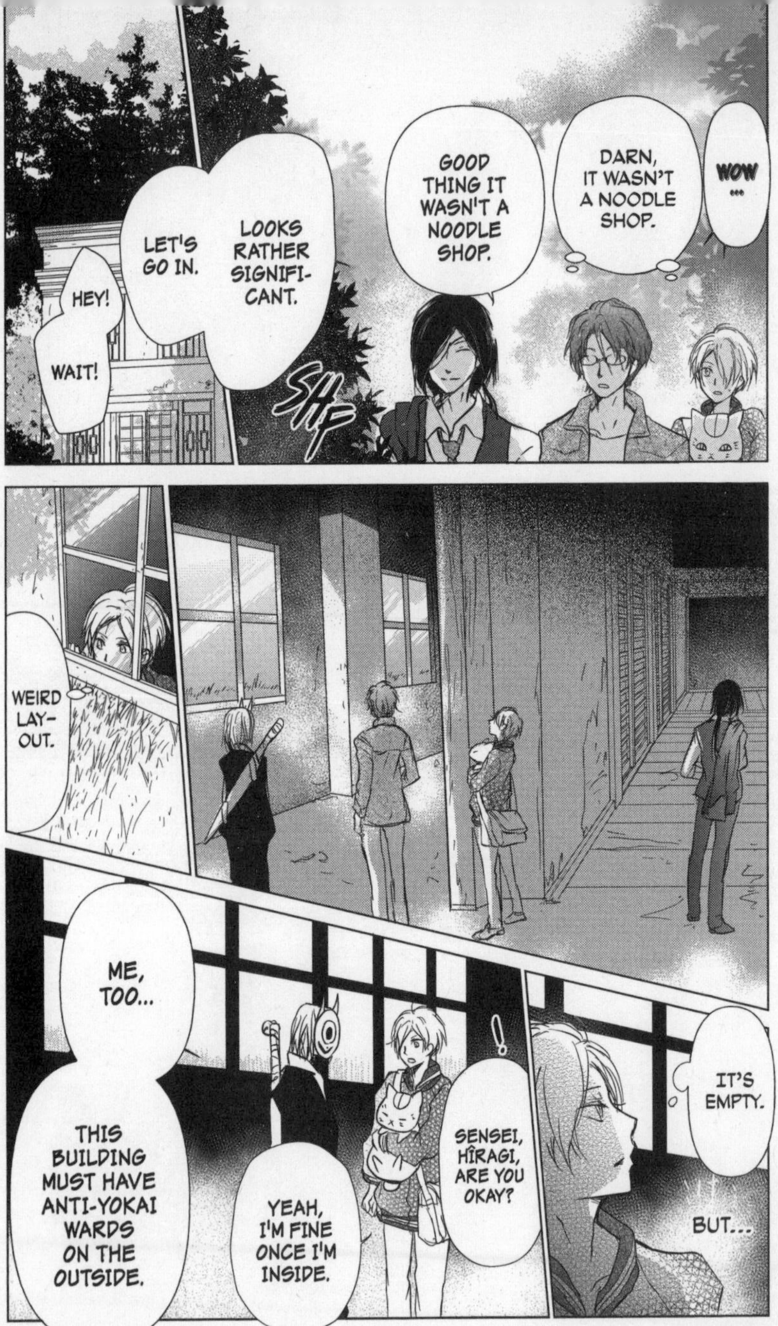
WOW...
DARN, IT WASN'T A NOODLE SHOP.
GOOD THING IT WASN'T A NOODLE SHOP.
LOOKS RATHER SIGNIFI-CANT.
LET'S GO IN.
SHF
HEY!
WAIT!
WEIRD LAY-OUT.
IT'S EMPTY.
BUT...
!
SENSEI, HÎRAGI, ARE YOU OKAY?
YEAH, I'M FINE ONCE I'M INSIDE.
ME, TOO...
THIS BUILDING MUST HAVE ANTI-YOKAI WARDS ON THE OUTSIDE.

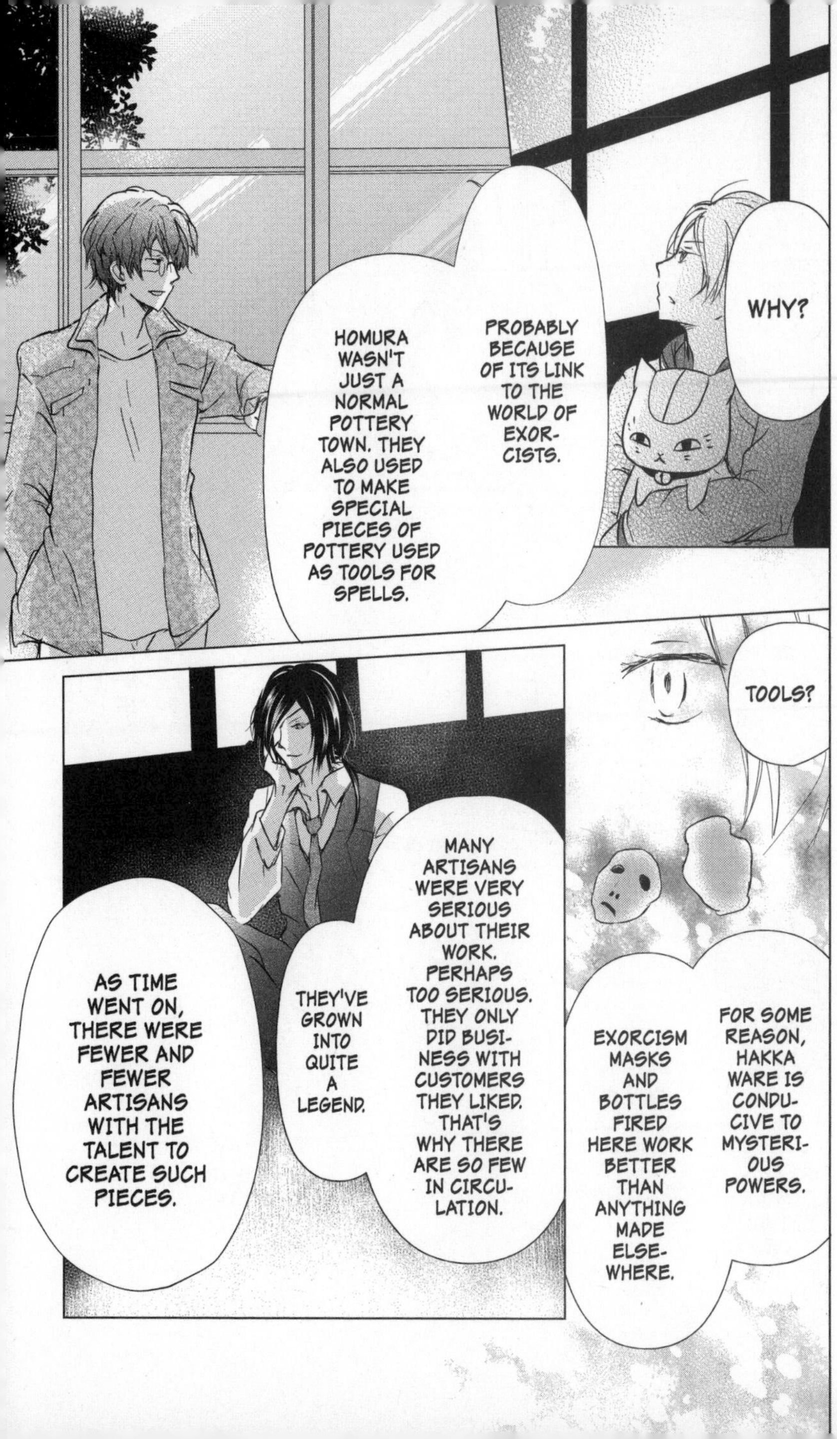
WHY?
PROBABLY BECAUSE OF ITS LINK TO THE WORLD OF EXOR-CISTS.
HOMURA WASN'T JUST A NORMAL POTTERY TOWN. THEY ALSO USED TO MAKE SPECIAL PIECES OF POTTERY USED AS TOOLS FOR SPELLS.
TOOLS?
FOR SOME REASON, HAKKA WARE IS CONDU-CIVE TO MYSTERI-OUS POWERS.
EXORCISM MASKS AND BOTTLES FIRED HERE WORK BETTER THAN ANYTHING MADE ELSE-WHERE.
MANY ARTISANS WERE VERY SERIOUS ABOUT THEIR WORK. PERHAPS TOO SERIOUS. THEY ONLY DID BUSI-NESS WITH CUSTOMERS THEY LIKED. THAT'S WHY THERE ARE SO FEW IN CIRCU-LATION.
THEY'VE GROWN INTO QUITE A LEGEND.
AS TIME WENT ON, THERE WERE FEWER AND FEWER ARTISANS WITH THE TALENT TO CREATE SUCH PIECES.

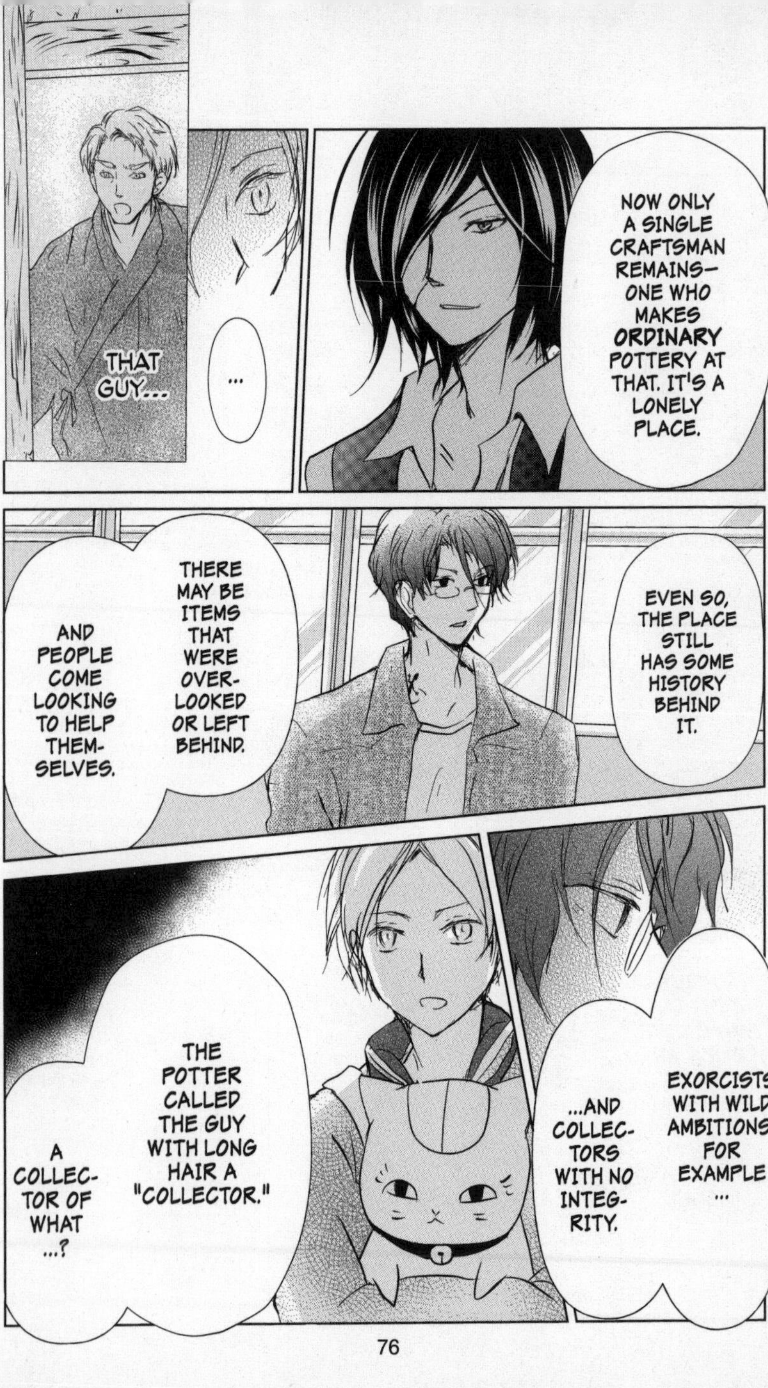
NOW ONLY A SINGLE CRAFTSMAN REMAINS—ONE WHO MAKES ORDINARY POTTERY AT THAT. IT'S A LONELY PLACE.
...
THAT GUY...
EVEN SO, THE PLACE STILL HAS SOME HISTORY BEHIND IT.
THERE MAY BE ITEMS THAT WERE OVERLOOKED OR LEFT BEHIND.
AND PEOPLE COME LOOKING TO HELP THEMSELVES.
EXORCISTS WITH WILD AMBITIONS, FOR EXAMPLE...
...AND COLLECTORS WITH NO INTEGRITY.
THE POTTER CALLED THE GUY WITH LONG HAIR A "COLLECTOR."
A COLLECTOR OF WHAT...?

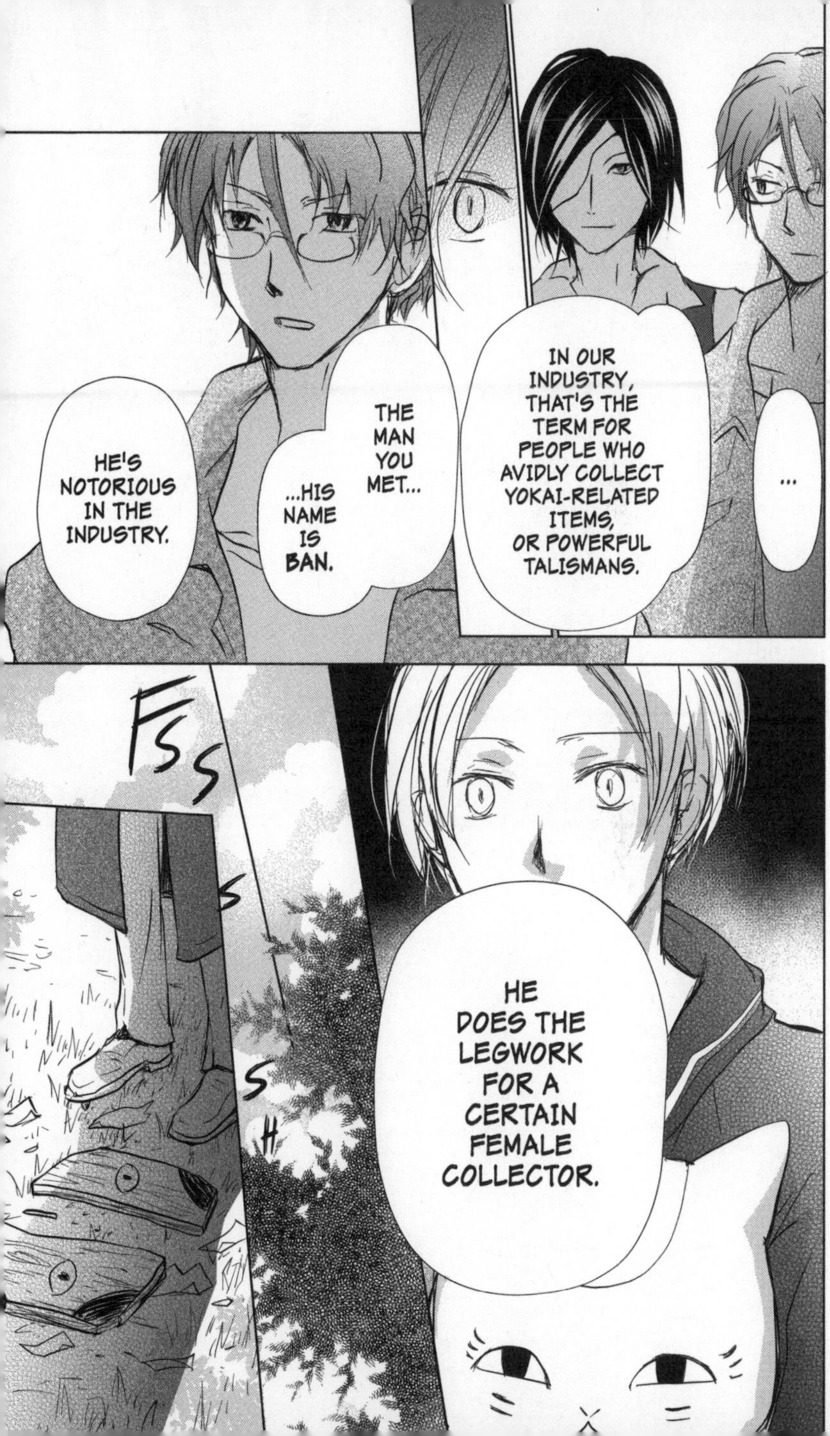
IN OUR INDUSTRY, THAT'S THE TERM FOR PEOPLE WHO AVIDLY COLLECT YOKAI-RELATED ITEMS, OR POWERFUL TALISMANS.
...
THE MAN YOU MET...
...HIS NAME IS BAN.
HE'S NOTORIOUS IN THE INDUSTRY.
HE DOES THE LEGWORK FOR A CERTAIN FEMALE COLLECTOR.
FSS

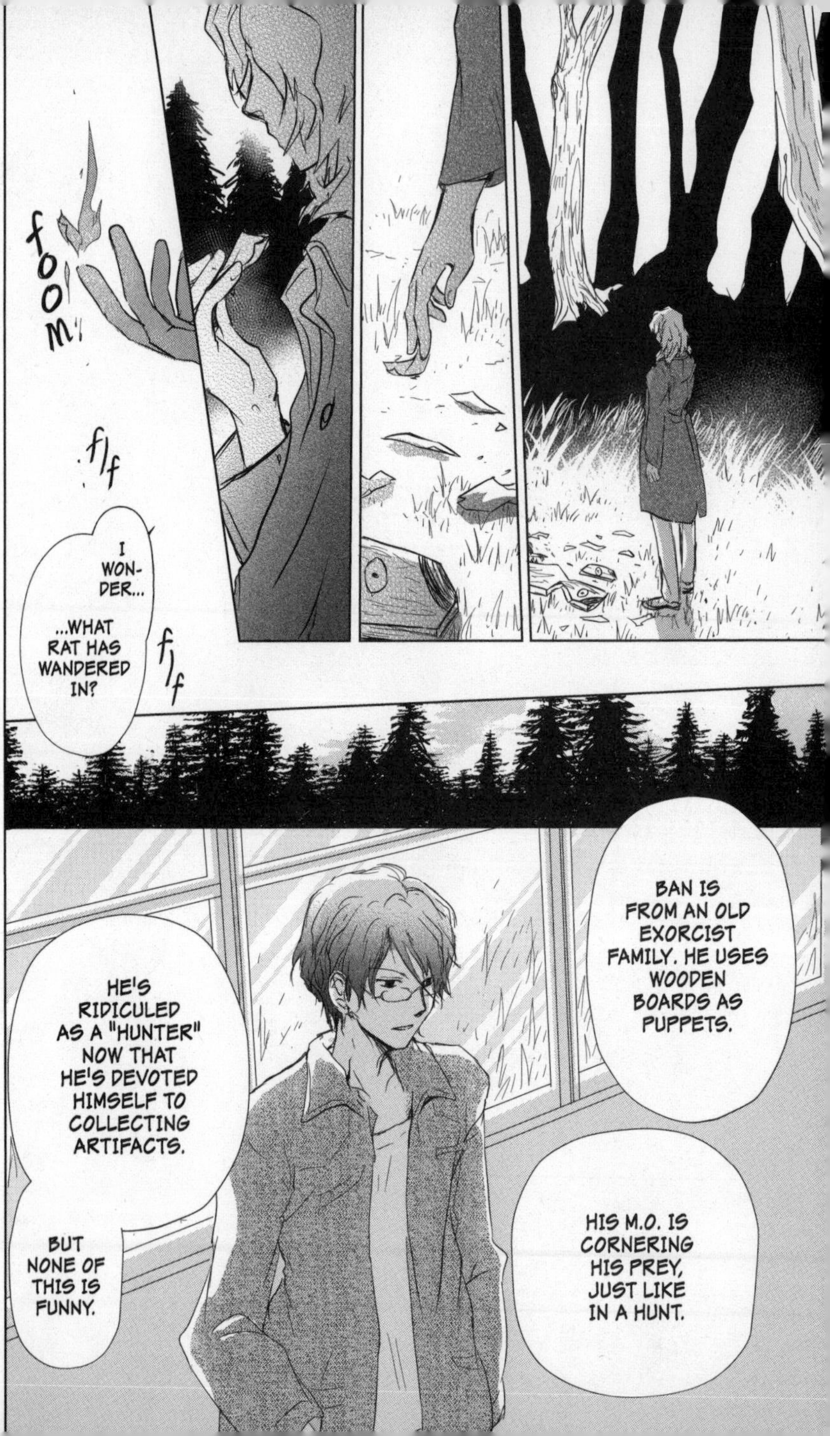
foom
fl f
I WONDER...
...WHAT RAT HAS WANDERED IN?
fl f
BAN IS FROM AN OLD EXORCIST FAMILY. HE USES WOODEN BOARDS AS PUPPETS.
HIS M.O. IS CORNERING HIS PREY, JUST LIKE IN A HUNT.
HE'S RIDICULED AS A "HUNTER" NOW THAT HE'S DEVOTED HIMSELF TO COLLECTING ARTIFACTS.
BUT NONE OF THIS IS FUNNY.

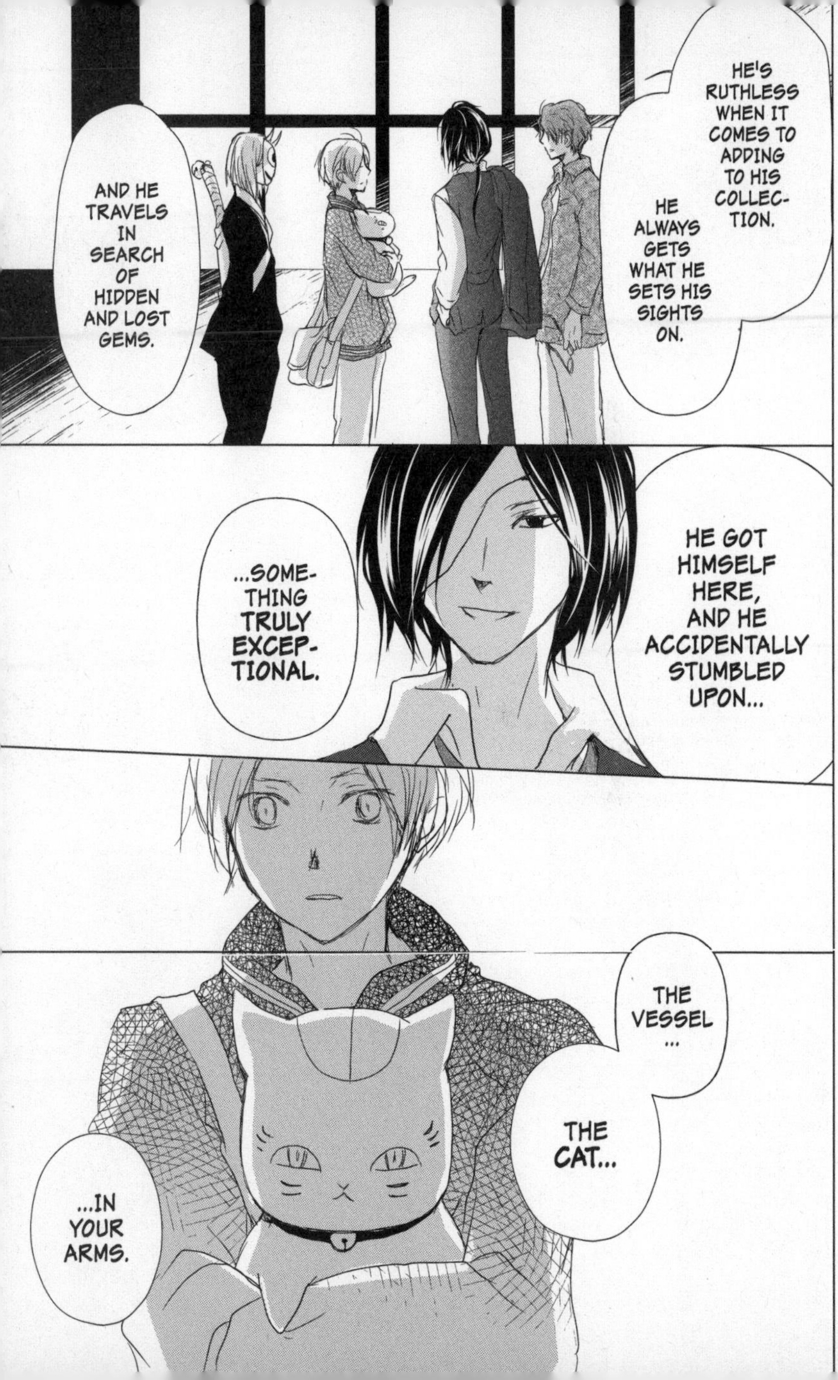
HE'S RUTHLESS WHEN IT COMES TO ADDING TO HIS COLLECTION.
HE ALWAYS GETS WHAT HE SETS HIS SIGHTS ON.
AND HE TRAVELS IN SEARCH OF HIDDEN AND LOST GEMS.
HE GOT HIMSELF HERE, AND HE ACCIDENTALLY STUMBLED UPON...
...SOMETHING TRULY EXCEPTIONAL.
THE VESSEL ...
THE CAT...
...IN YOUR ARMS.

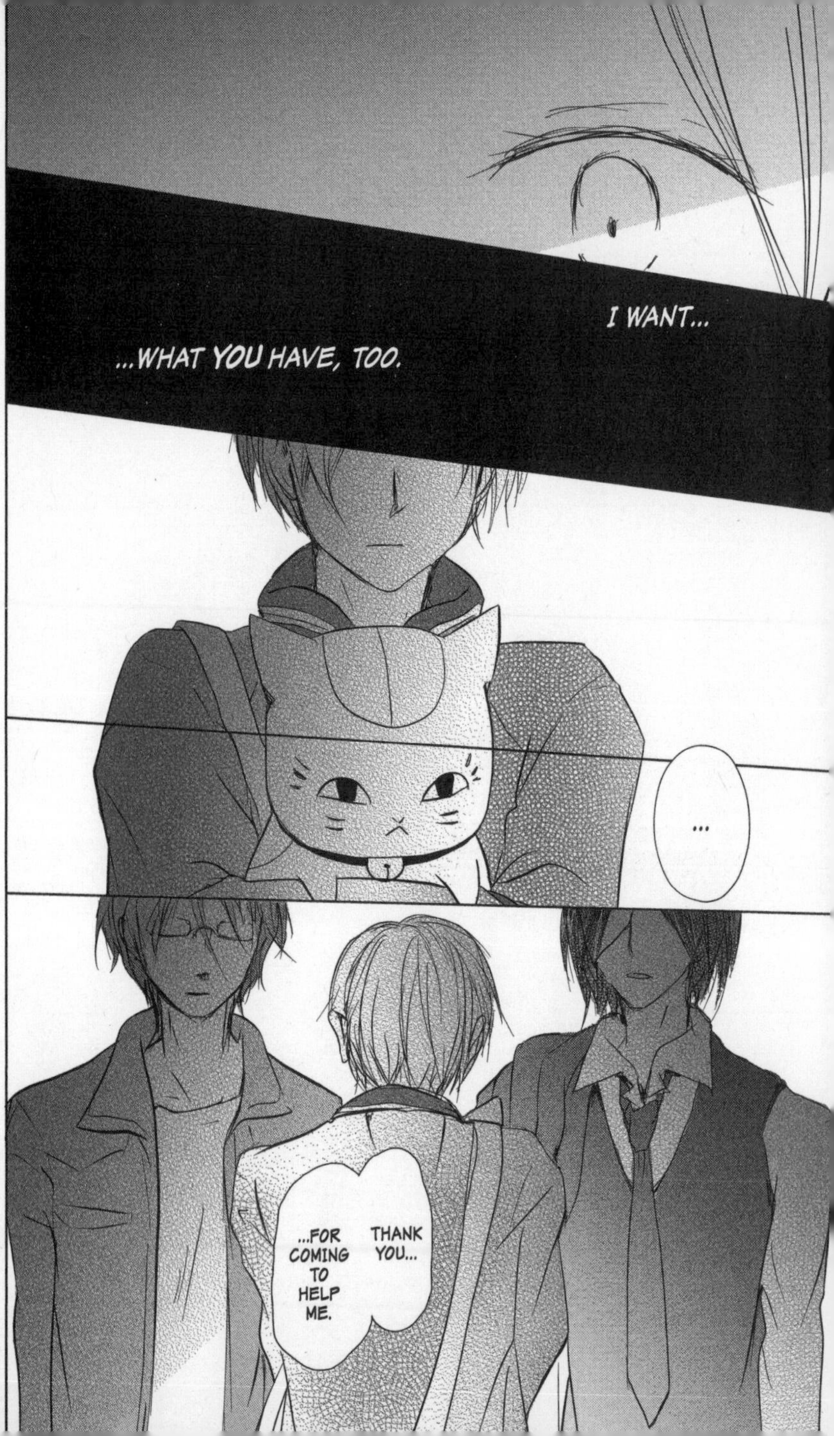
I WANT...
...WHAT YOU HAVE, TOO.
...
THANK YOU...
...FOR COMING TO HELP ME.

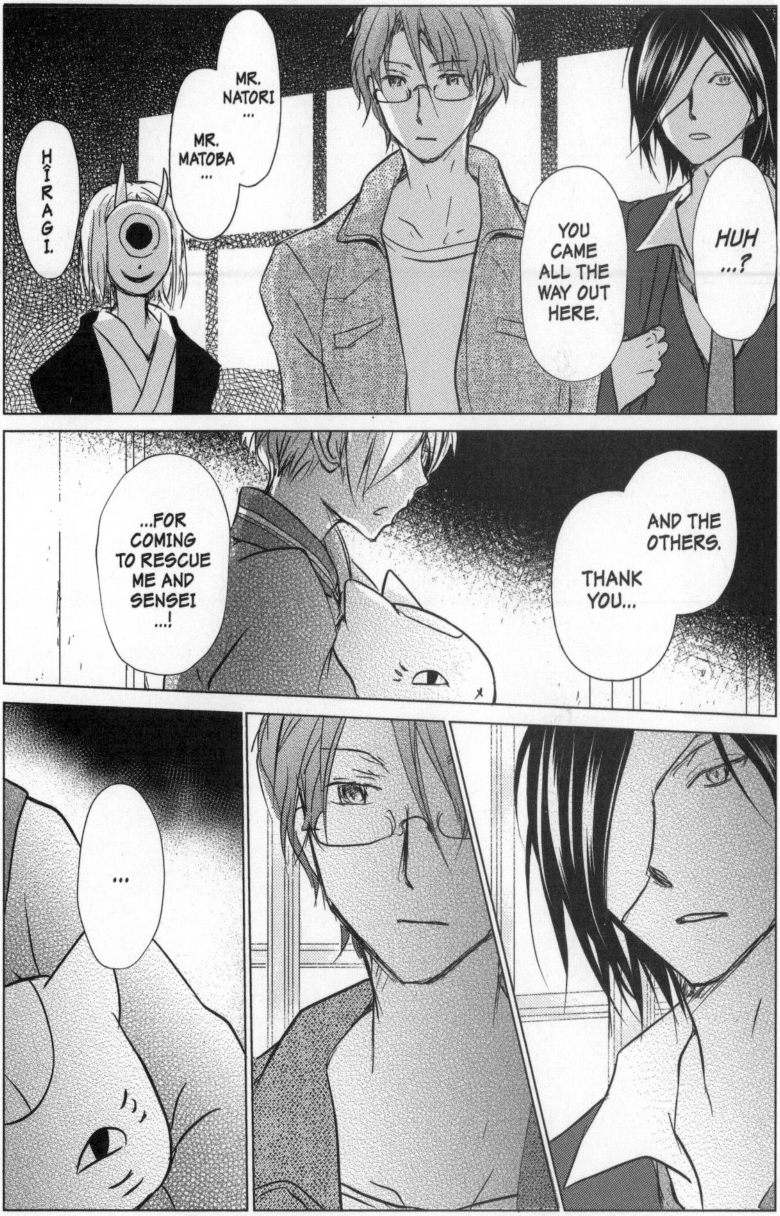
HUH ...?
YOU CAME ALL THE WAY OUT HERE.
MR. NATORI ...
MR. MATOBA ...
HÎRAGI.
AND THE OTHERS.
THANK YOU...
...FOR COMING TO RESCUE ME AND SENSEI ...!
...

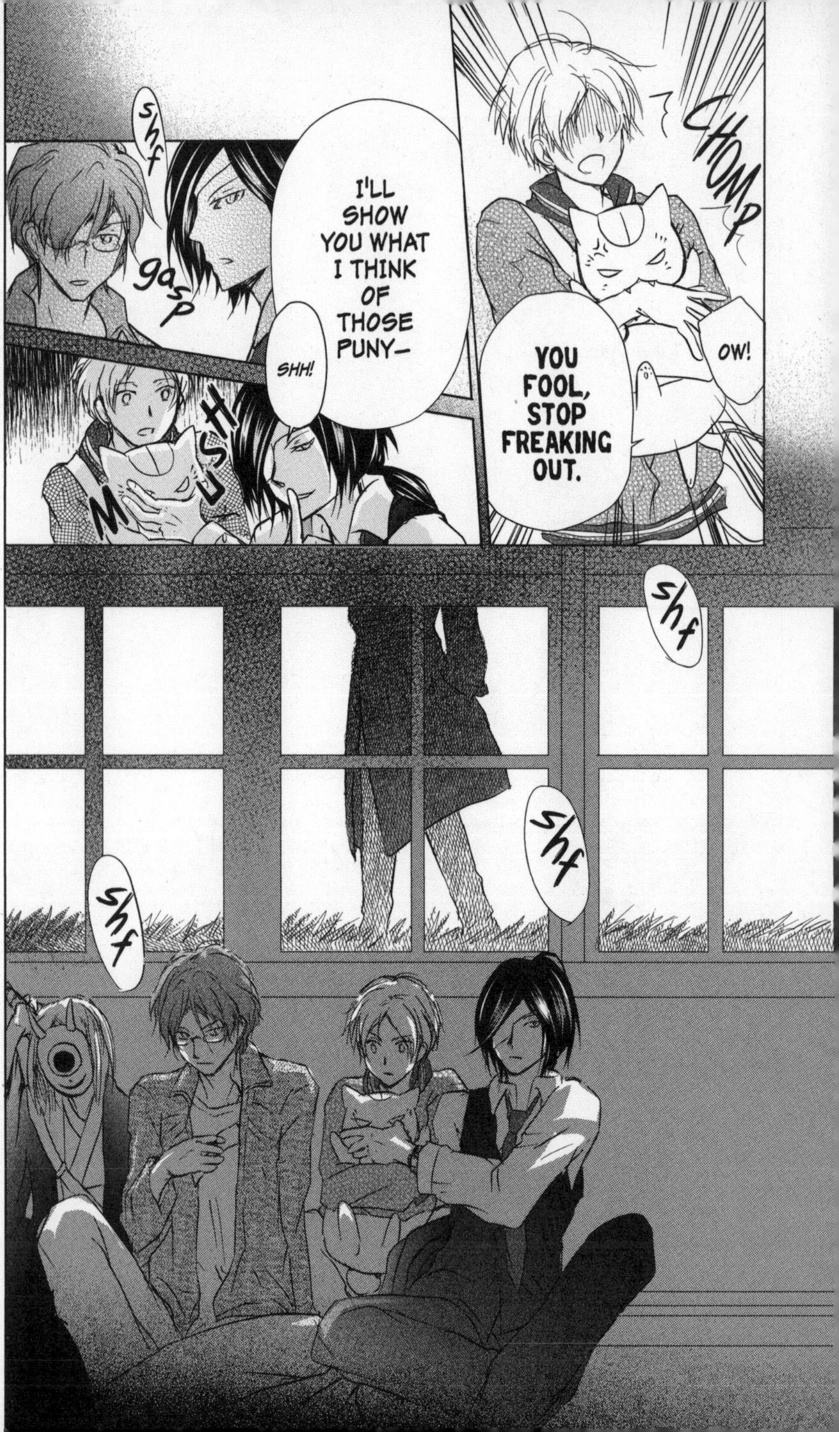
CHOMP
OW!
YOU FOOL, STOP FREAKING OUT.
I'LL SHOW YOU WHAT I THINK OF THOSE PUNY—
shf
gasp
SHH!
MUSH
shf
shf
shf

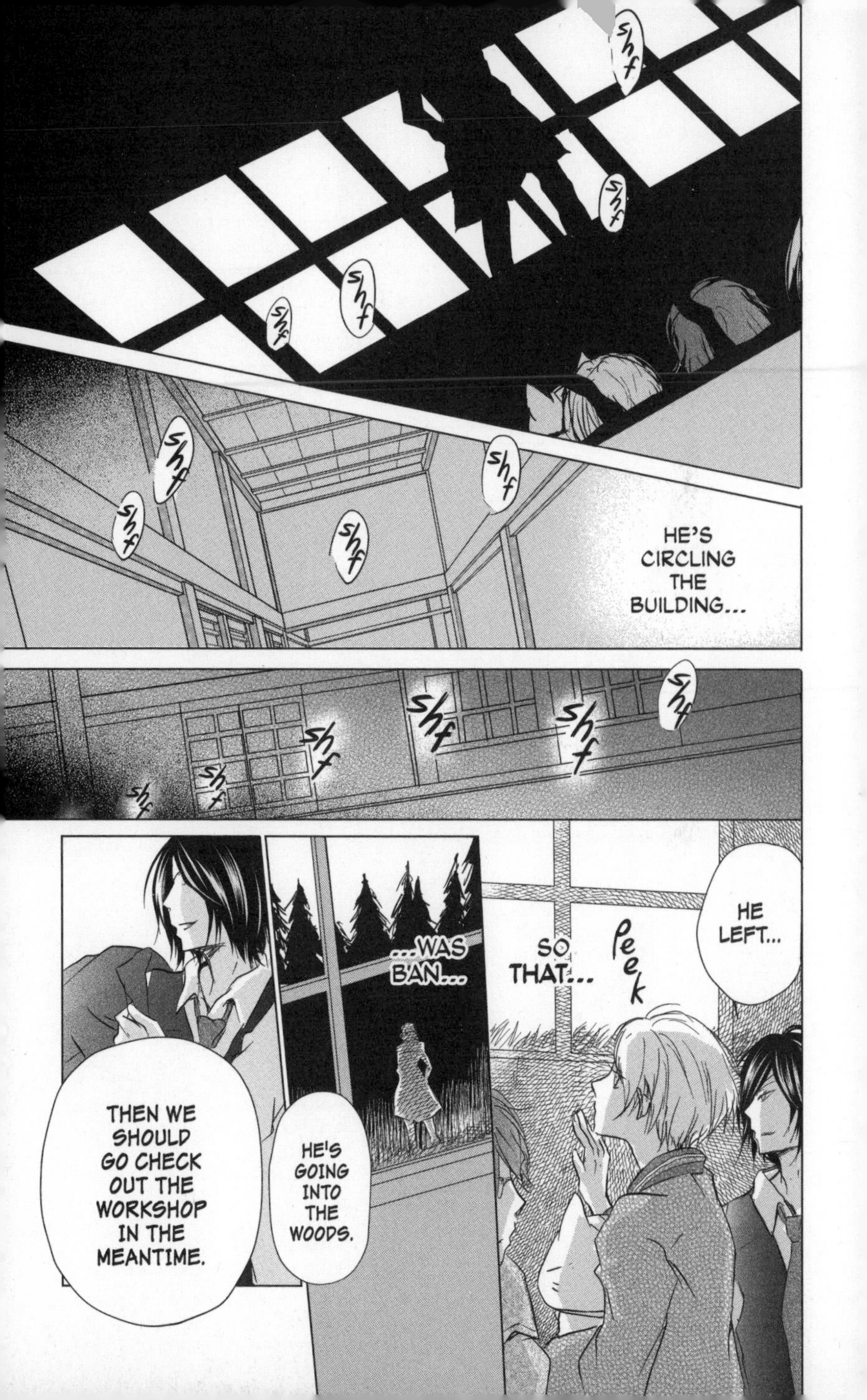
shf
shf
shf
shf
shf
shf
shf
shf
HE'S CIRCLING THE BUILDING...
shf
shf
shf
shf
shf
shf
HE LEFT...
Peek
SO THAT...
...WAS BAN...
HE'S GOING INTO THE WOODS.
THEN WE SHOULD GO CHECK OUT THE WORKSHOP IN THE MEANTIME.

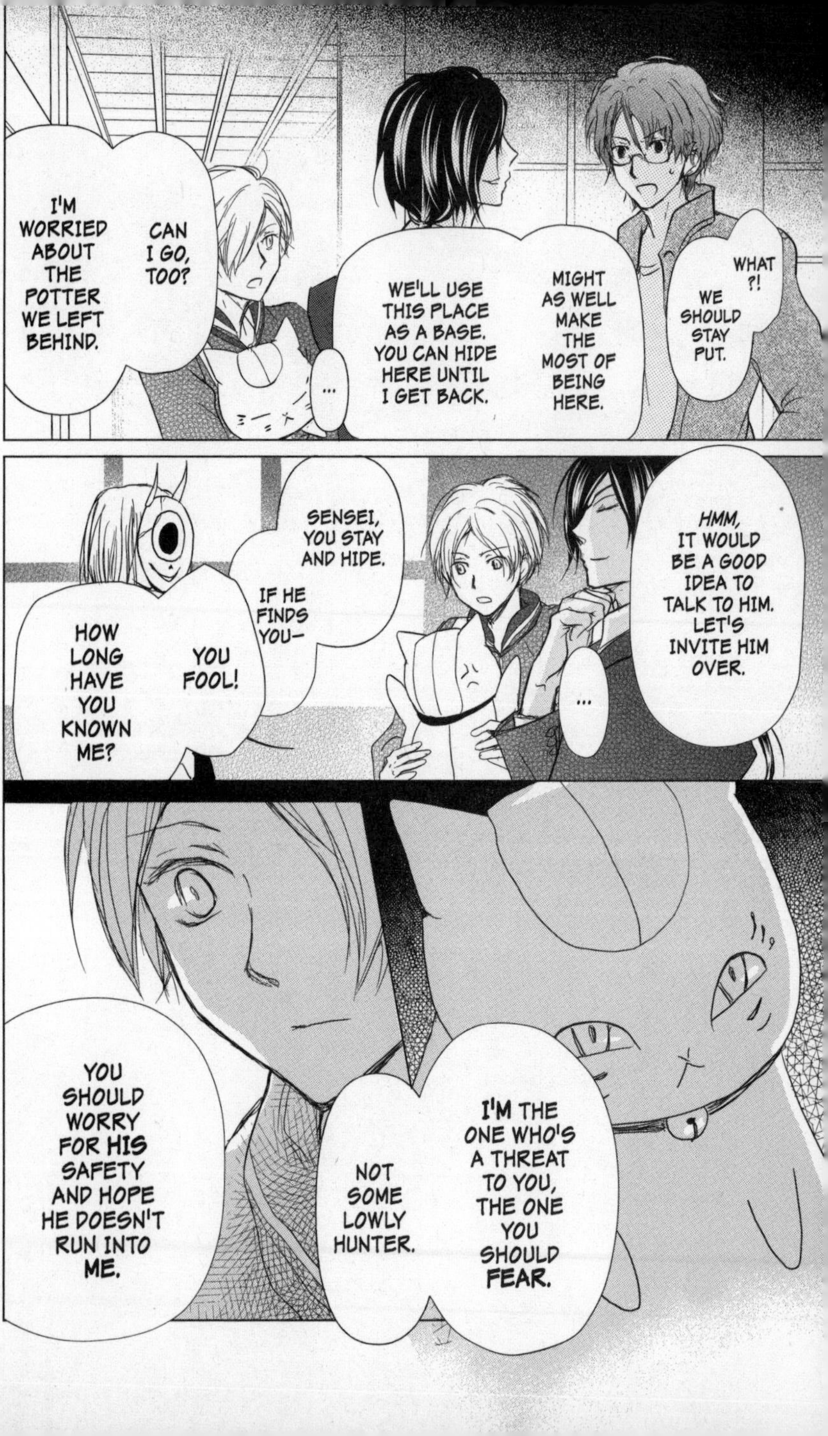
WHAT?!
WE SHOULD STAY PUT.
MIGHT AS WELL MAKE THE MOST OF BEING HERE.
WE'LL USE THIS PLACE AS A BASE. YOU CAN HIDE HERE UNTIL I GET BACK.
...
CAN I GO, TOO?
I'M WORRIED ABOUT THE POTTER WE LEFT BEHIND.
HMM, IT WOULD BE A GOOD IDEA TO TALK TO HIM. LET'S INVITE HIM OVER.
...
SENSEI, YOU STAY AND HIDE.
IF HE FINDS YOU—
YOU FOOL!
HOW LONG HAVE YOU KNOWN ME?
I'M THE ONE WHO'S A THREAT TO YOU, THE ONE YOU SHOULD **FEAR.**
NOT SOME LOWLY HUNTER.
YOU SHOULD WORRY FOR **HIS** SAFETY AND HOPE HE DOESN'T RUN INTO **ME.**

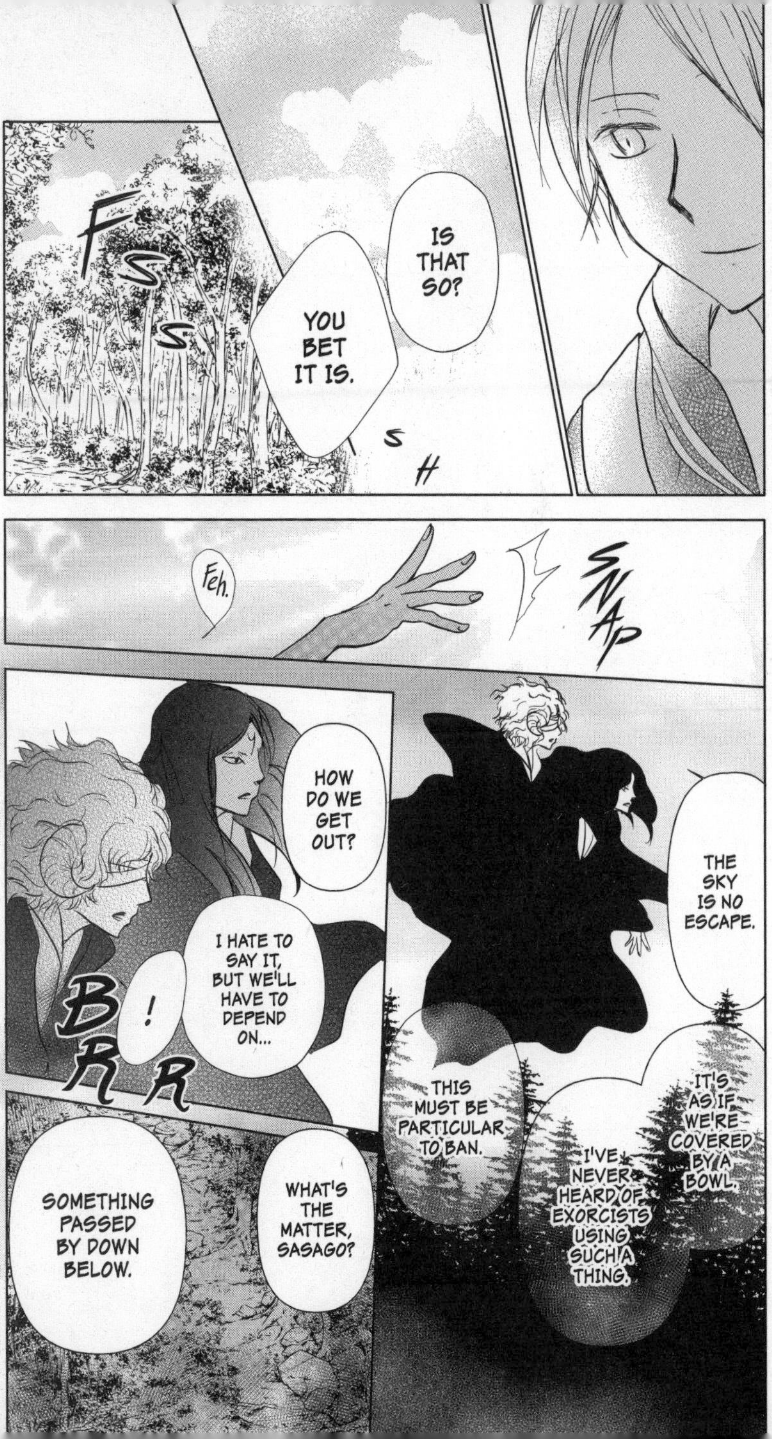
IS THAT SO?
YOU BET IT IS.
SH
FSS
SNAP
Feh.
THE SKY IS NO ESCAPE.
IT'S AS IF WE'RE COVERED BY A BOWL.
I'VE NEVER HEARD OF EXORCISTS USING SUCH A THING.
THIS MUST BE PARTICULAR TO BAN.
HOW DO WE GET OUT?
I HATE TO SAY IT, BUT WE'LL HAVE TO DEPEND ON...
!
BRR
WHAT'S THE MATTER, SASAGO?
SOMETHING PASSED BY DOWN BELOW.

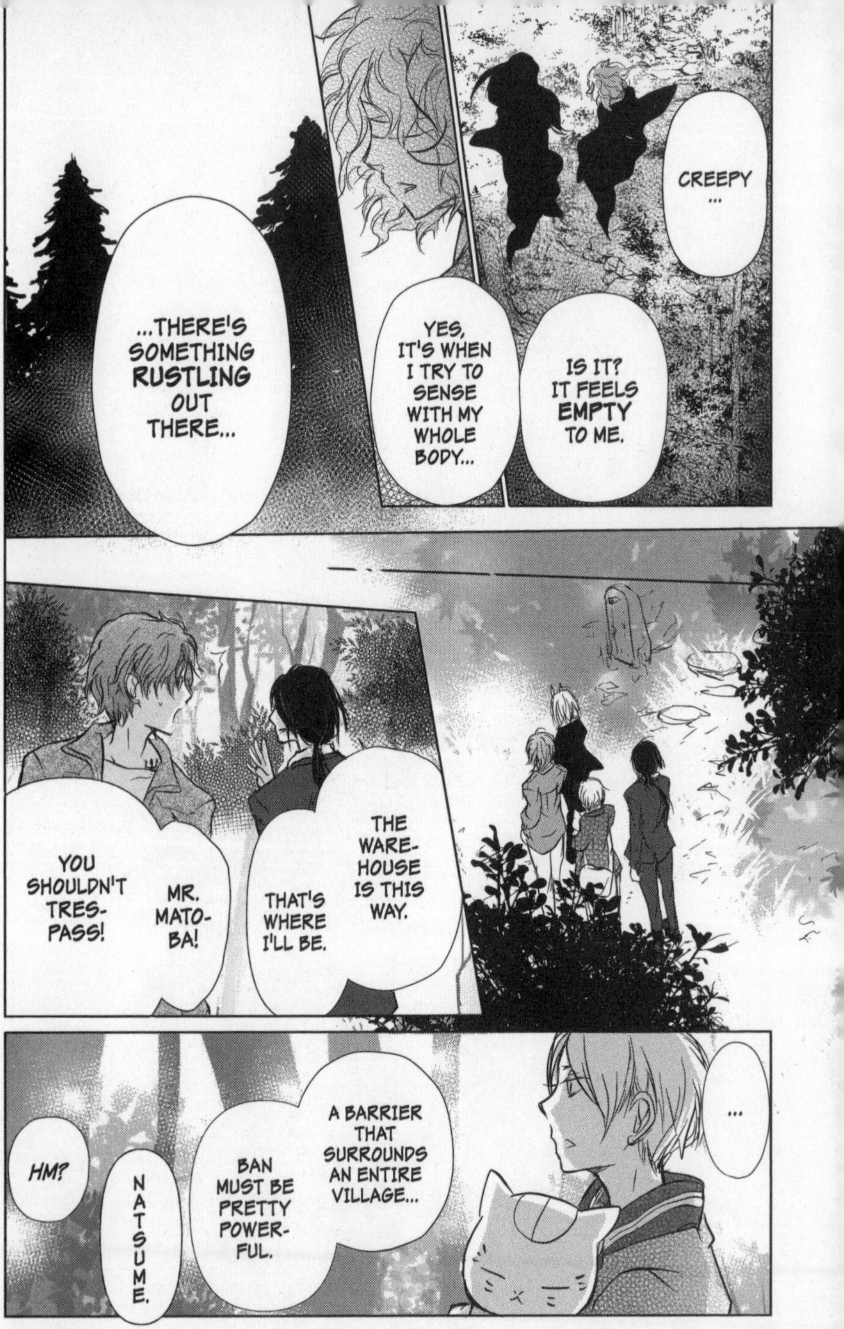
CREEPY...
IS IT? IT FEELS EMPTY TO ME.
YES, IT'S WHEN I TRY TO SENSE WITH MY WHOLE BODY...
...THERE'S SOMETHING RUSTLING OUT THERE...
THE WAREHOUSE IS THIS WAY.
THAT'S WHERE I'LL BE.
MR. MATOBA!
YOU SHOULDN'T TRESPASS!
...
A BARRIER THAT SURROUNDS AN ENTIRE VILLAGE...
BAN MUST BE PRETTY POWERFUL.
NATSUME.
HM?

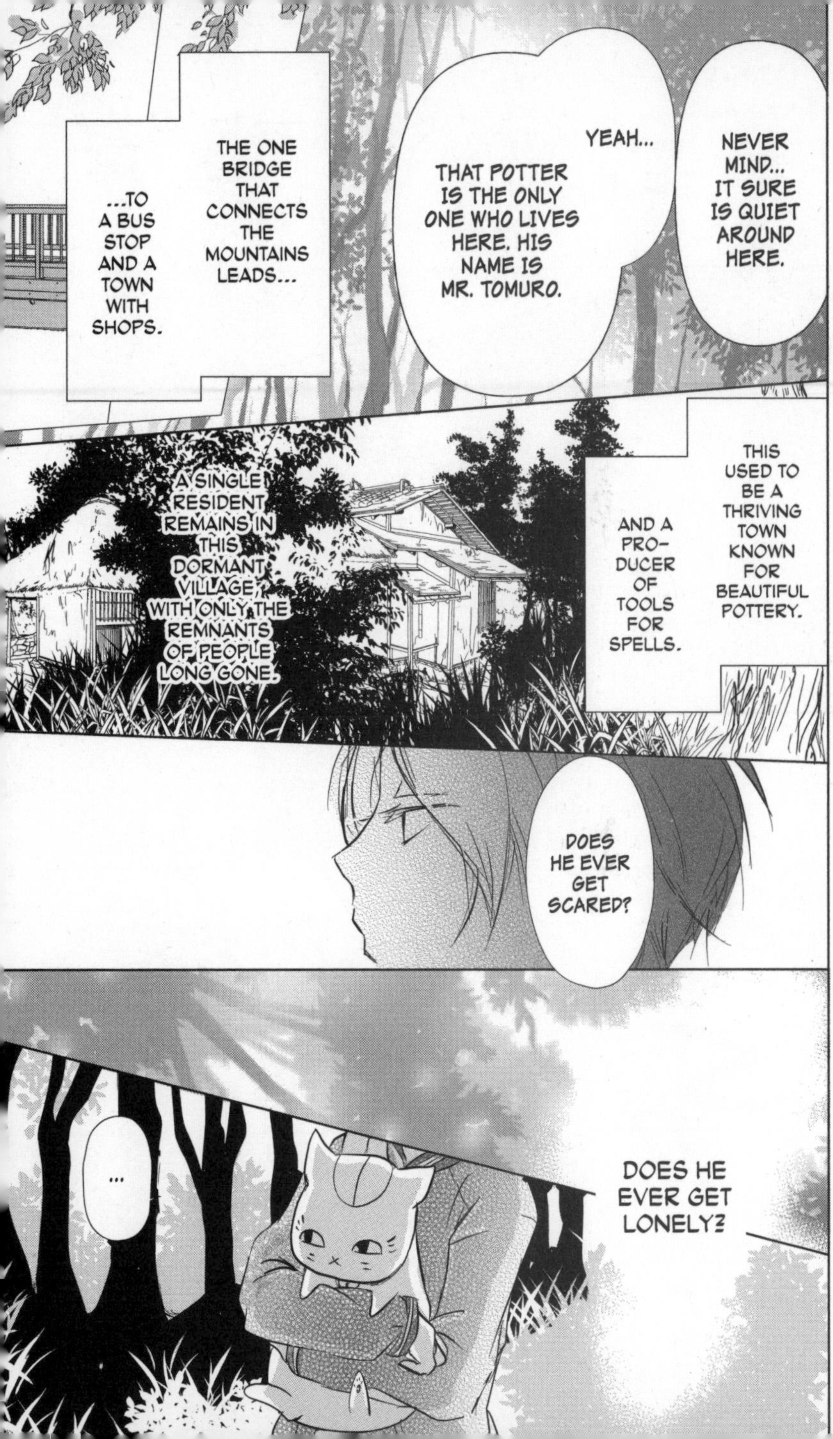
NEVER MIND... IT SURE IS QUIET AROUND HERE.
YEAH...
THAT POTTER IS THE ONLY ONE WHO LIVES HERE. HIS NAME IS MR. TOMURO.
THE ONE BRIDGE THAT CONNECTS THE MOUNTAINS LEADS...
...TO A BUS STOP AND A TOWN WITH SHOPS.
THIS USED TO BE A THRIVING TOWN KNOWN FOR BEAUTIFUL POTTERY.
AND A PRO-DUCER OF TOOLS FOR SPELLS.
A SINGLE RESIDENT REMAINS IN THIS DORMANT VILLAGE, WITH ONLY THE REMNANTS OF PEOPLE LONG GONE.
DOES HE EVER GET SCARED?
DOES HE EVER GET LONELY?
...

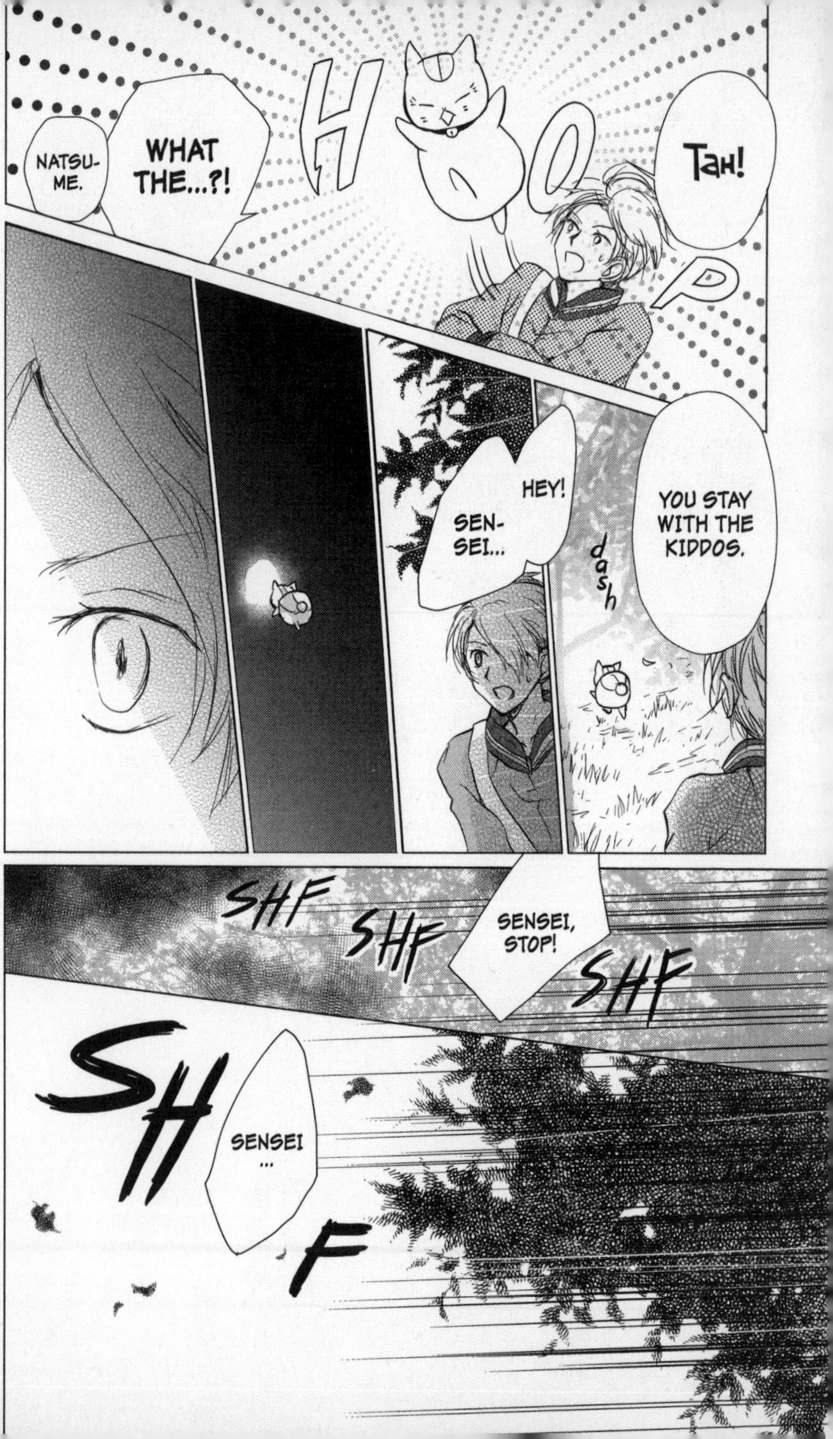
TAH!
HOOP
WHAT THE...?!
NATSU-ME.
YOU STAY WITH THE KIDDOS.
dash
HEY!
SEN-SEI...
SHF
SENSEI, STOP!
SHF
SHF
SENSEI...
SHF

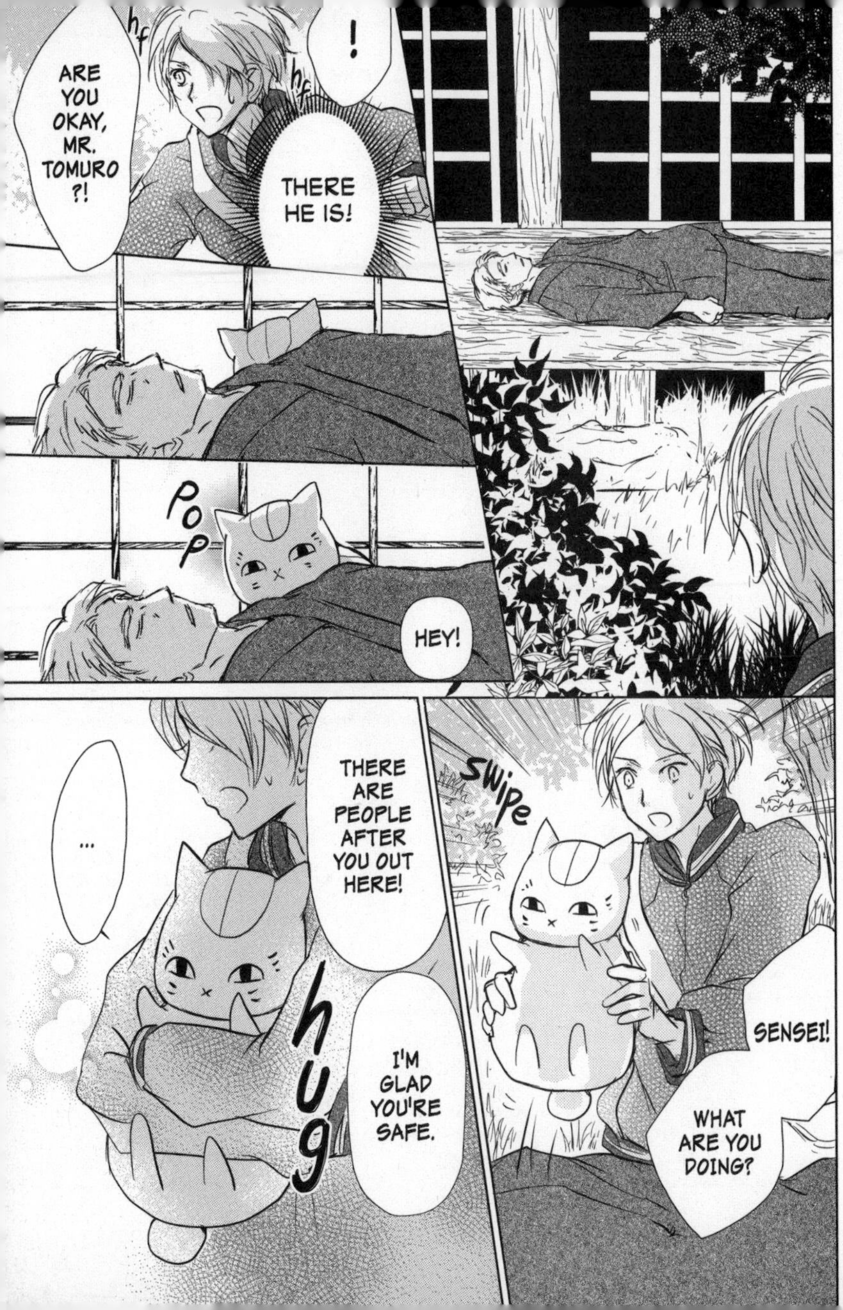

!
hf
hf
THERE HE IS!
ARE YOU OKAY, MR. TOMURO?!
HEY!
POP
swipe
SENSEI!
WHAT ARE YOU DOING?
THERE ARE PEOPLE AFTER YOU OUT HERE!
...
I'M GLAD YOU'RE SAFE.
hug

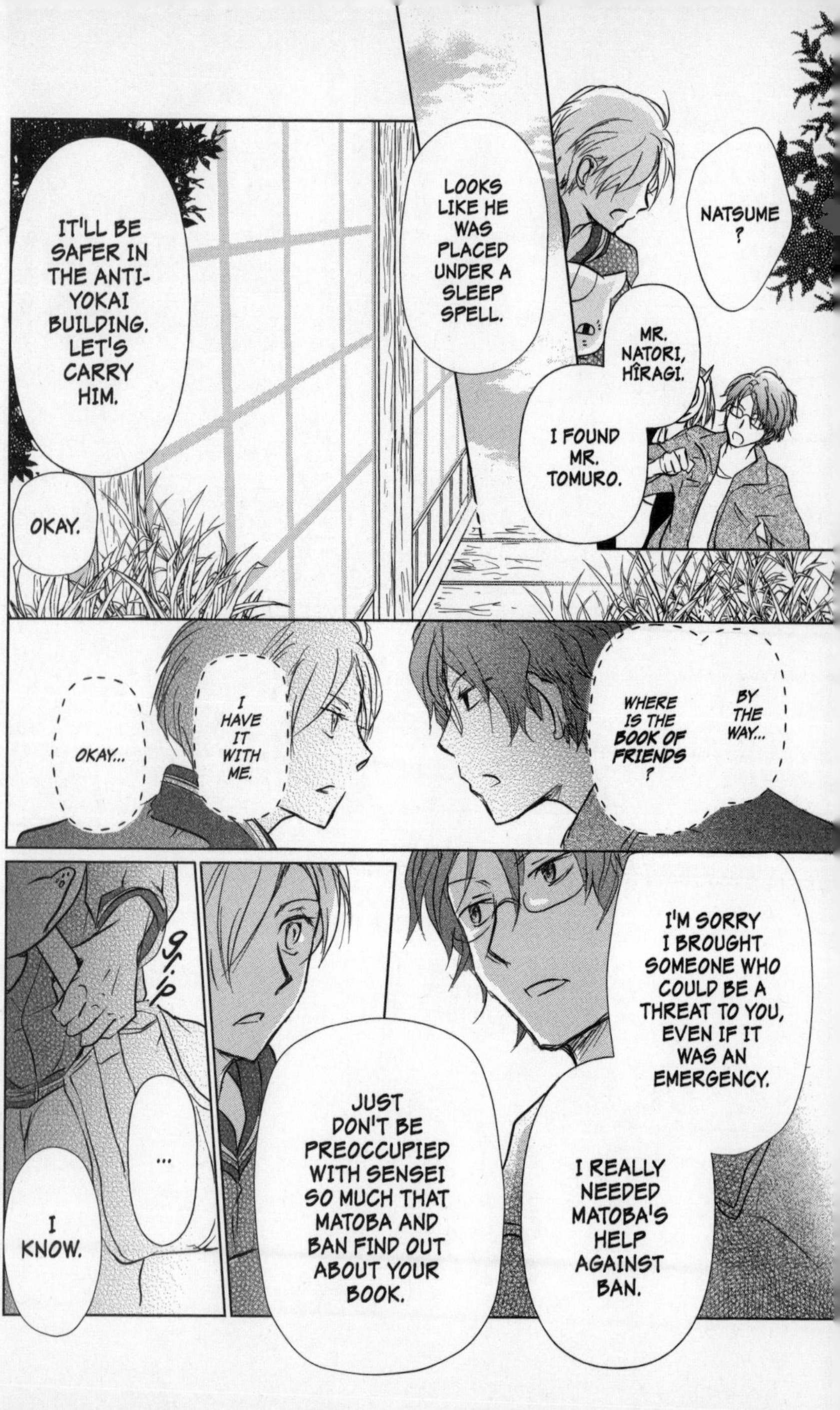
NATSUME?
MR. NATORI, HÎRAGI.
I FOUND MR. TOMURO.
LOOKS LIKE HE WAS PLACED UNDER A SLEEP SPELL.
IT'LL BE SAFER IN THE ANTI-YOKAI BUILDING. LET'S CARRY HIM.
OKAY.
BY THE WAY...
WHERE IS THE BOOK OF FRIENDS?
I HAVE IT WITH ME.
OKAY...
I'M SORRY I BROUGHT SOMEONE WHO COULD BE A THREAT TO YOU, EVEN IF IT WAS AN EMERGENCY.
I REALLY NEEDED MATOBA'S HELP AGAINST BAN.
JUST DON'T BE PREOCCUPIED WITH SENSEI SO MUCH THAT MATOBA AND BAN FIND OUT ABOUT YOUR BOOK.
...
grip
I KNOW.

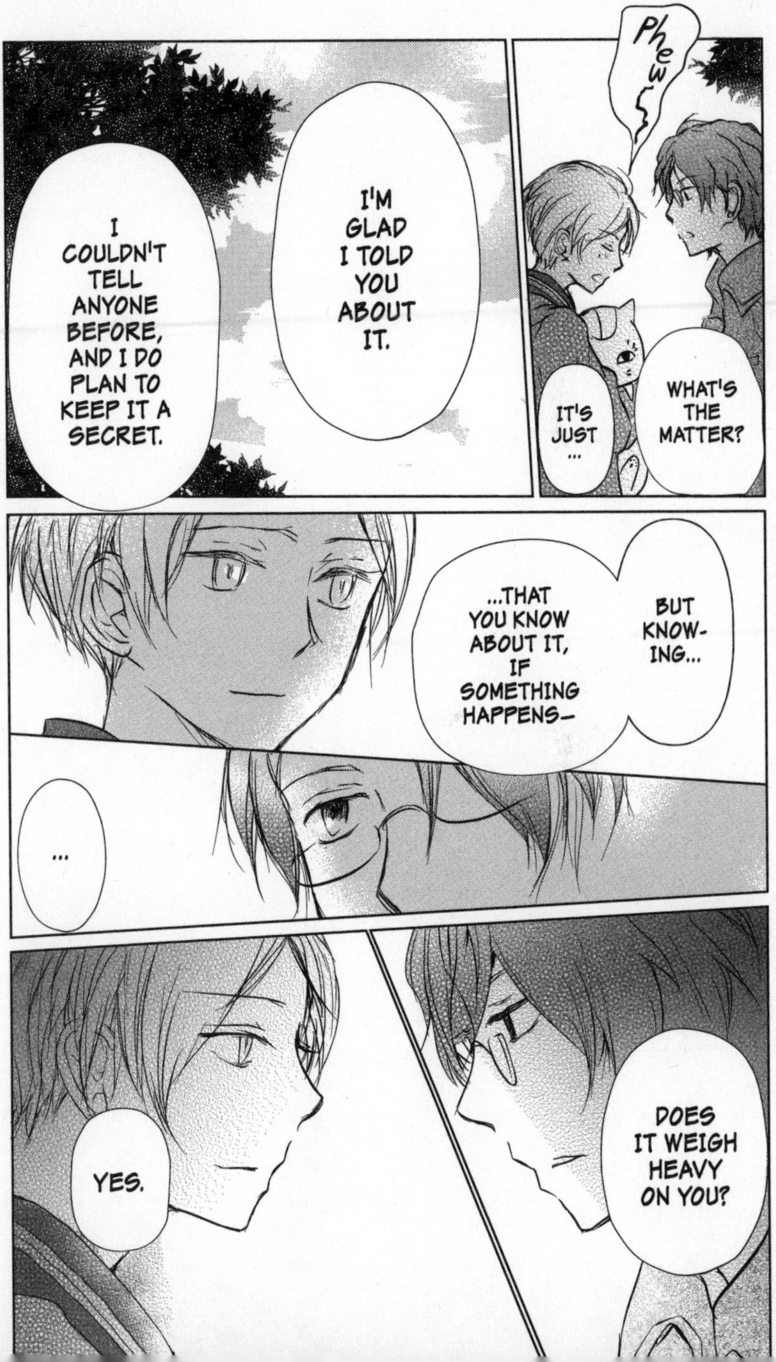
Phew
WHAT'S THE MATTER?
IT'S JUST ...
I'M GLAD I TOLD YOU ABOUT IT.
I COULDN'T TELL ANYONE BEFORE, AND I DO PLAN TO KEEP IT A SECRET.
BUT KNOWING...
...THAT YOU KNOW ABOUT IT, IF SOMETHING HAPPENS—
...
DOES IT WEIGH HEAVY ON YOU?
YES.

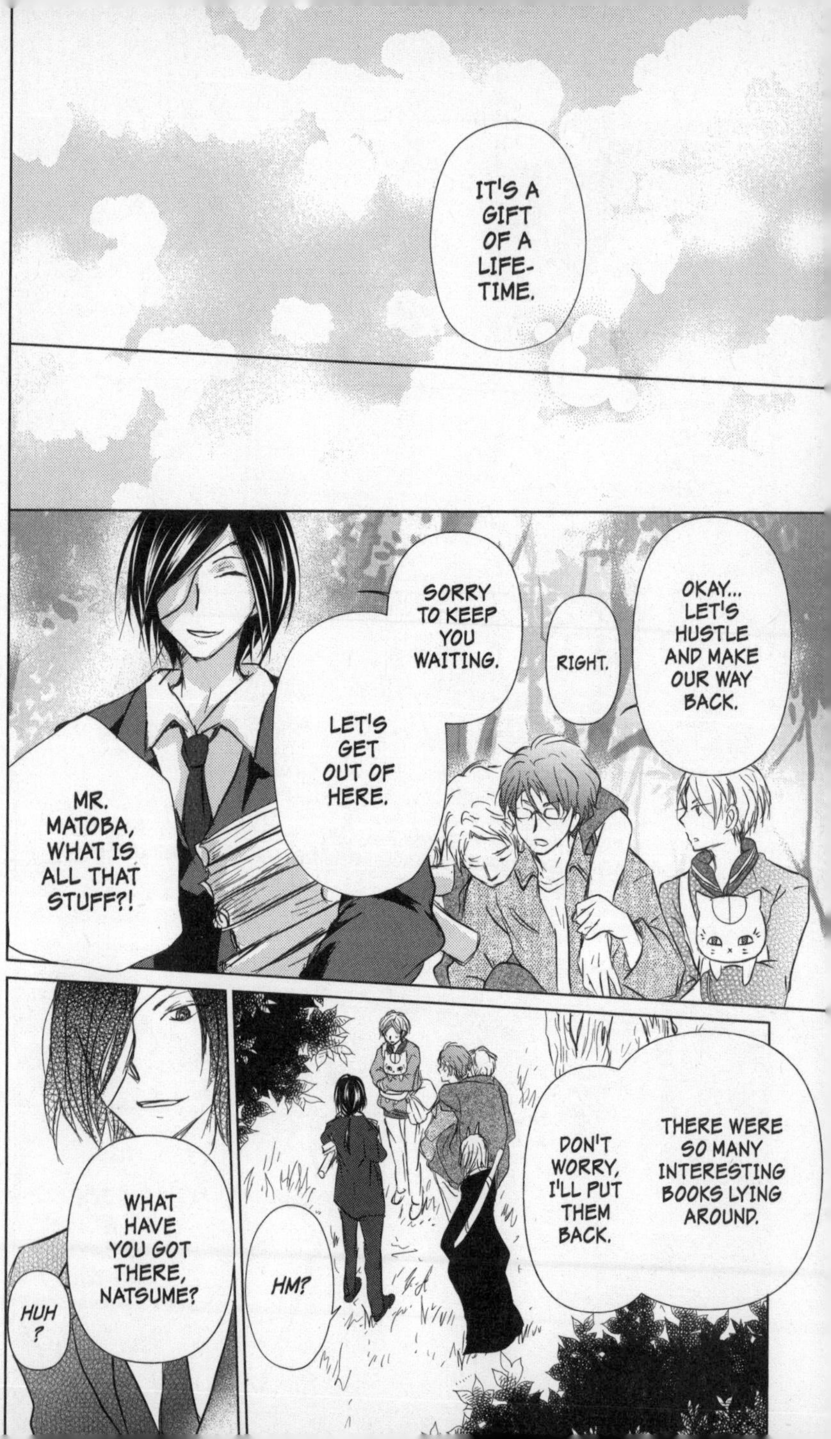
IT'S A GIFT OF A LIFE-TIME.
OKAY... LET'S HUSTLE AND MAKE OUR WAY BACK.
RIGHT.
SORRY TO KEEP YOU WAITING.
LET'S GET OUT OF HERE.
MR. MATOBA, WHAT IS ALL THAT STUFF?!
THERE WERE SO MANY INTERESTING BOOKS LYING AROUND.
DON'T WORRY, I'LL PUT THEM BACK.
HM?
WHAT HAVE YOU GOT THERE, NATSUME?
HUH?

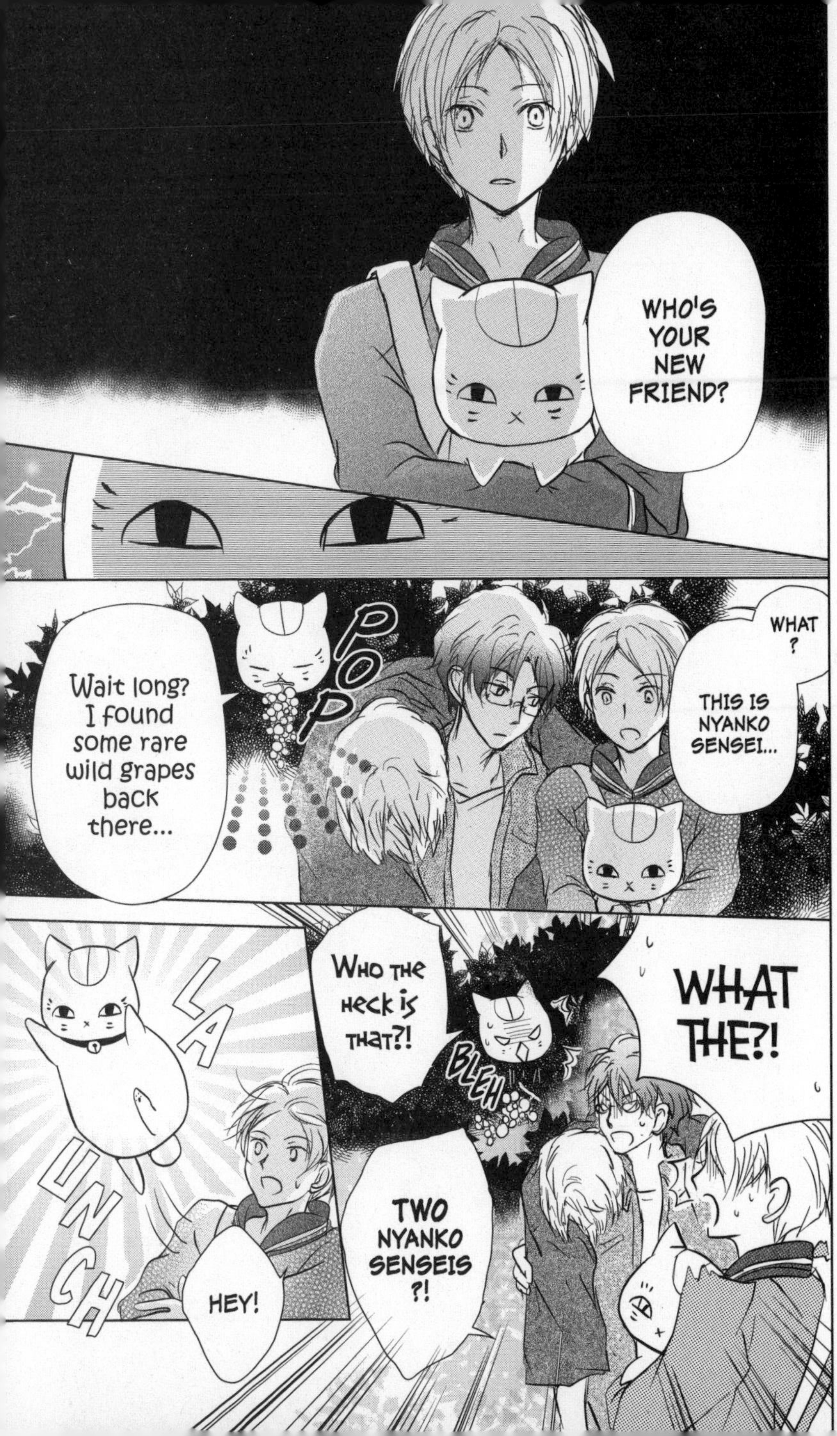
WHO'S YOUR NEW FRIEND?
WHAT?
THIS IS NYANKO SENSEI...
POP
Wait long? I found some rare wild grapes back there...
WHAT THE?!
Who the heck is that?!
BLEH
TWO NYANKO SENSEIS?!
LAUNCH
HEY!

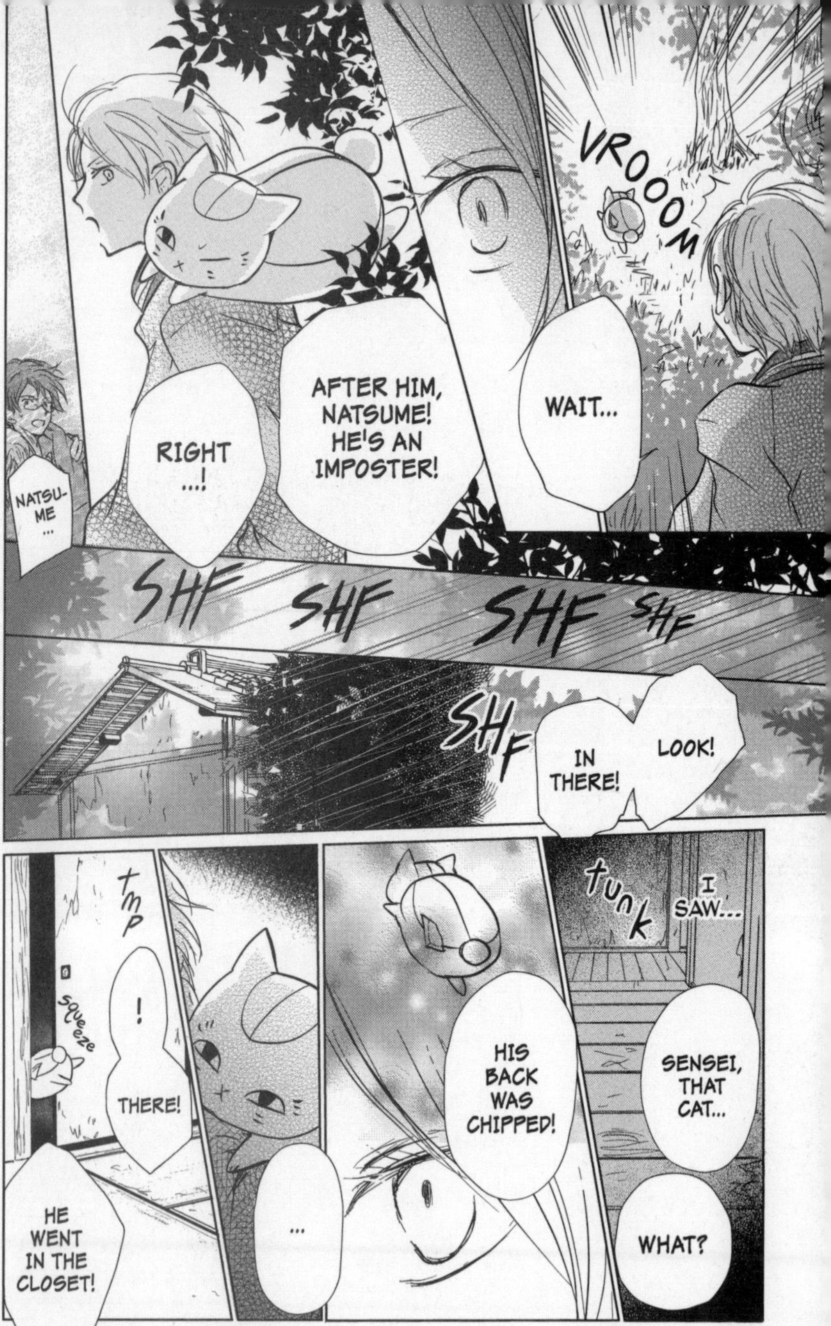
VROOOM
WAIT...
AFTER HIM, NATSUME! HE'S AN IMPOSTER!
RIGHT ...!
NATSU-ME ...
SHF SHF SHF SHF
SHF
LOOK!
IN THERE!
tunk
I SAW...
SENSEI, THAT CAT...
WHAT?
HIS BACK WAS CHIPPED!
...
tmp
!
squeeze
THERE!
HE WENT IN THE CLOSET!

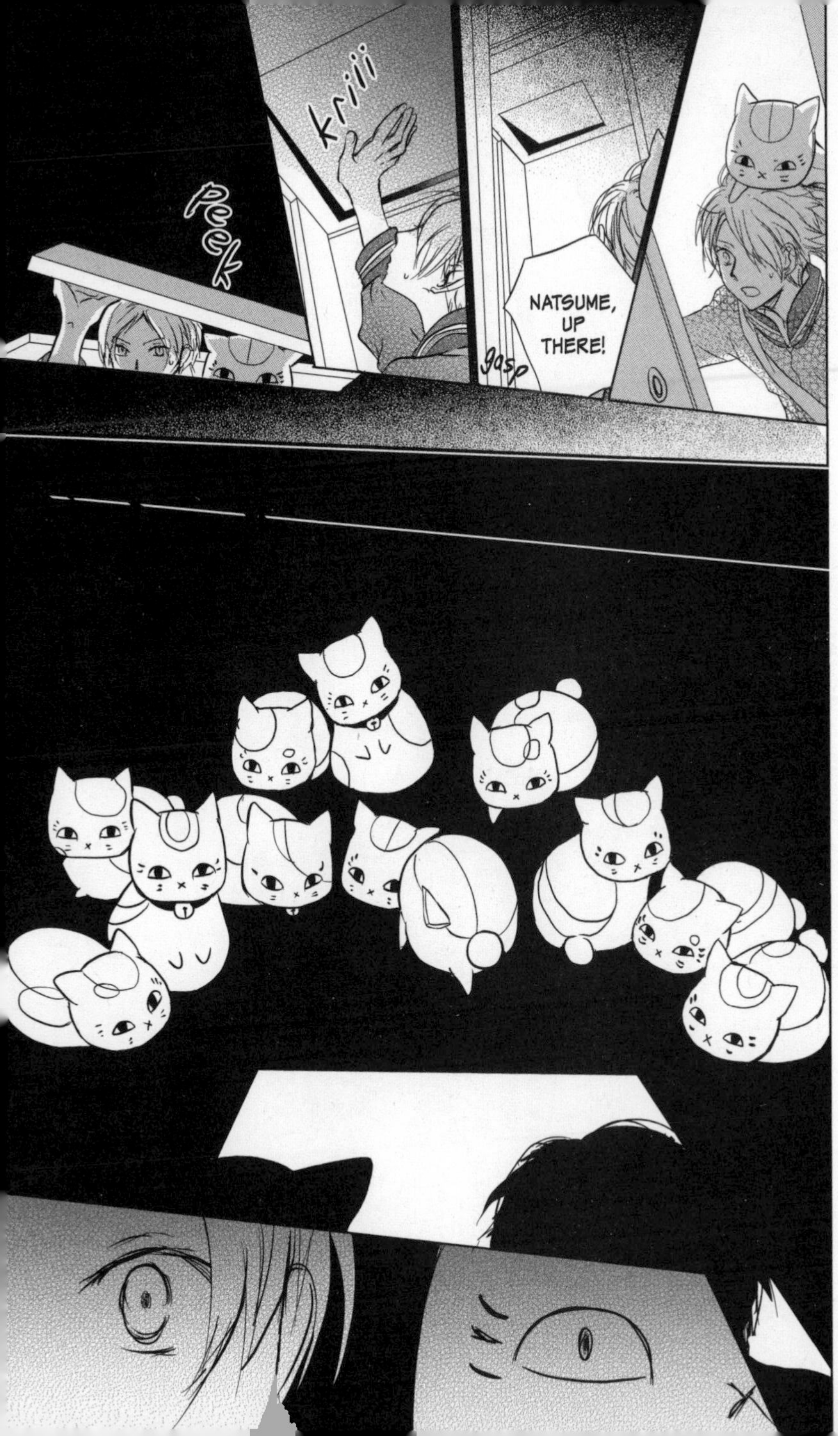
NATSUME, UP THERE!
gasp
kriii
Peek

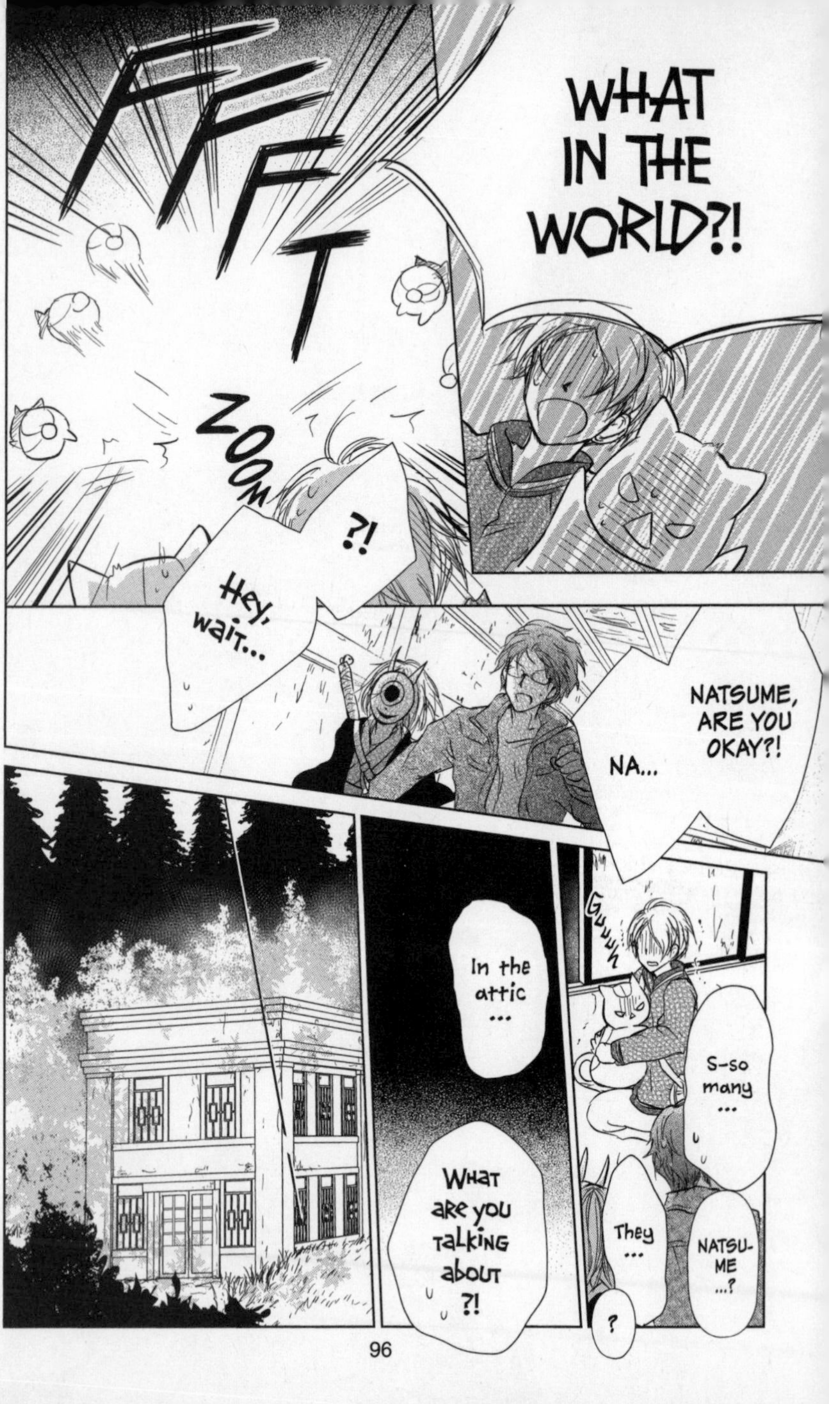
WHAT IN THE WORLD?!
FFFT
ZOOM
?!
Hey, wait...
NATSUME, ARE YOU OKAY?!
NA...
GUUUH
S-so many...
NATSU-ME...?
They...
?
In the attic...
WHAT are you talking about?!

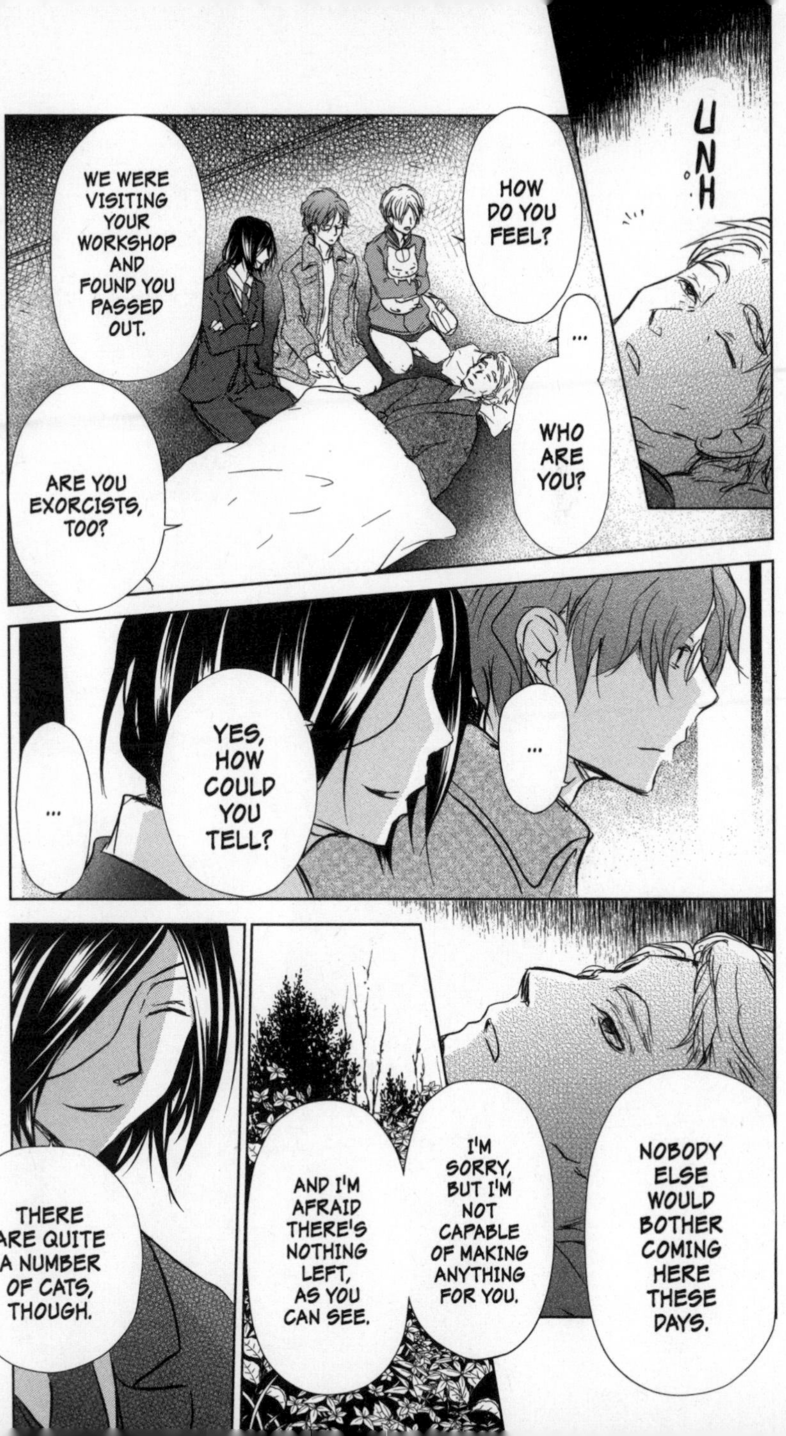
UNH
HOW DO YOU FEEL?
WE WERE VISITING YOUR WORKSHOP AND FOUND YOU PASSED OUT.
...
WHO ARE YOU?
ARE YOU EXORCISTS, TOO?
...
YES, HOW COULD YOU TELL?
...
NOBODY ELSE WOULD BOTHER COMING HERE THESE DAYS.
I'M SORRY, BUT I'M NOT CAPABLE OF MAKING ANYTHING FOR YOU.
AND I'M AFRAID THERE'S NOTHING LEFT, AS YOU CAN SEE.
THERE ARE QUITE A NUMBER OF CATS, THOUGH.

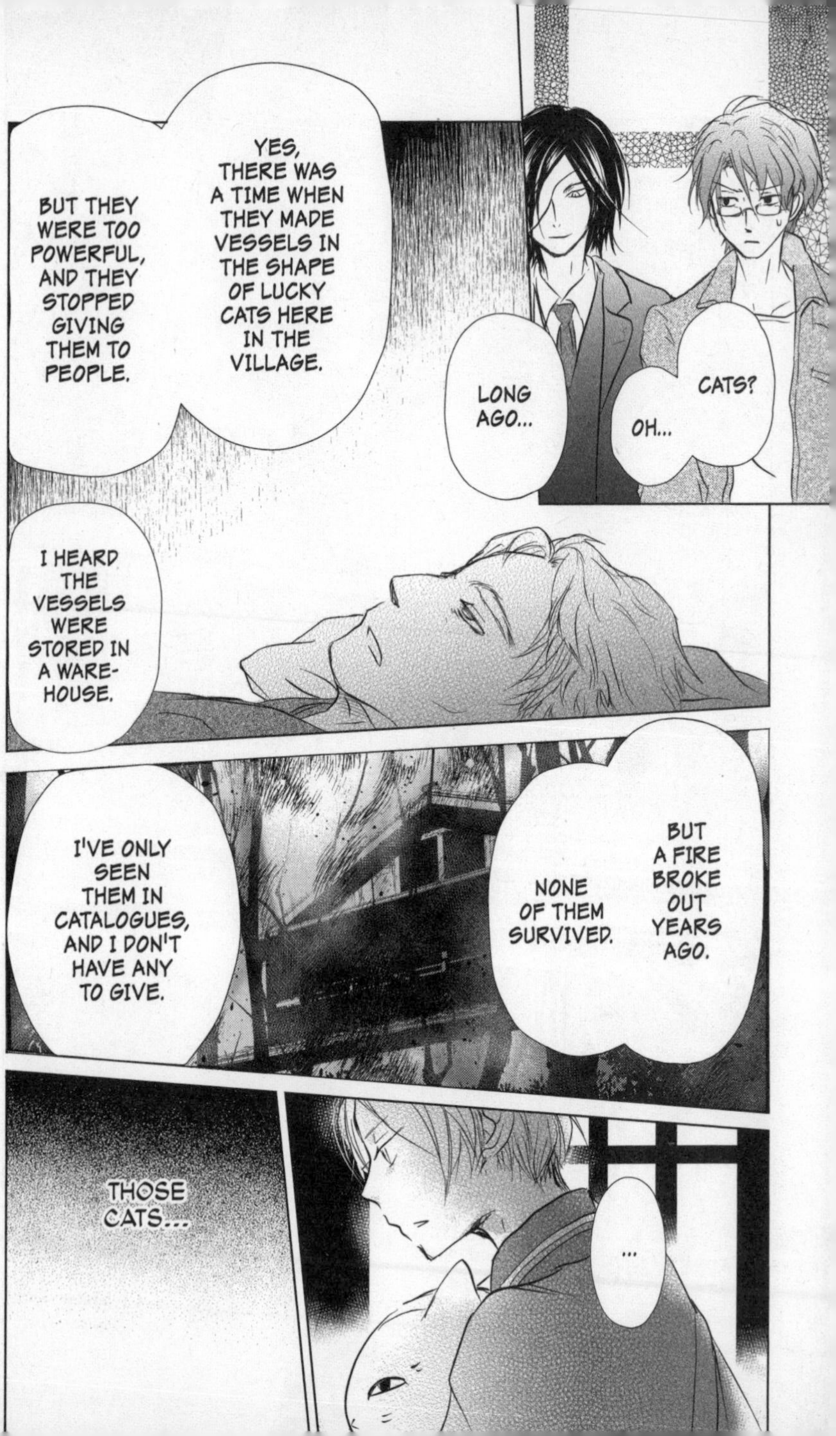
CATS? OH...
LONG AGO...
YES, THERE WAS A TIME WHEN THEY MADE VESSELS IN THE SHAPE OF LUCKY CATS HERE IN THE VILLAGE.
BUT THEY WERE TOO POWERFUL, AND THEY STOPPED GIVING THEM TO PEOPLE.
I HEARD THE VESSELS WERE STORED IN A WARE-HOUSE.
BUT A FIRE BROKE OUT YEARS AGO.
NONE OF THEM SURVIVED.
I'VE ONLY SEEN THEM IN CATALOGUES, AND I DON'T HAVE ANY TO GIVE.
...
THOSE CATS...

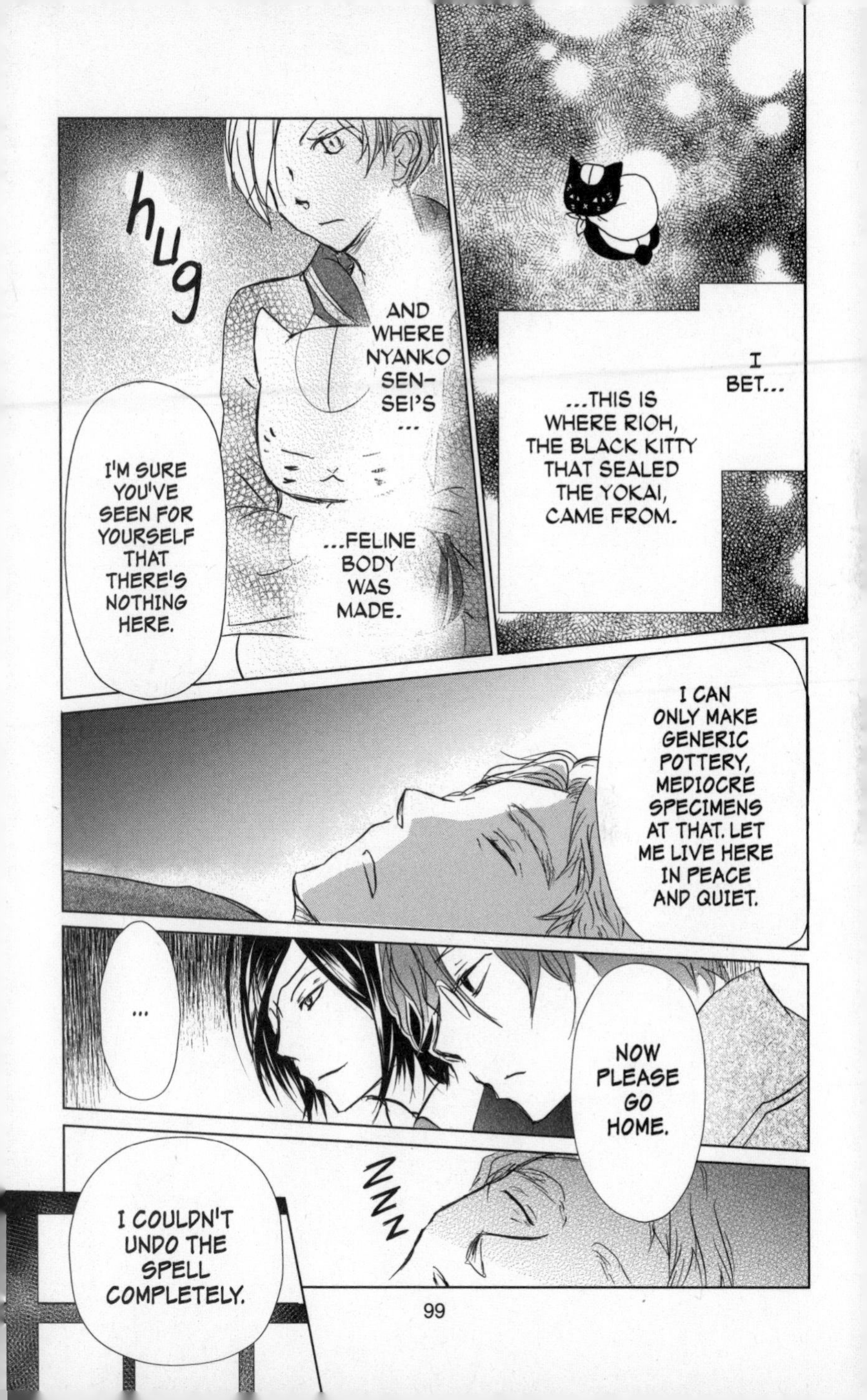
I BET...
...THIS IS WHERE RIOH, THE BLACK KITTY THAT SEALED THE YOKAI, CAME FROM.
hug
AND WHERE NYANKO SEN-SEI'S ...
...FELINE BODY WAS MADE.
I'M SURE YOU'VE SEEN FOR YOURSELF THAT THERE'S NOTHING HERE.
I CAN ONLY MAKE GENERIC POTTERY, MEDIOCRE SPECIMENS AT THAT. LET ME LIVE HERE IN PEACE AND QUIET.
NOW PLEASE GO HOME.
...
NNN
I COULDN'T UNDO THE SPELL COMPLETELY.

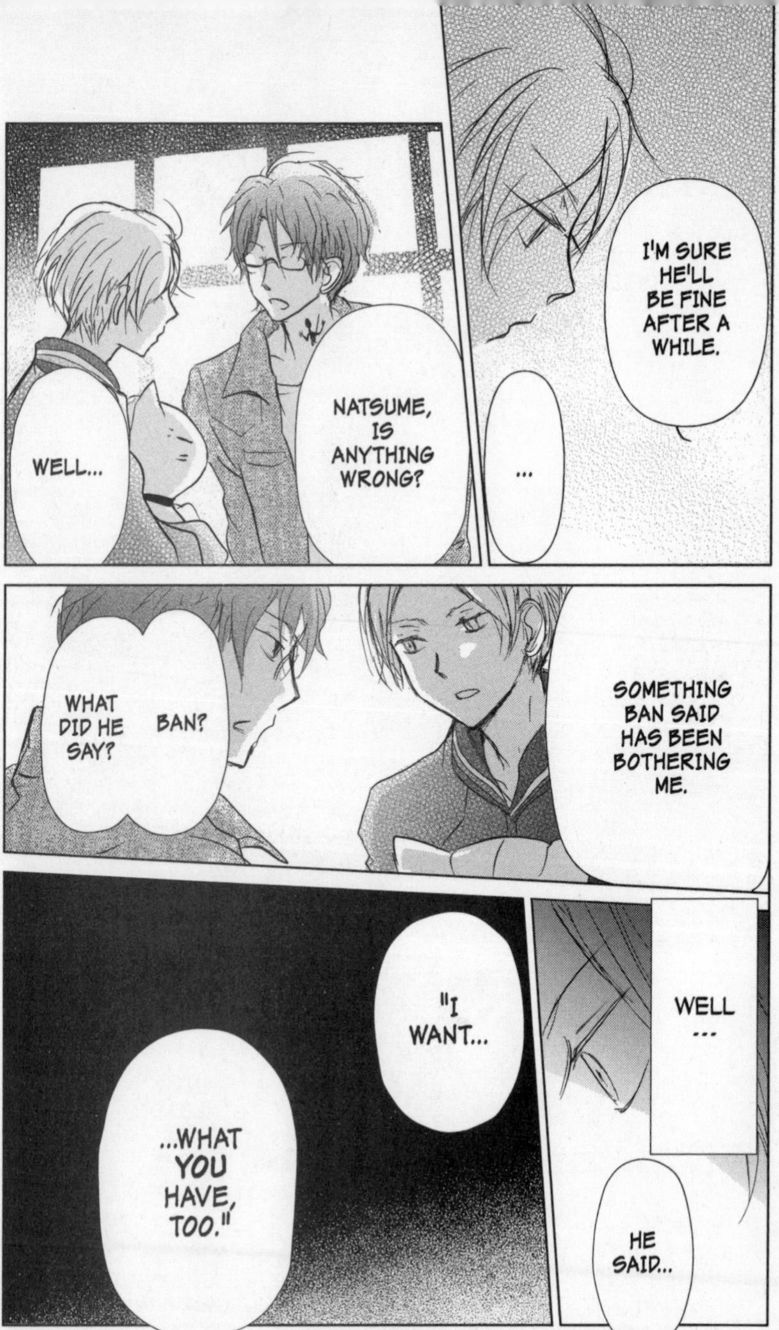
I'M SURE HE'LL BE FINE AFTER A WHILE.
...
NATSUME, IS ANYTHING WRONG?
WELL...
SOMETHING BAN SAID HAS BEEN BOTHERING ME.
BAN? WHAT DID HE SAY?
WELL ...
HE SAID...
"I WANT...
...WHAT YOU HAVE, TOO."

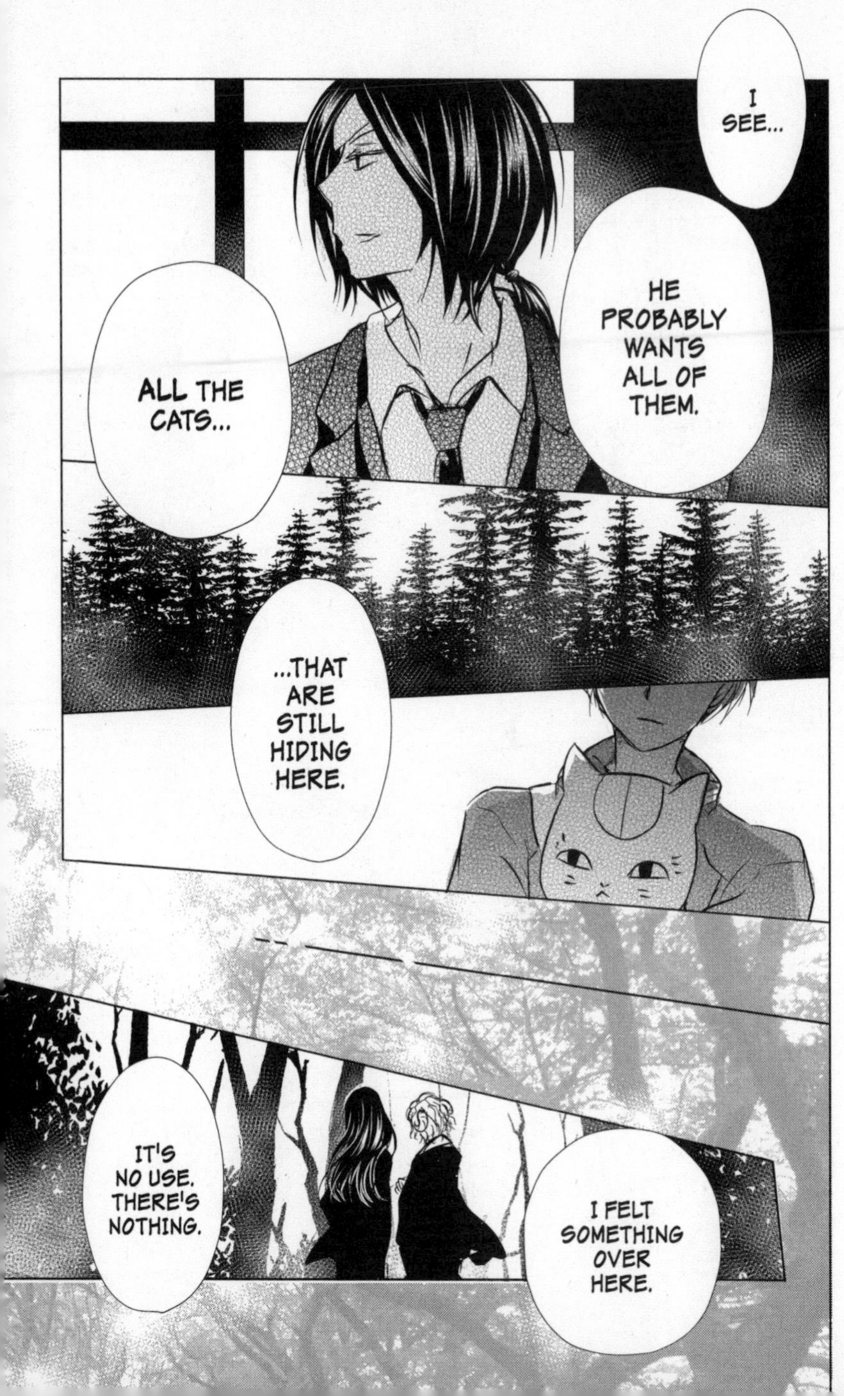
I SEE...
HE PROBABLY WANTS ALL OF THEM.
ALL THE CATS...
...THAT ARE STILL HIDING HERE.
I FELT SOMETHING OVER HERE.
IT'S NO USE. THERE'S NOTHING.

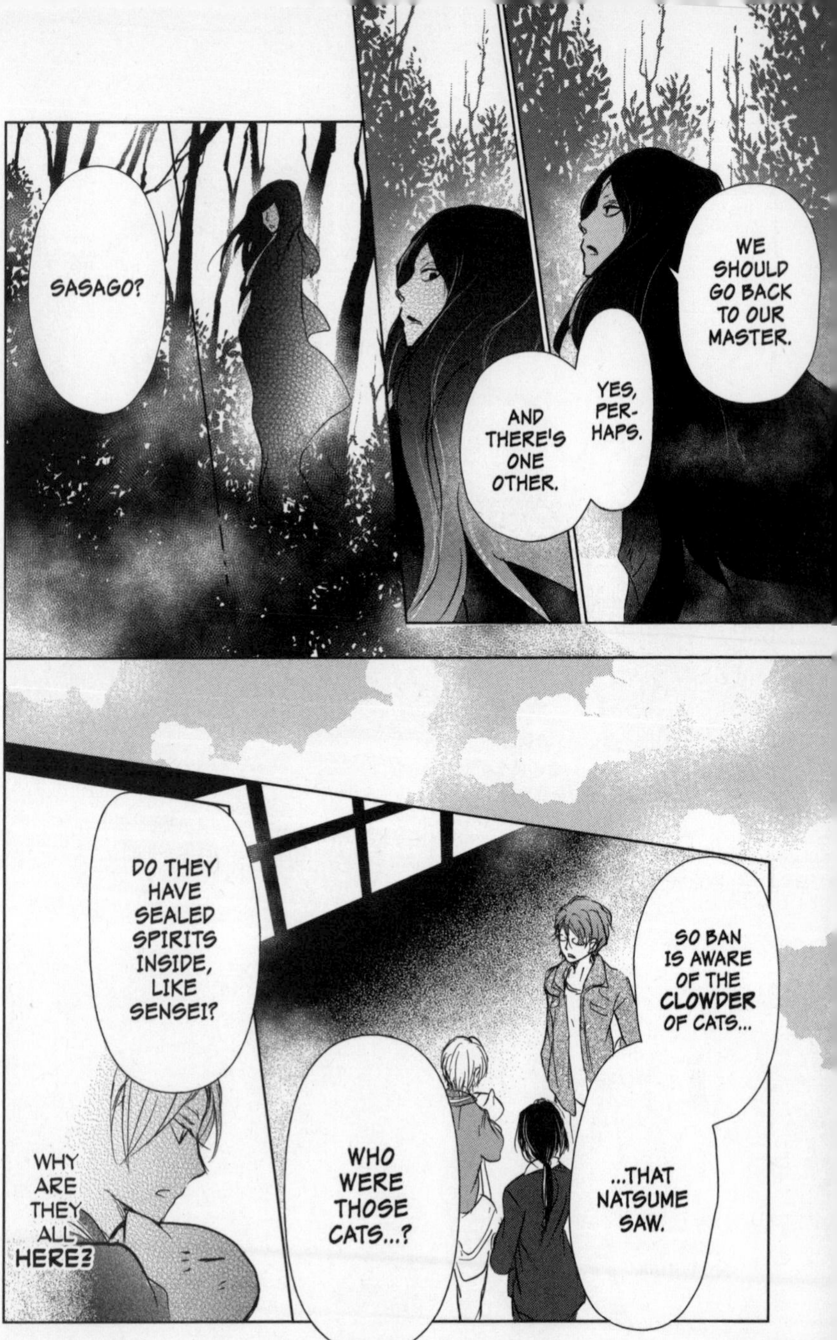
WE SHOULD GO BACK TO OUR MASTER.
YES, PER-HAPS.
AND THERE'S ONE OTHER.
SASAGO?
SO BAN IS AWARE OF THE CLOWDER OF CATS...
...THAT NATSUME SAW.
WHO WERE THOSE CATS...?
DO THEY HAVE SEALED SPIRITS INSIDE, LIKE SENSEI?
WHY ARE THEY ALL HERE?

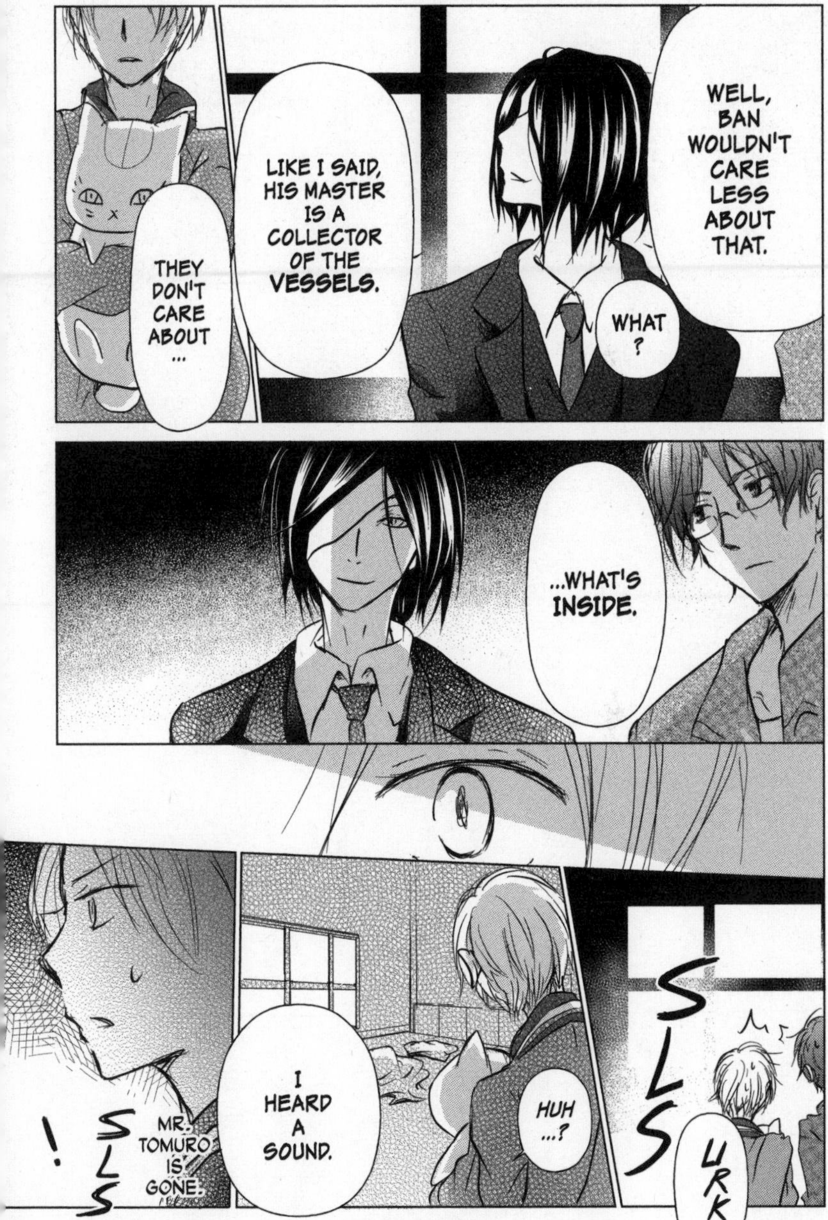
WELL, BAN WOULDN'T CARE LESS ABOUT THAT.
WHAT?
LIKE I SAID, HIS MASTER IS A COLLECTOR OF THE VESSELS.
THEY DON'T CARE ABOUT...
...WHAT'S INSIDE.
SLS
URK
HUH...?
I HEARD A SOUND.
MR. TOMURO IS GONE.
SLS
!

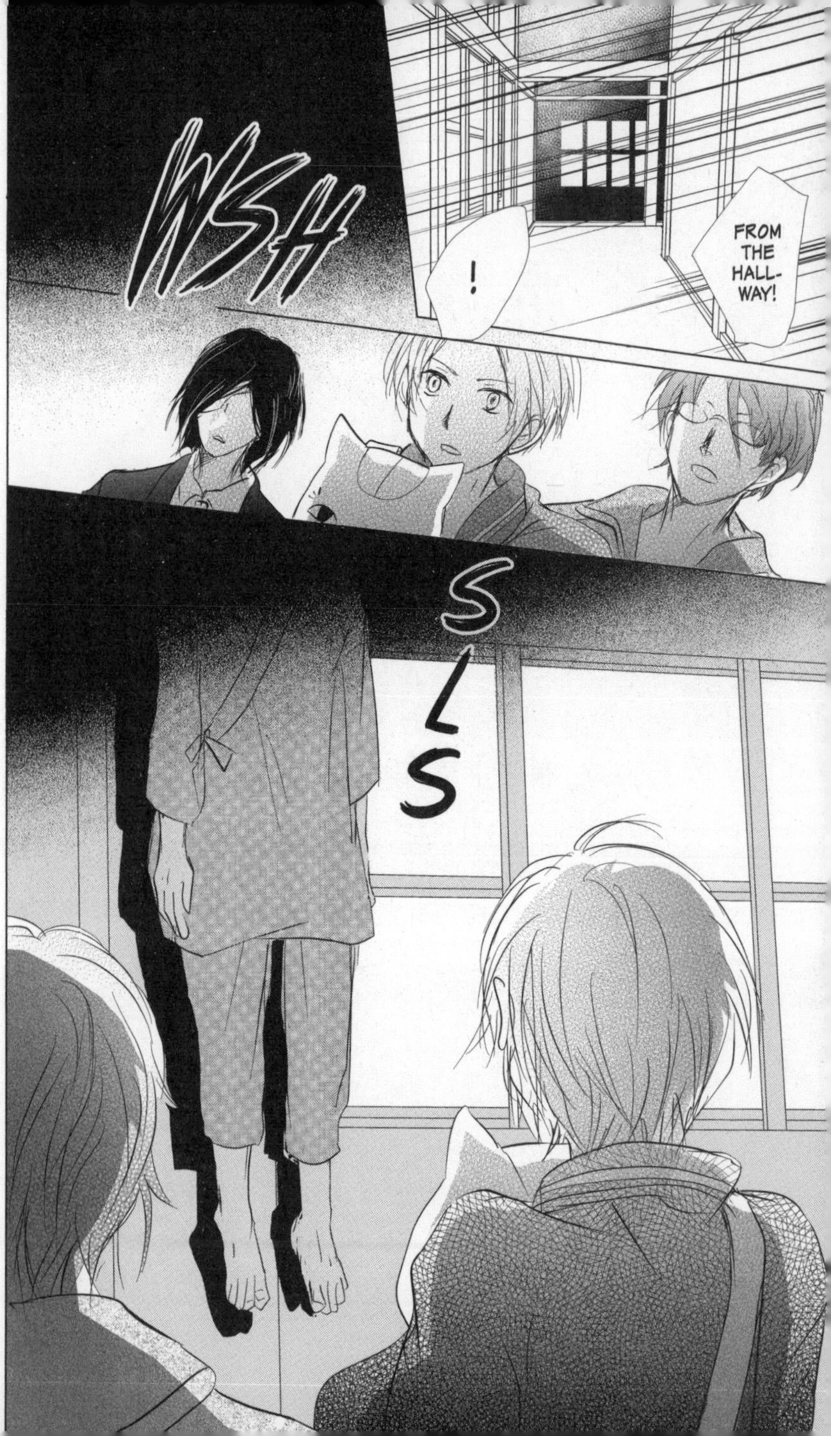
FROM THE HALL-WAY!
!
WSH
SLS

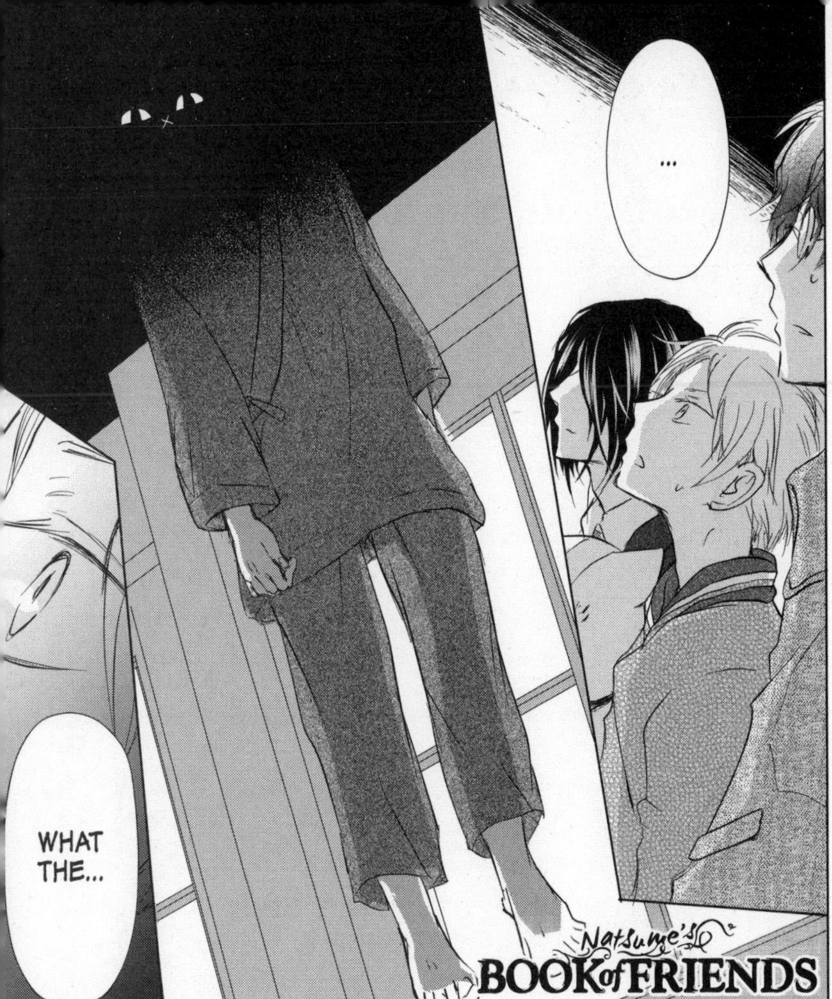
...
WHAT THE...
Natsume's
BOOK of FRIENDS

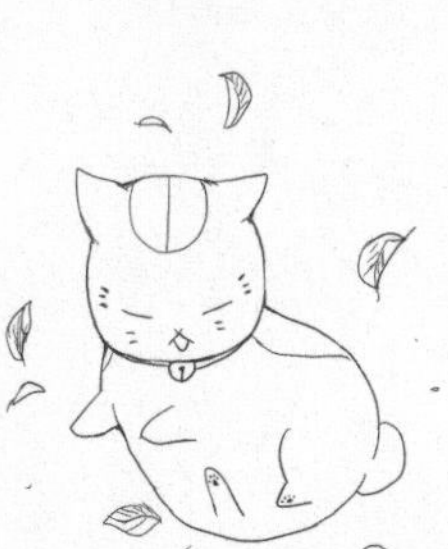

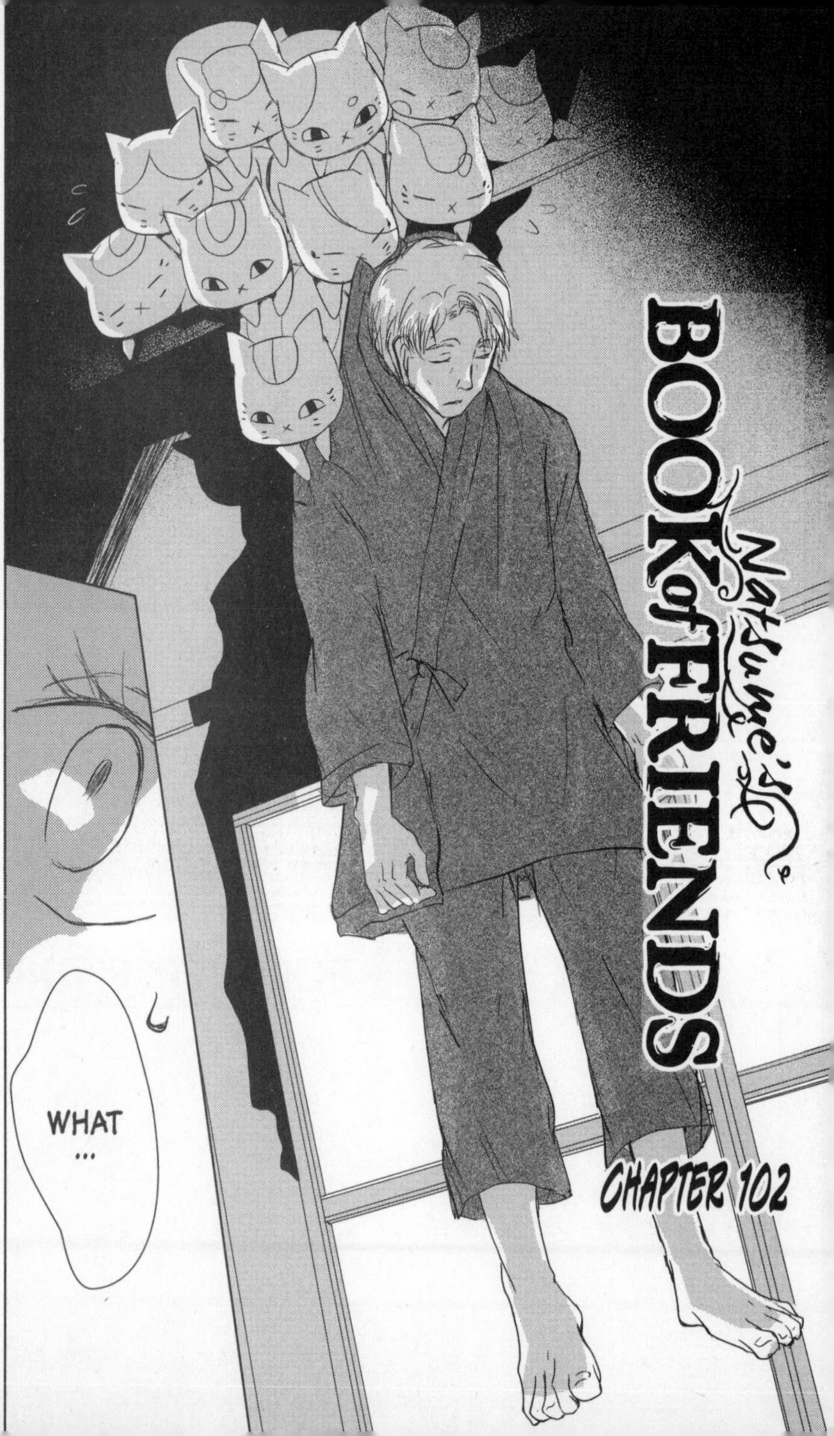
Natsume's BOOK of FRIENDS
CHAPTER 102
WHAT ...

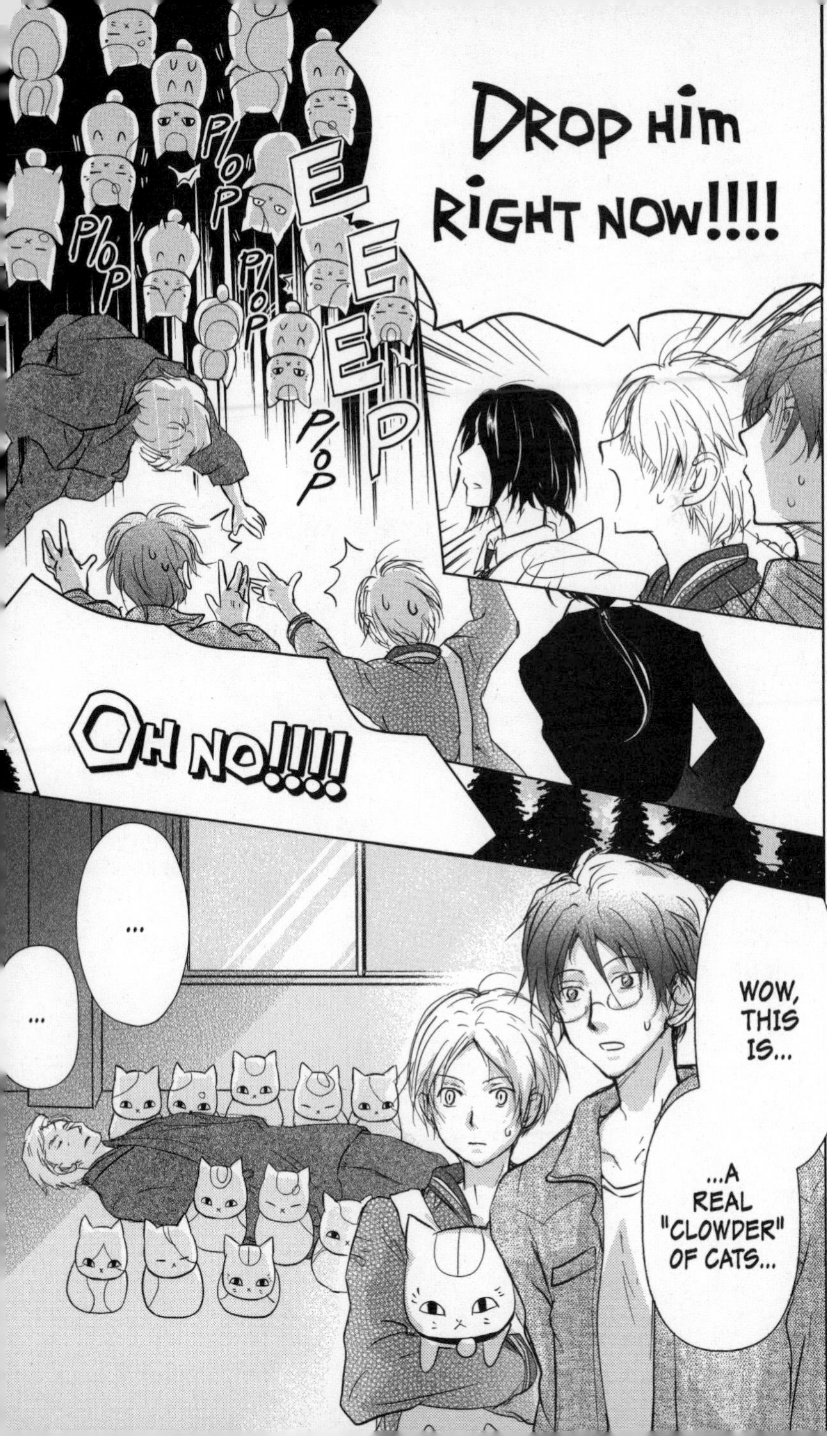
DROP HIM RIGHT NOW!!!!
EEEEP
PLOP
PLOP
PLOP
PLOP
OH NO!!!!
WOW, THIS IS...
...A REAL "CLOWDER" OF CATS...
...
...

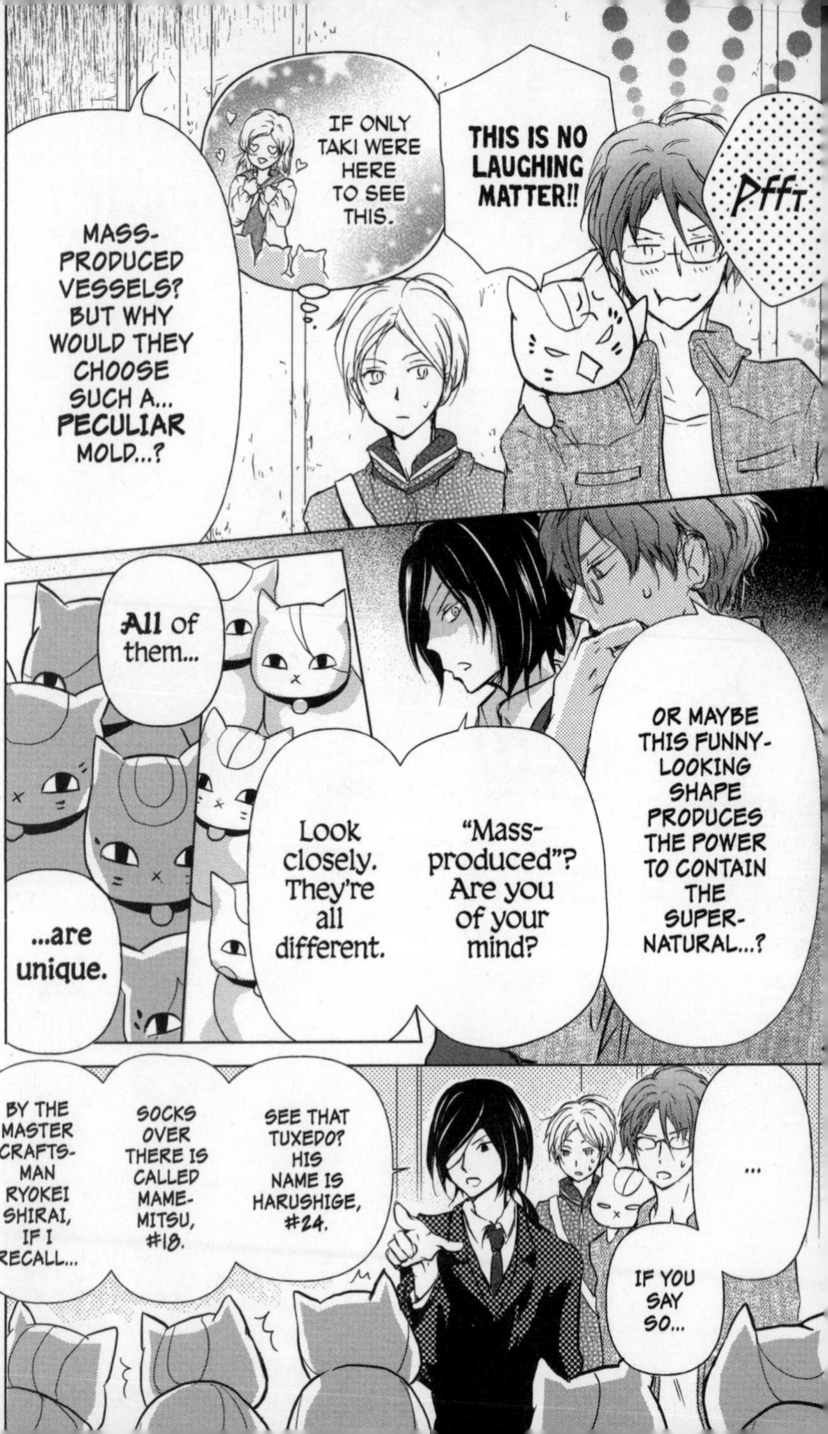
PFFFT
THIS IS NO LAUGHING MATTER!!
IF ONLY TAKI WERE HERE TO SEE THIS.
MASS-PRODUCED VESSELS? BUT WHY WOULD THEY CHOOSE SUCH A... PECULIAR MOLD...?
OR MAYBE THIS FUNNY-LOOKING SHAPE PRODUCES THE POWER TO CONTAIN THE SUPER-NATURAL...?
“Mass-produced”? Are you of your mind?
Look closely. They're all different.
All of them...
...are unique.
...
IF YOU SAY SO...
SEE THAT TUXEDO? HIS NAME IS HARUSHIGE, #24.
SOCKS OVER THERE IS CALLED MAME-MITSU, #18.
BY THE MASTER CRAFTS-MAN RYOKEI SHIRAI, IF I RECALL...

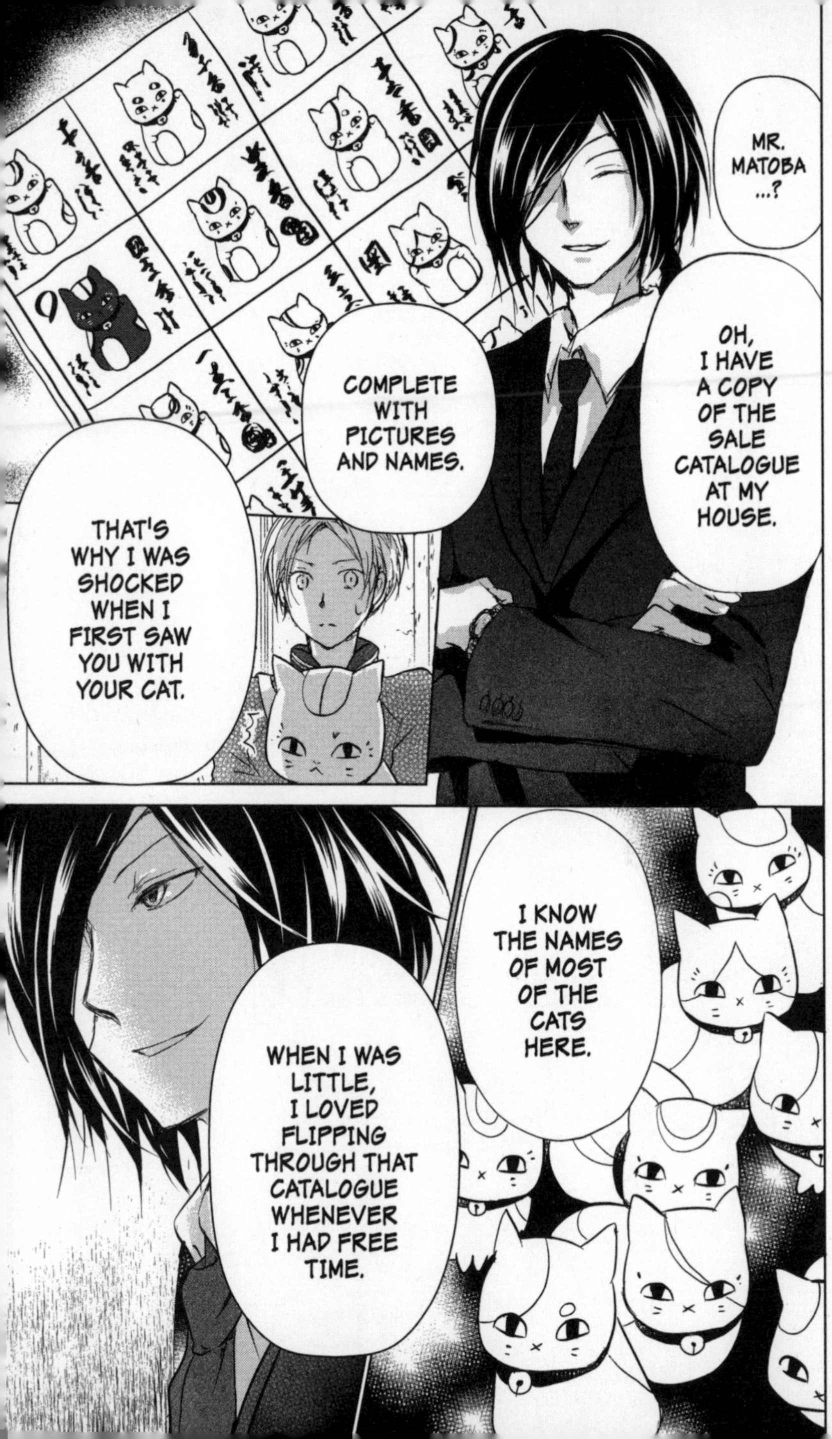
MR. MATOBA ...?
OH, I HAVE A COPY OF THE SALE CATALOGUE AT MY HOUSE.
COMPLETE WITH PICTURES AND NAMES.
THAT'S WHY I WAS SHOCKED WHEN I FIRST SAW YOU WITH YOUR CAT.
I KNOW THE NAMES OF MOST OF THE CATS HERE.
WHEN I WAS LITTLE, I LOVED FLIPPING THROUGH THAT CATALOGUE WHENEVER I HAD FREE TIME.

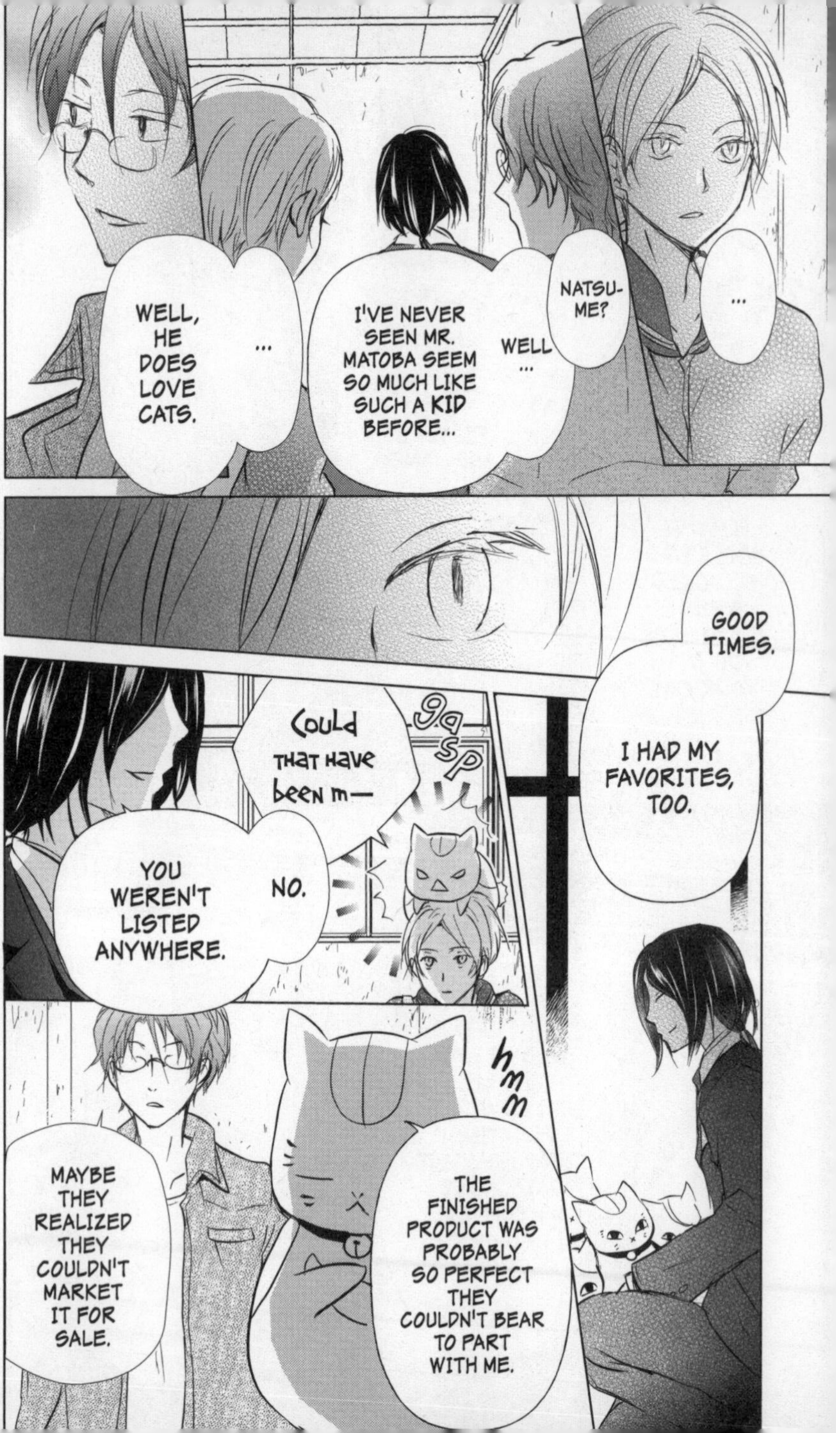
...
NATSU-ME?
WELL ...
I'VE NEVER SEEN MR. MATOBA SEEM SO MUCH LIKE SUCH A KID BEFORE...
...
WELL, HE DOES LOVE CATS.
GOOD TIMES.
I HAD MY FAVORITES, TOO.
gasp
Could that have been m—
NO.
YOU WEREN'T LISTED ANYWHERE.
hmm
THE FINISHED PRODUCT WAS PROBABLY SO PERFECT THEY COULDN'T BEAR TO PART WITH ME.
MAYBE THEY REALIZED THEY COULDN'T MARKET IT FOR SALE.

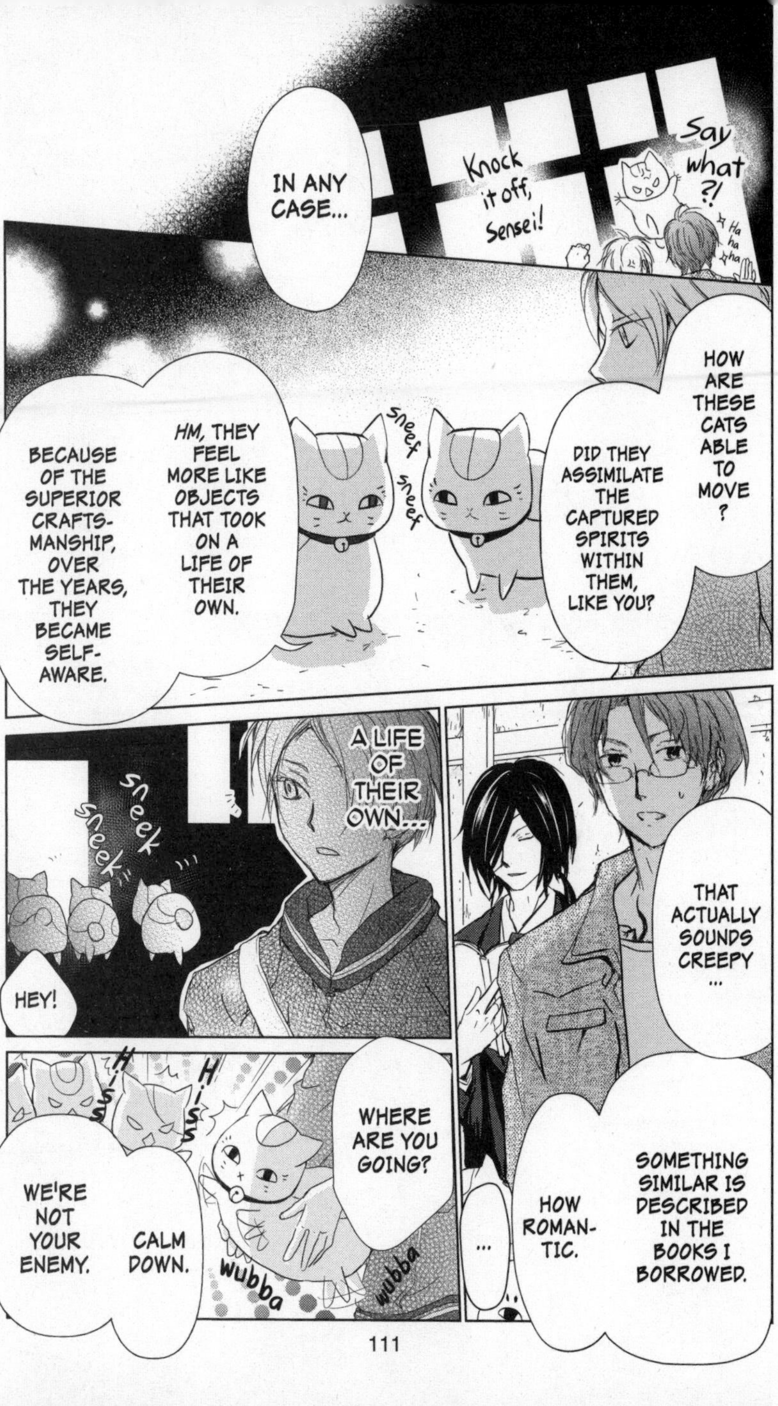

Say what ?!
Ha ha ha
Knock it off, Sensei!
IN ANY CASE...
HOW ARE THESE CATS ABLE TO MOVE ?
DID THEY ASSIMILATE THE CAPTURED SPIRITS WITHIN THEM, LIKE YOU?
sneef sneef
HM, THEY FEEL MORE LIKE OBJECTS THAT TOOK ON A LIFE OF THEIR OWN.
BECAUSE OF THE SUPERIOR CRAFTS-MANSHIP, OVER THE YEARS, THEY BECAME SELF-AWARE.
THAT ACTUALLY SOUNDS CREEPY ...
A LIFE OF THEIR OWN...
sneek sneek
HEY!
SOMETHING SIMILAR IS DESCRIBED IN THE BOOKS I BORROWED.
HOW ROMAN-TIC.
...
WHERE ARE YOU GOING?
Hiss Hiss
CALM DOWN.
WE'RE NOT YOUR ENEMY.
wubba wubba

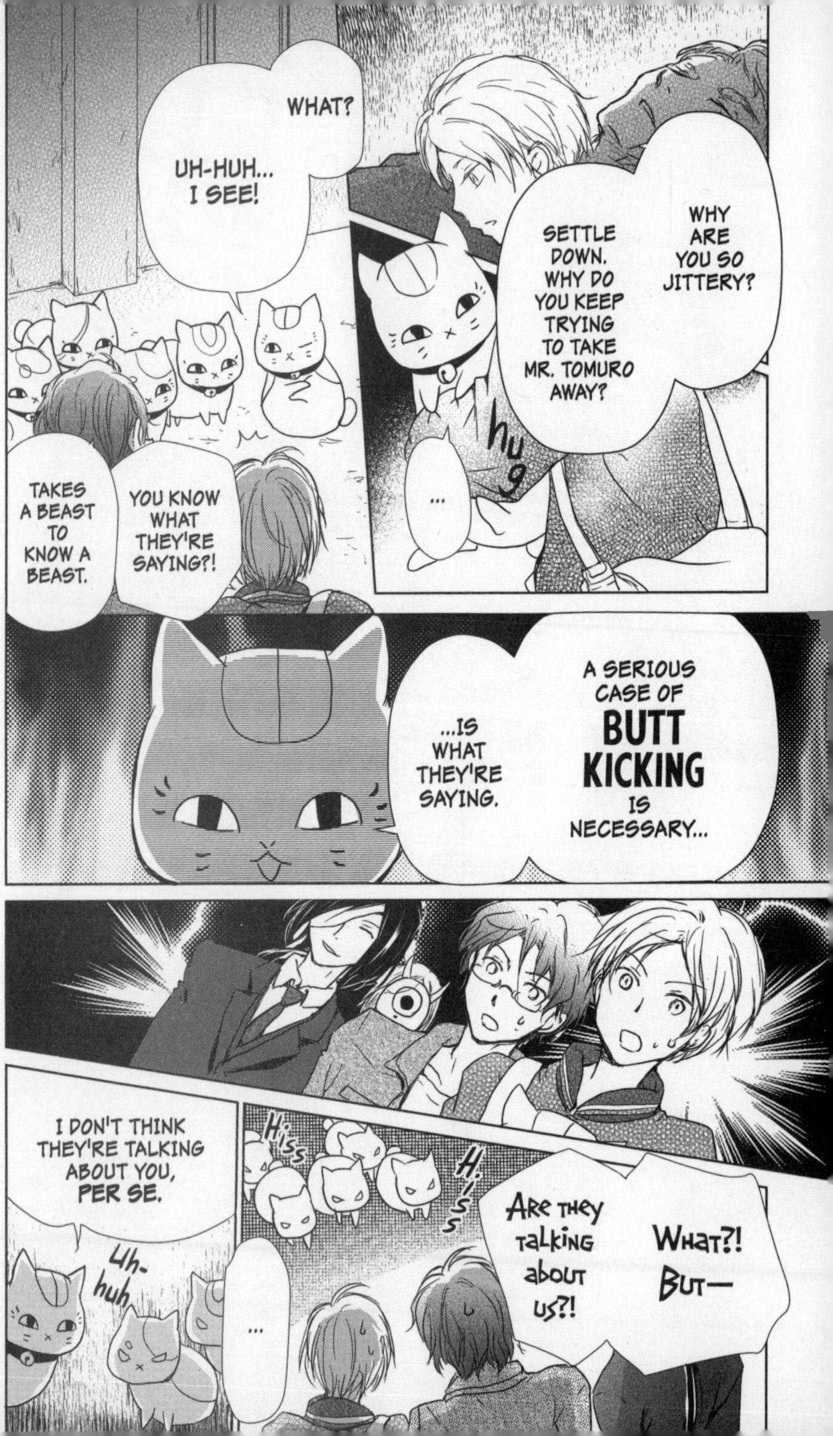
WHY ARE YOU SO JITTERY?
SETTLE DOWN. WHY DO YOU KEEP TRYING TO TAKE MR. TOMURO AWAY?
hug
...
WHAT?
UH-HUH... I SEE!
YOU KNOW WHAT THEY'RE SAYING?!
TAKES A BEAST TO KNOW A BEAST.
A SERIOUS CASE OF **BUTT KICKING** IS NECESSARY...
...IS WHAT THEY'RE SAYING.
WHAT?! BUT—
ARE THEY TALKING ABOUT US?!
HISS
HISS
...
UH-HUH
I DON'T THINK THEY'RE TALKING ABOUT YOU, **PER SE.**

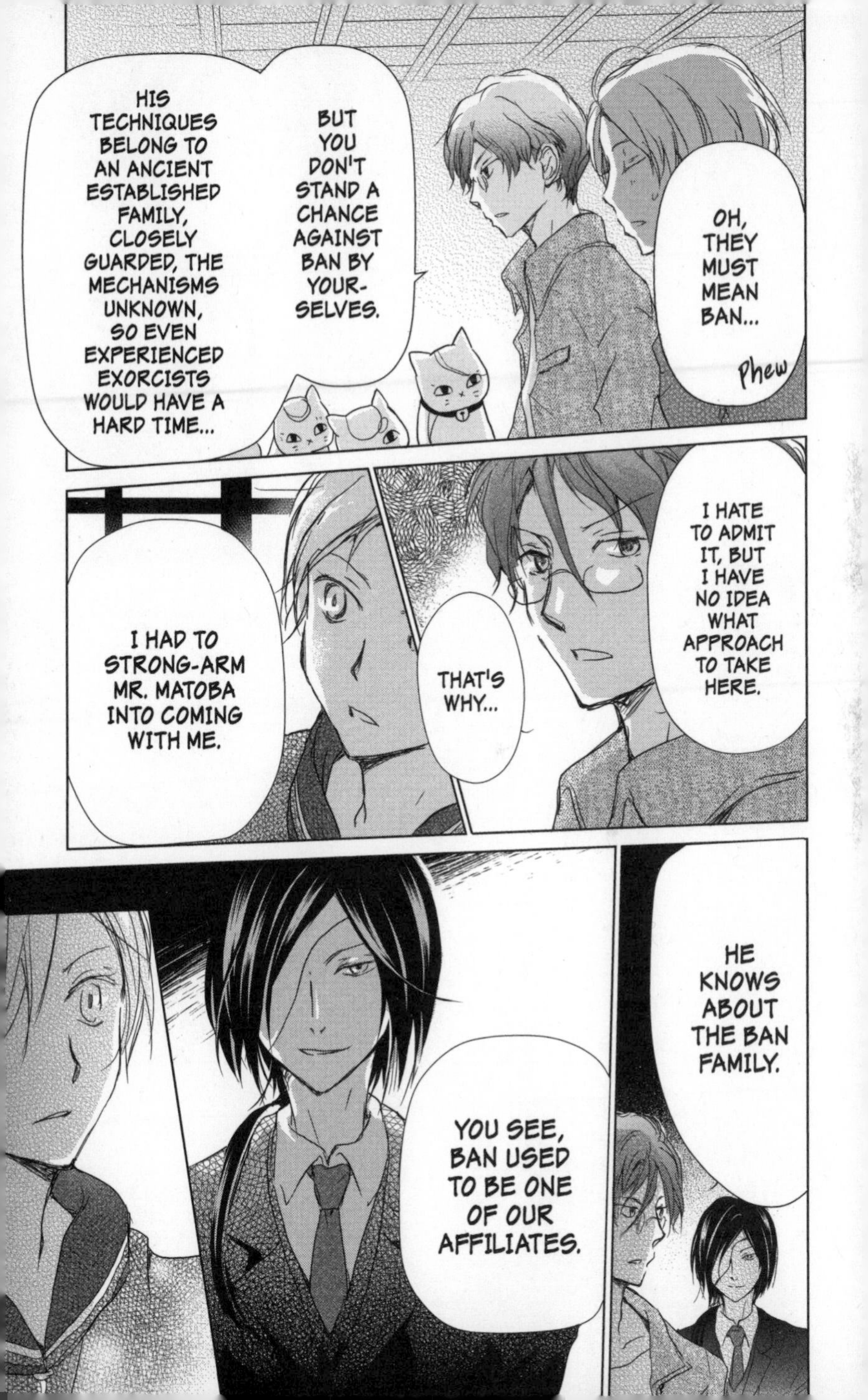
OH, THEY MUST MEAN BAN...
Phew
HIS TECHNIQUES BELONG TO AN ANCIENT ESTABLISHED FAMILY, CLOSELY GUARDED, THE MECHANISMS UNKNOWN, SO EVEN EXPERIENCED EXORCISTS WOULD HAVE A HARD TIME...
BUT YOU DON'T STAND A CHANCE AGAINST BAN BY YOUR-SELVES.
I HATE TO ADMIT IT, BUT I HAVE NO IDEA WHAT APPROACH TO TAKE HERE.
THAT'S WHY...
I HAD TO STRONG-ARM MR. MATOBA INTO COMING WITH ME.
HE KNOWS ABOUT THE BAN FAMILY.
YOU SEE, BAN USED TO BE ONE OF OUR AFFILIATES.

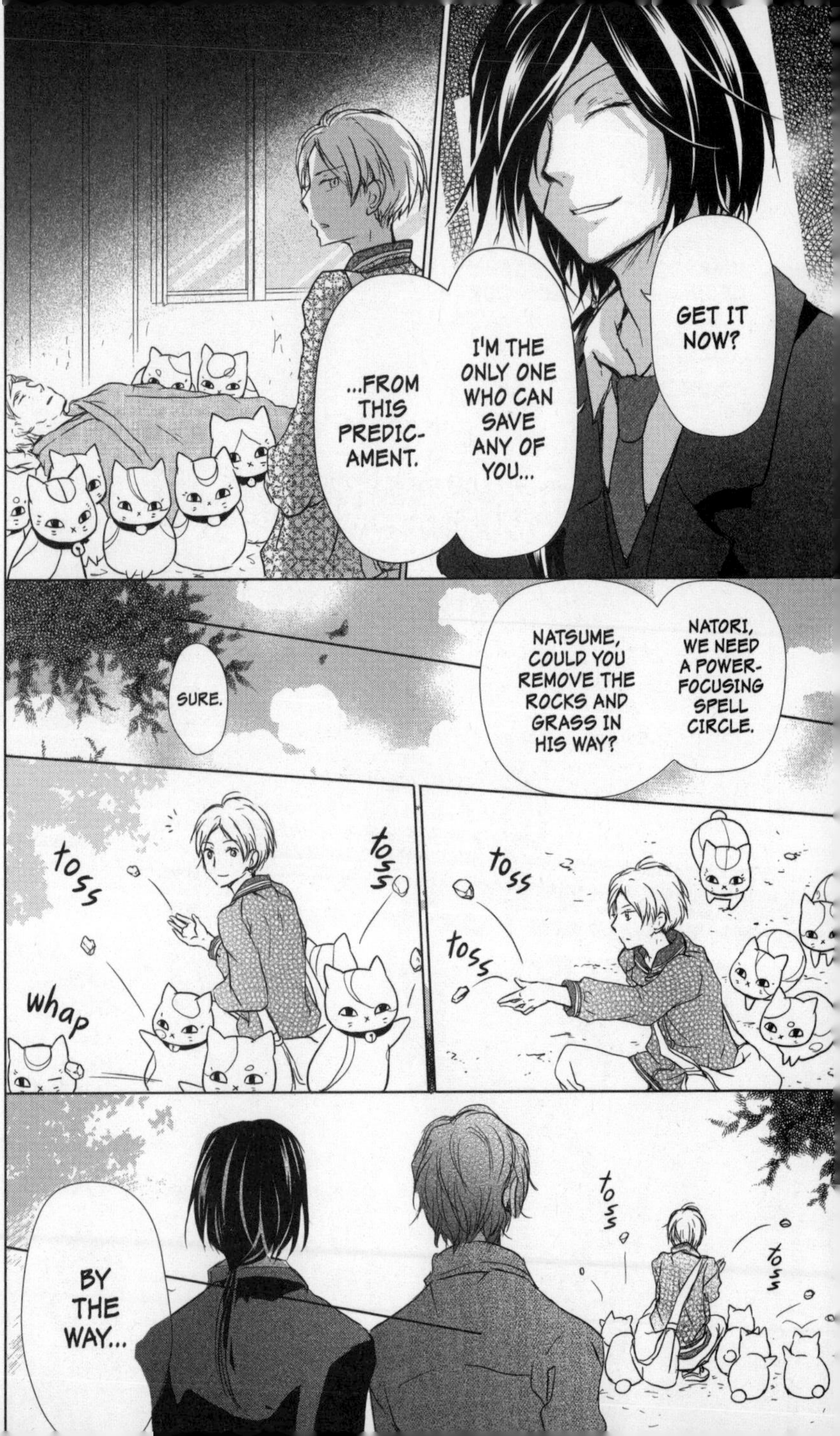
GET IT NOW?
I'M THE ONLY ONE WHO CAN SAVE ANY OF YOU...
...FROM THIS PREDICAMENT.
NATORI, WE NEED A POWER-FOCUSING SPELL CIRCLE.
NATSUME, COULD YOU REMOVE THE ROCKS AND GRASS IN HIS WAY?
SURE.
toss
toss
toss
toss
whap
toss
toss
BY THE WAY...

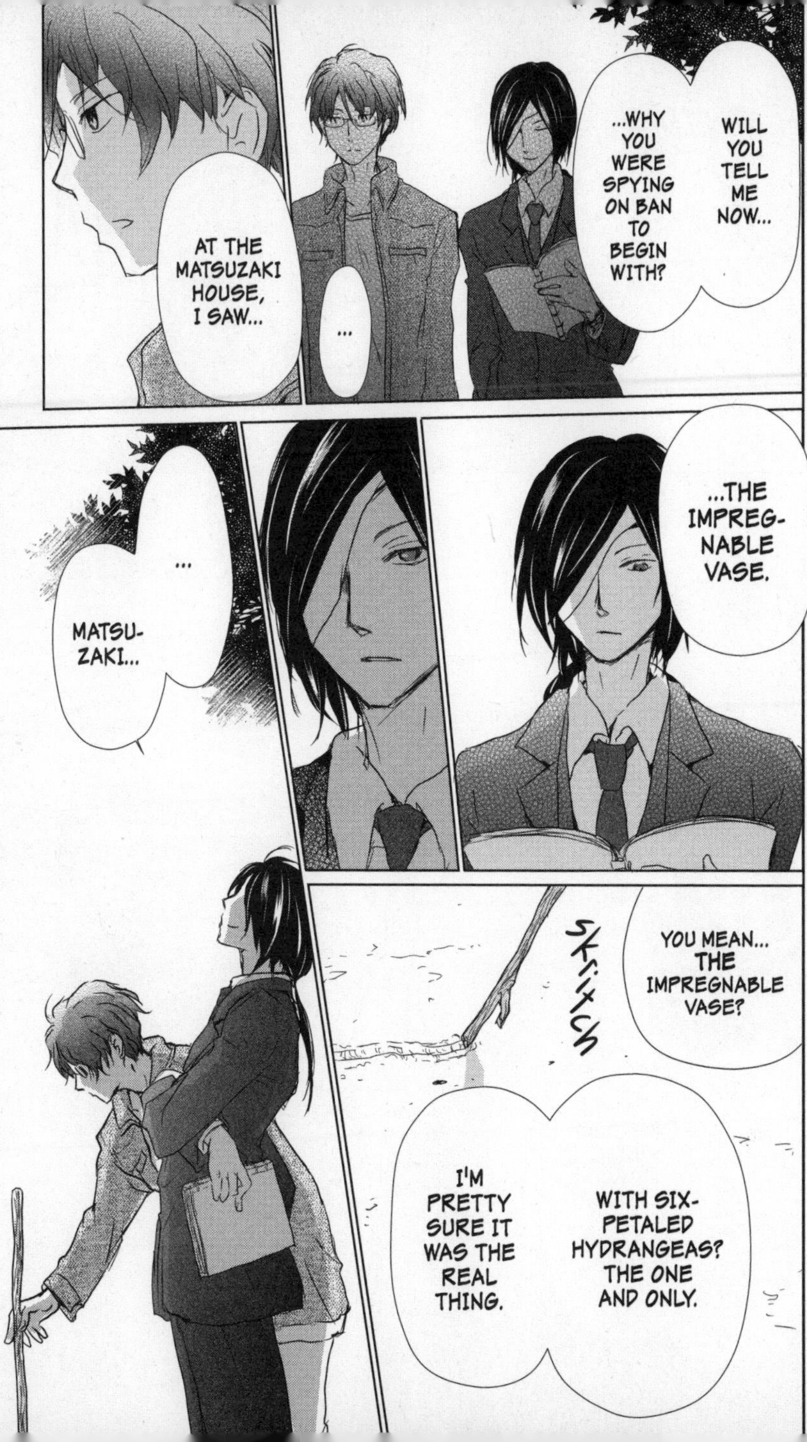
WILL YOU TELL ME NOW...
...WHY YOU WERE SPYING ON BAN TO BEGIN WITH?
...
AT THE MATSUZAKI HOUSE, I SAW...
...THE IMPREG-NABLE VASE.
...
MATSU-ZAKI...
YOU MEAN... THE IMPREGNABLE VASE?
SKRITCH
WITH SIX-PETALED HYDRANGEAS? THE ONE AND ONLY.
I'M PRETTY SURE IT WAS THE REAL THING.

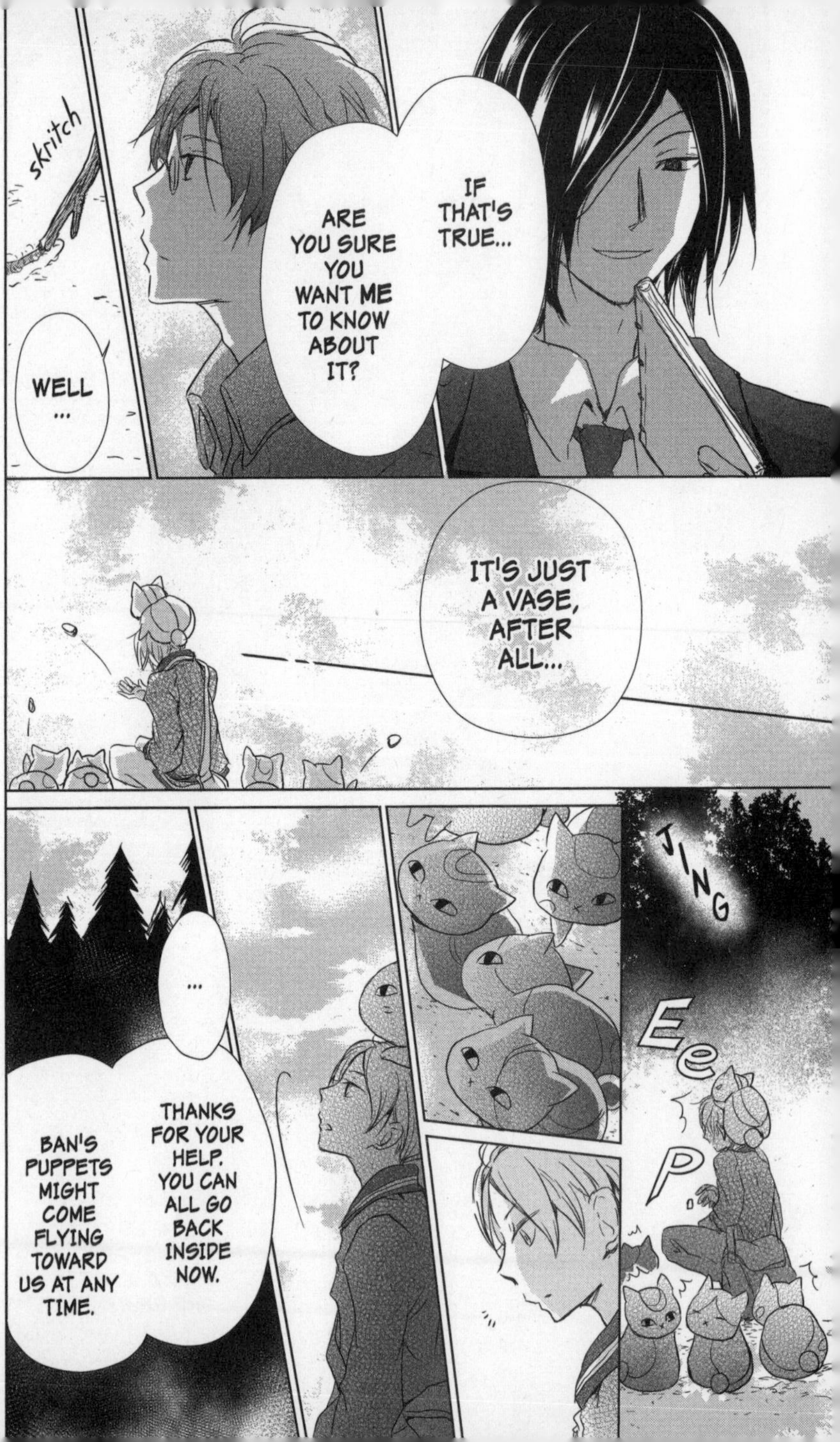
IF THAT'S TRUE...
ARE YOU SURE YOU WANT ME TO KNOW ABOUT IT?
skritch
WELL ...
IT'S JUST A VASE, AFTER ALL...
JING
EeP
...
THANKS FOR YOUR HELP. YOU CAN ALL GO BACK INSIDE NOW.
BAN'S PUPPETS MIGHT COME FLYING TOWARD US AT ANY TIME.

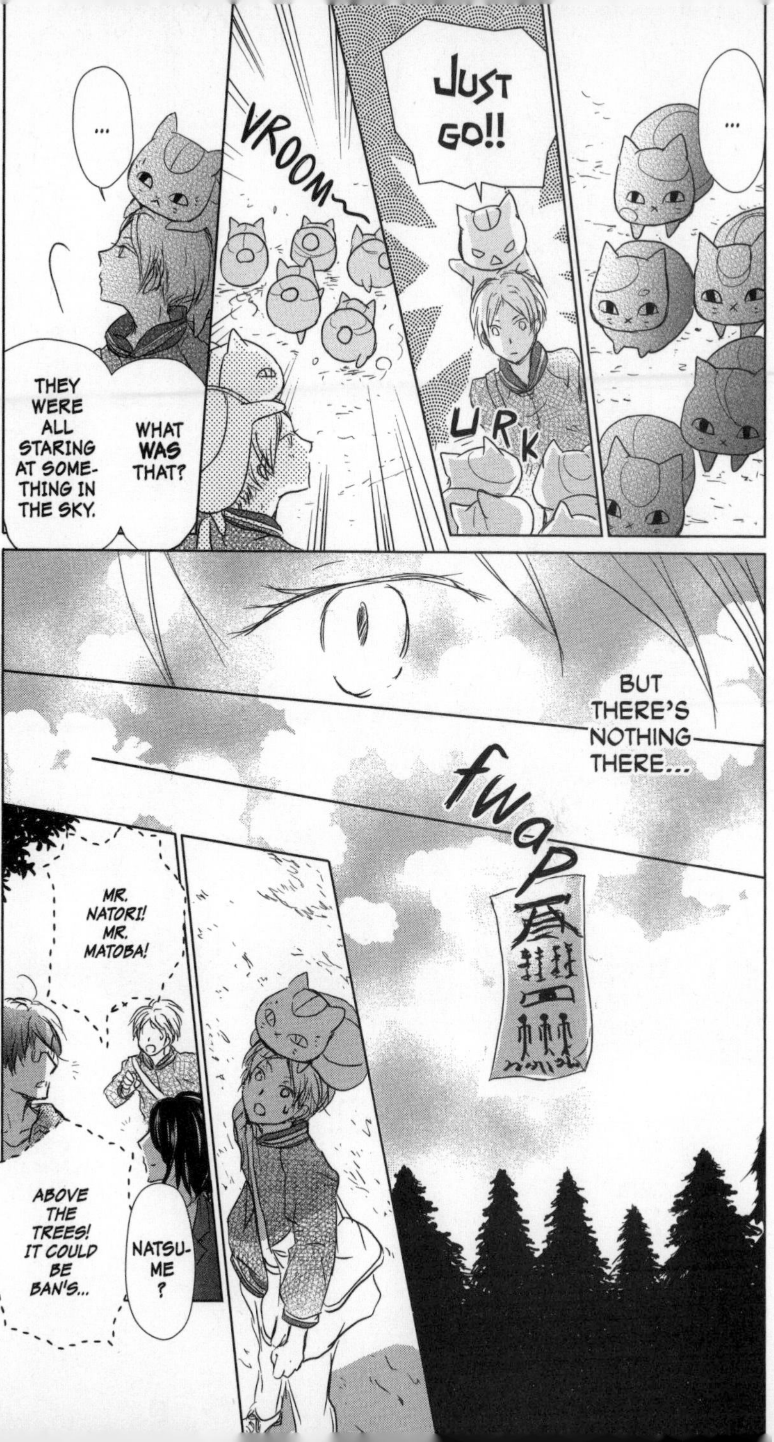
...
JUST GO!!
URK
VROOM~
...
WHAT WAS THAT?
THEY WERE ALL STARING AT SOME-THING IN THE SKY.
BUT THERE'S NOTHING THERE...
fwap
MR. NATORI! MR. MATOBA!
NATSU-ME?
ABOVE THE TREES! IT COULD BE BAN'S...

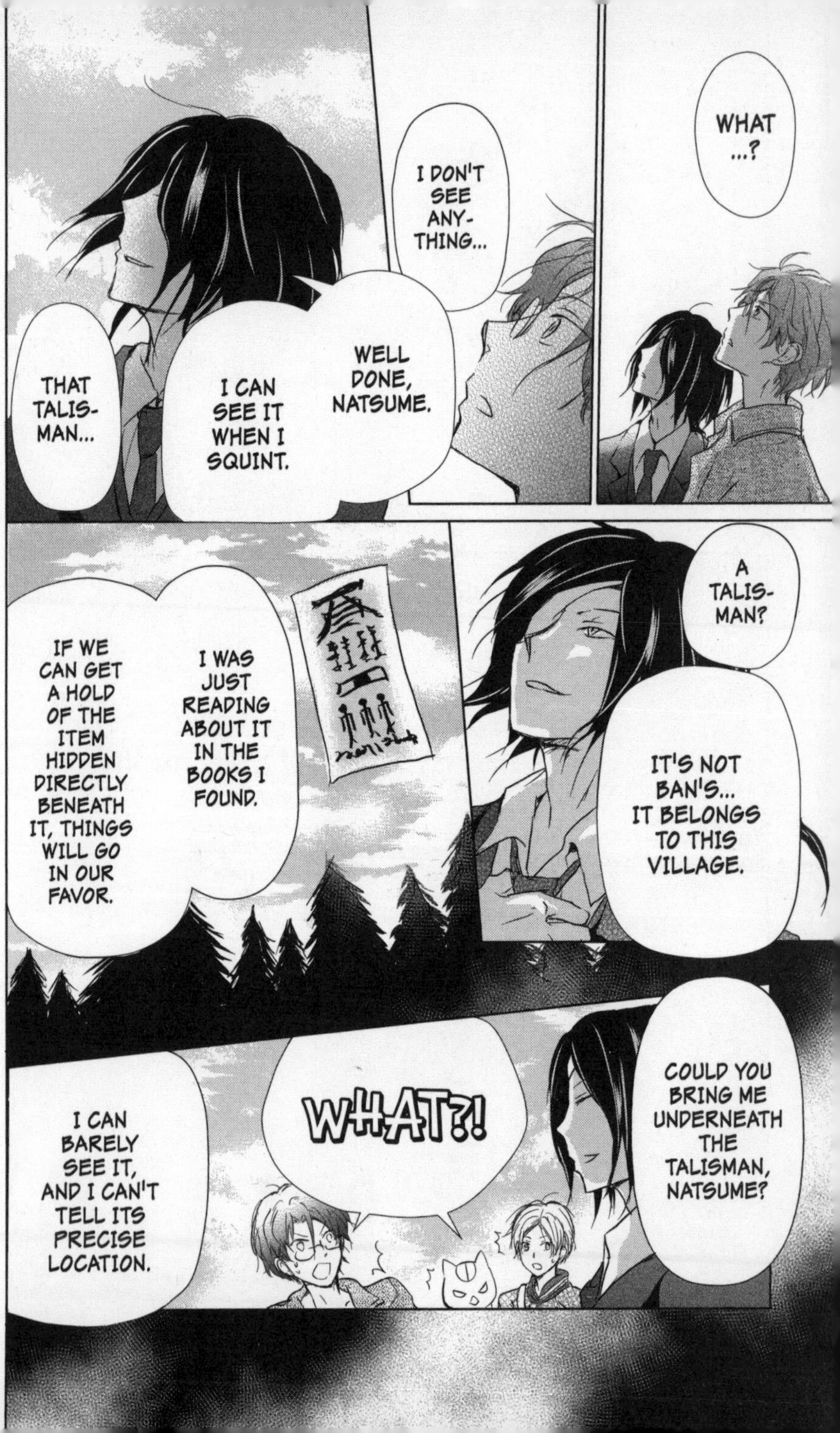
WHAT ...?
I DON'T SEE ANY-THING...
WELL DONE, NATSUME.
I CAN SEE IT WHEN I SQUINT.
THAT TALIS-MAN...
A TALIS-MAN?
IT'S NOT BAN'S... IT BELONGS TO THIS VILLAGE.
I WAS JUST READING ABOUT IT IN THE BOOKS I FOUND.
IF WE CAN GET A HOLD OF THE ITEM HIDDEN DIRECTLY BENEATH IT, THINGS WILL GO IN OUR FAVOR.
COULD YOU BRING ME UNDERNEATH THE TALISMAN, NATSUME?
WHAT?!
I CAN BARELY SEE IT, AND I CAN'T TELL ITS PRECISE LOCATION.

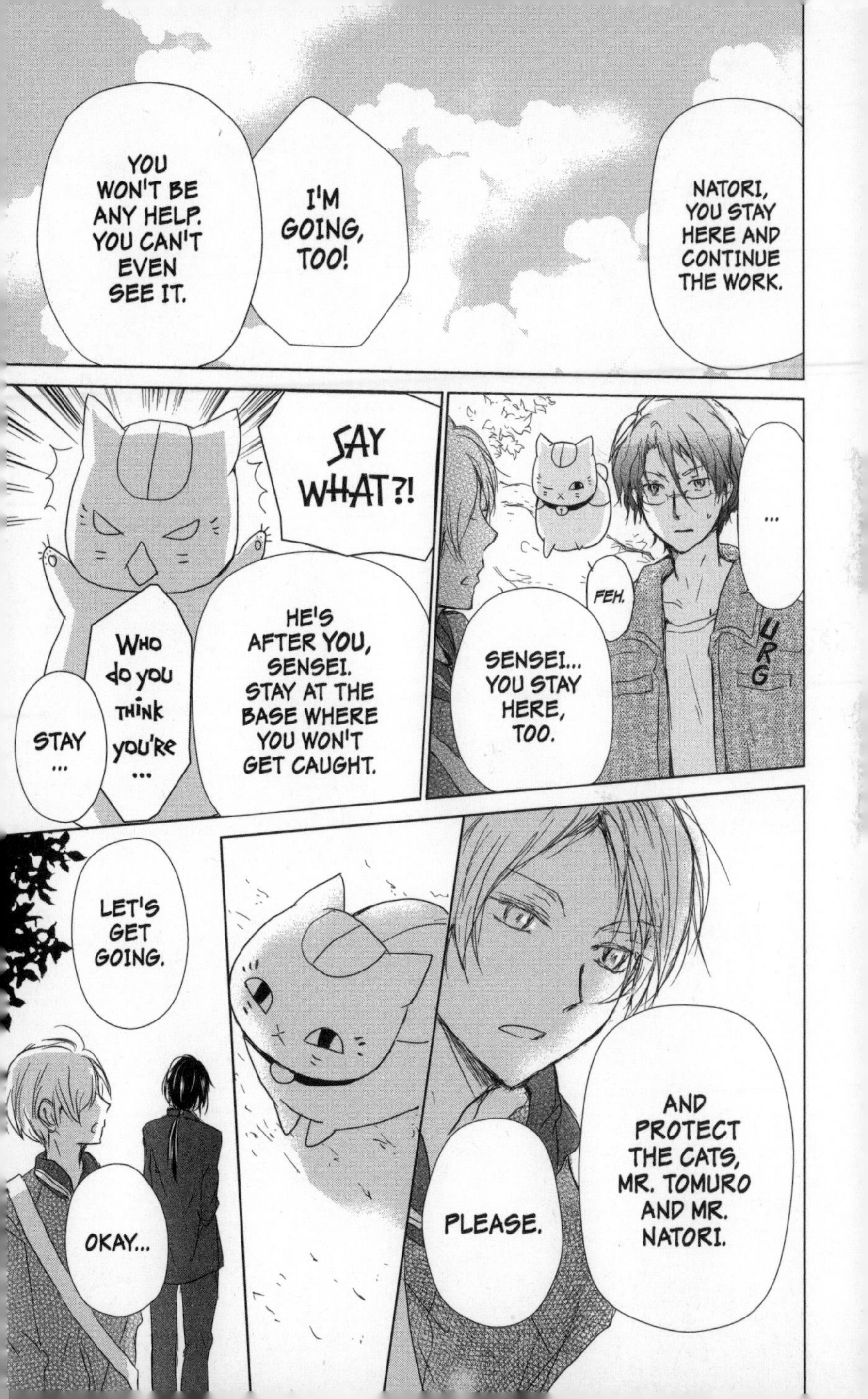
NATORI, YOU STAY HERE AND CONTINUE THE WORK.
I'M GOING, TOO!
YOU WON'T BE ANY HELP. YOU CAN'T EVEN SEE IT.
...
FEH.
SENSEI... YOU STAY HERE, TOO.
URG
SAY WHAT?!
HE'S AFTER YOU, SENSEI. STAY AT THE BASE WHERE YOU WON'T GET CAUGHT.
Who do you think you're ...
STAY ...
AND PROTECT THE CATS, MR. TOMURO AND MR. NATORI.
PLEASE.
LET'S GET GOING.
OKAY...

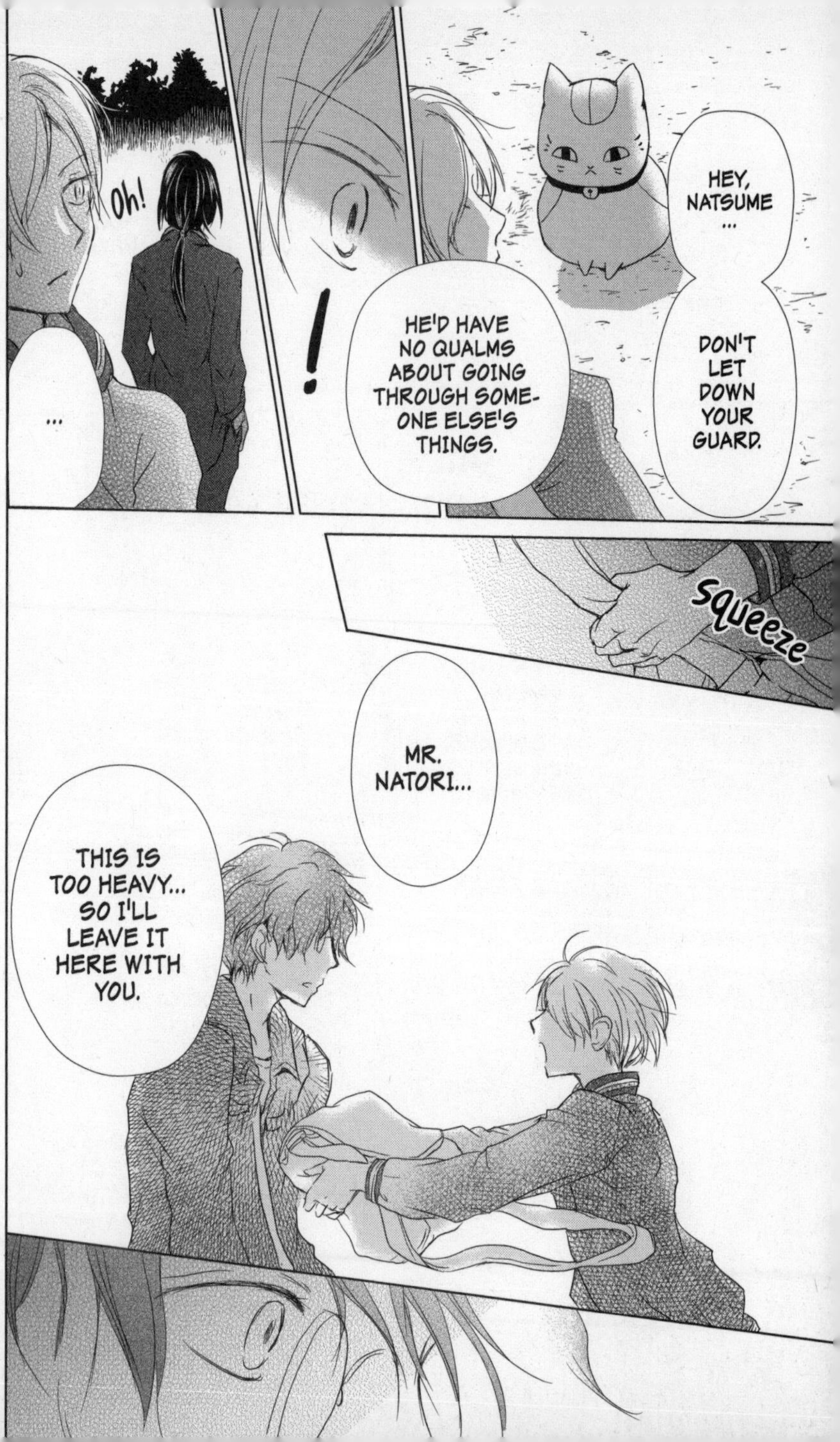
HEY, NATSUME...
DON'T LET DOWN YOUR GUARD.
HE'D HAVE NO QUALMS ABOUT GOING THROUGH SOMEONE ELSE'S THINGS.
!
Oh!
...
squeeze
MR. NATORI...
THIS IS TOO HEAVY... SO I'LL LEAVE IT HERE WITH YOU.

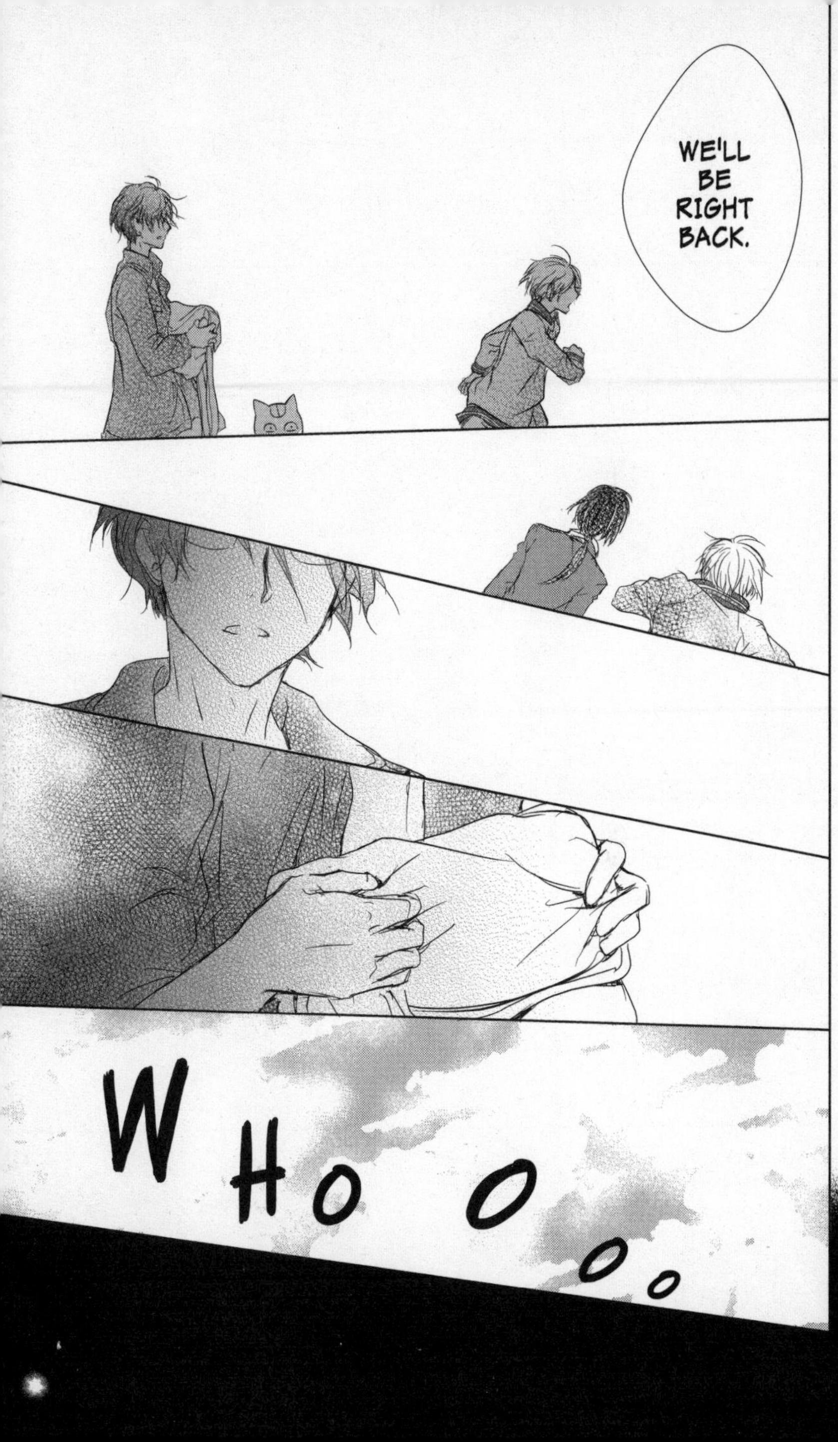
WE'LL BE RIGHT BACK.
WHOOOO...

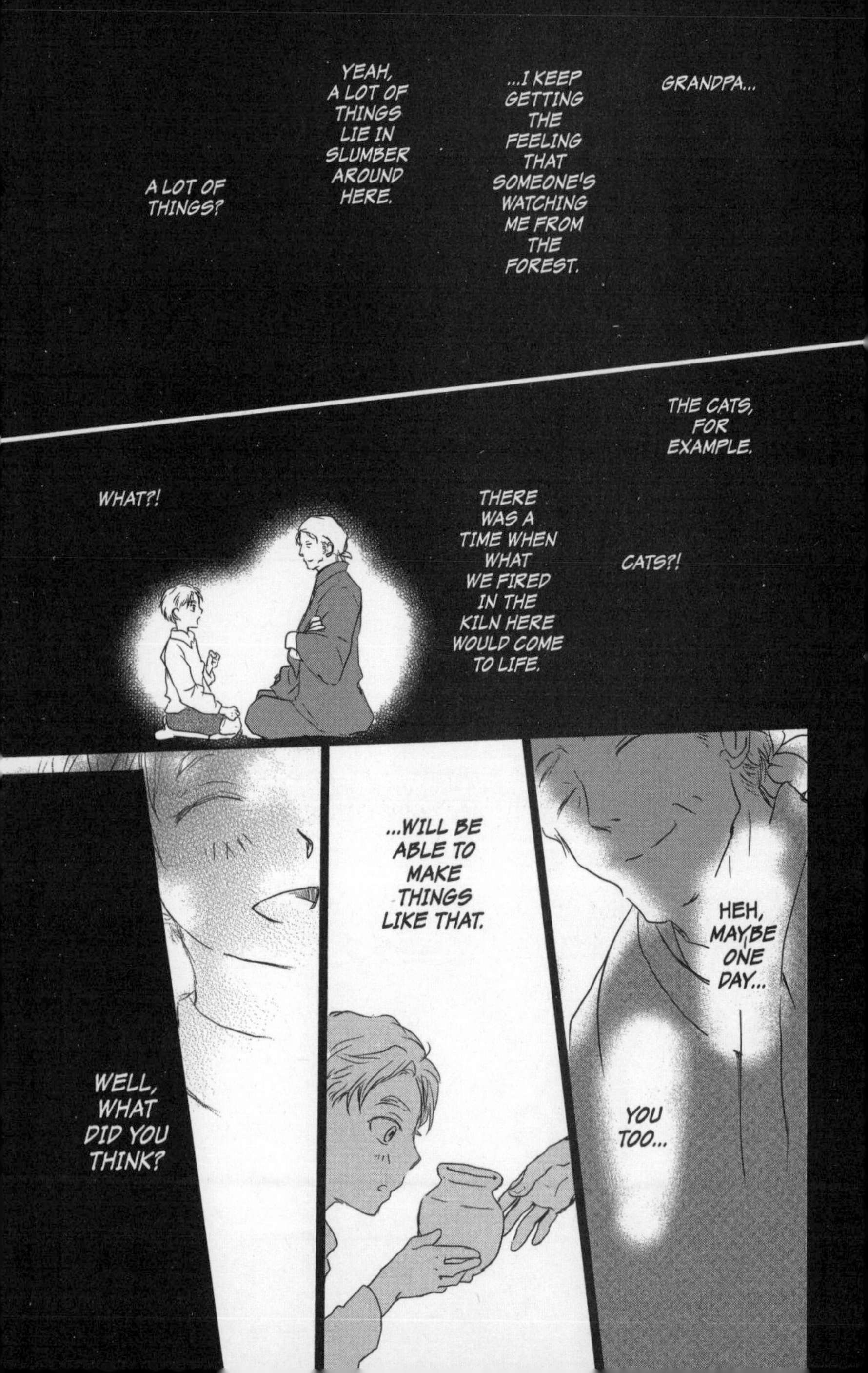
GRANDPA...
...I KEEP GETTING THE FEELING THAT SOMEONE'S WATCHING ME FROM THE FOREST.
YEAH, A LOT OF THINGS LIE IN SLUMBER AROUND HERE.
A LOT OF THINGS?
THE CATS, FOR EXAMPLE.
CATS?!
THERE WAS A TIME WHEN WHAT WE FIRED IN THE KILN HERE WOULD COME TO LIFE.
WHAT?!
HEH, MAYBE ONE DAY...
YOU TOO...
...WILL BE ABLE TO MAKE THINGS LIKE THAT.
WELL, WHAT DID YOU THINK?

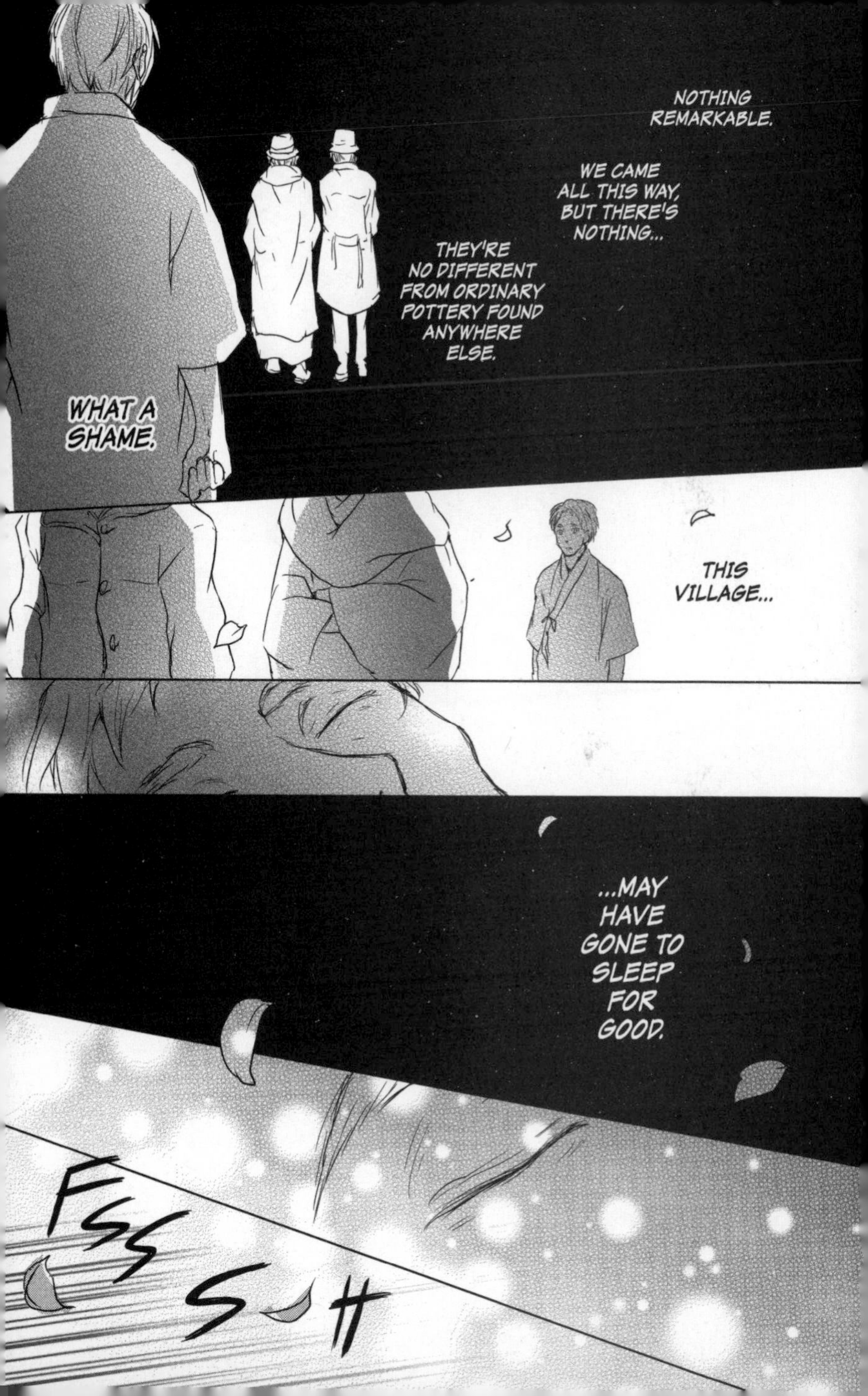
NOTHING REMARKABLE.
WE CAME ALL THIS WAY, BUT THERE'S NOTHING...
THEY'RE NO DIFFERENT FROM ORDINARY POTTERY FOUND ANYWHERE ELSE.
WHAT A SHAME.
THIS VILLAGE...
...MAY HAVE GONE TO SLEEP FOR GOOD.
FSSSH

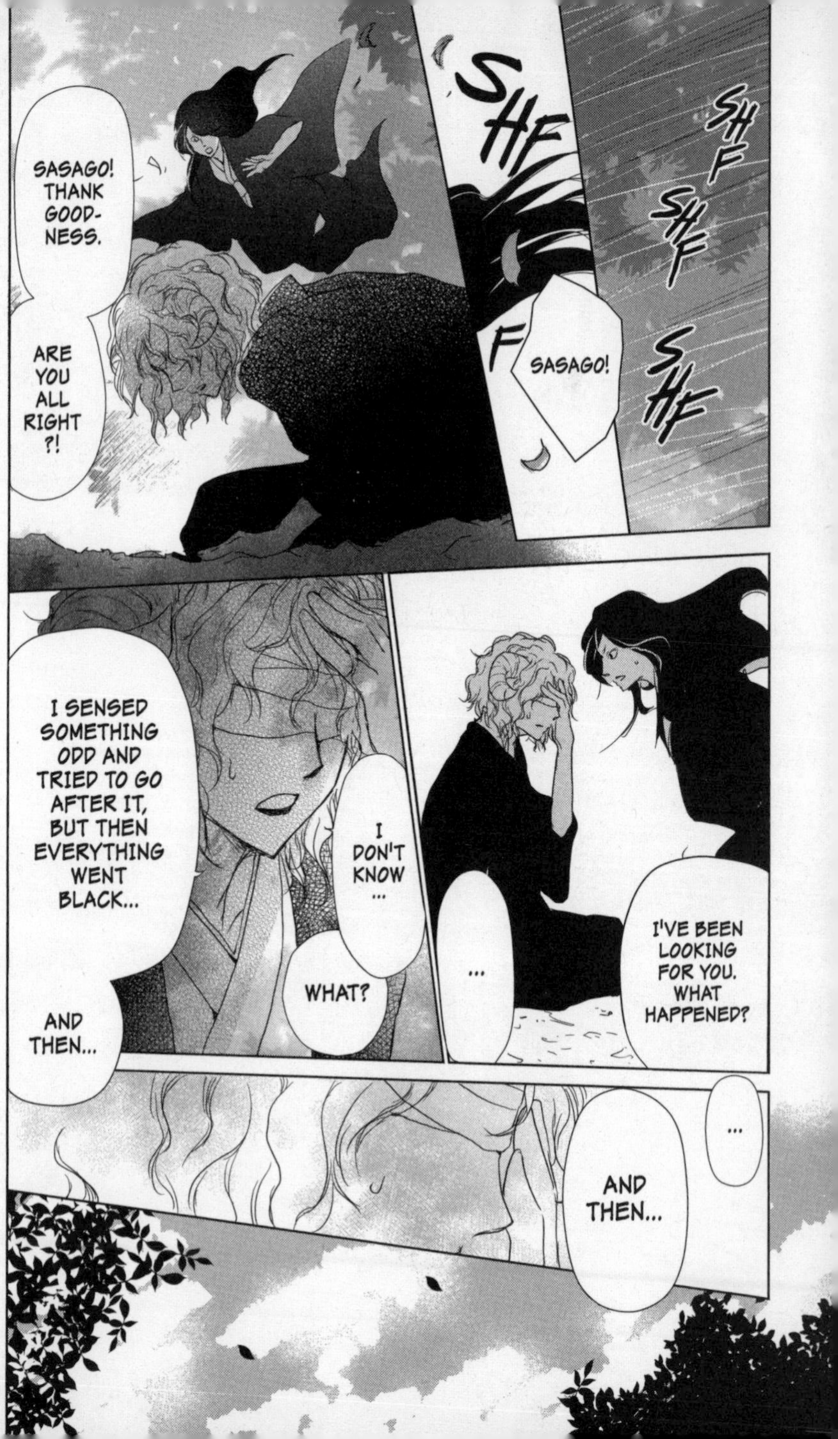
SHF
SHF
SHF
SHF
F
SASAGO!
SASAGO! THANK GOODNESS.
ARE YOU ALL RIGHT ?!
I'VE BEEN LOOKING FOR YOU. WHAT HAPPENED?
...
I DON'T KNOW ...
WHAT?
I SENSED SOMETHING ODD AND TRIED TO GO AFTER IT, BUT THEN EVERYTHING WENT BLACK...
AND THEN...
...
AND THEN...

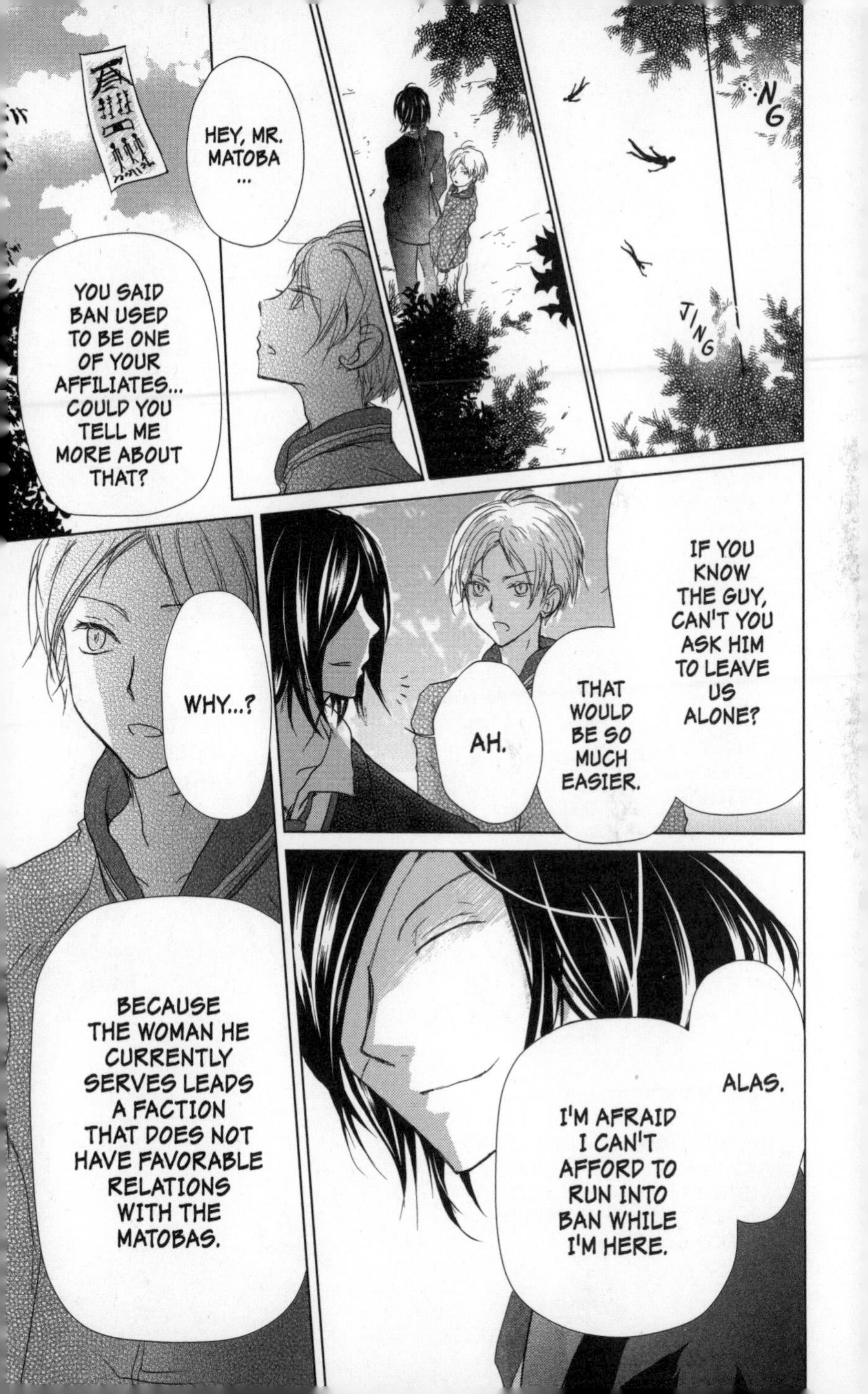

...NG
JING
HEY, MR. MATOBA ...
YOU SAID BAN USED TO BE ONE OF YOUR AFFILIATES... COULD YOU TELL ME MORE ABOUT THAT?
IF YOU KNOW THE GUY, CAN'T YOU ASK HIM TO LEAVE US ALONE?
THAT WOULD BE SO MUCH EASIER.
AH.
ALAS.
I'M AFRAID I CAN'T AFFORD TO RUN INTO BAN WHILE I'M HERE.
WHY...?
BECAUSE THE WOMAN HE CURRENTLY SERVES LEADS A FACTION THAT DOES NOT HAVE FAVORABLE RELATIONS WITH THE MATOBAS.

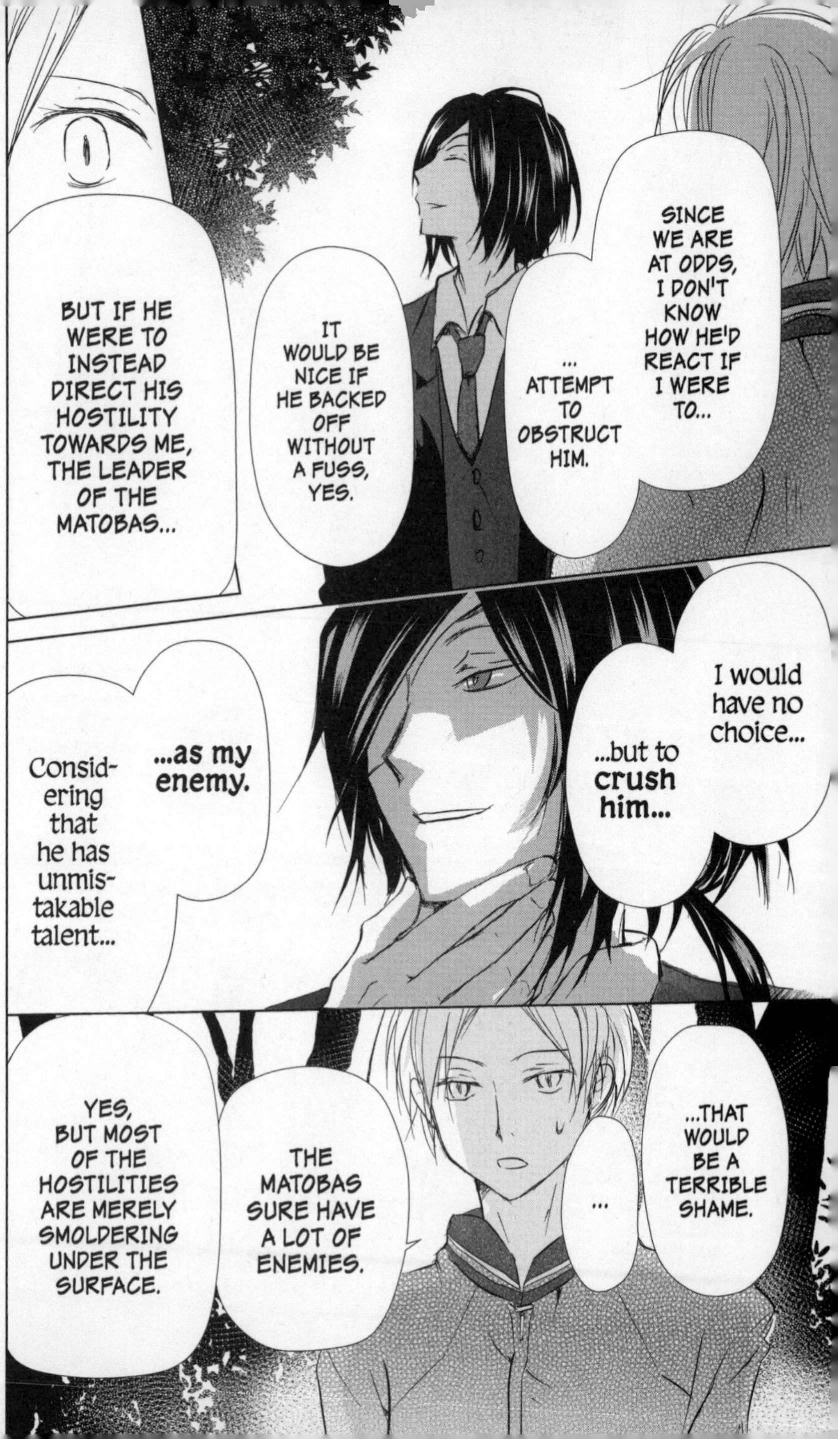
SINCE WE ARE AT ODDS, I DON'T KNOW HOW HE'D REACT IF I WERE TO...
... ATTEMPT TO OBSTRUCT HIM.
IT WOULD BE NICE IF HE BACKED OFF WITHOUT A FUSS, YES.
BUT IF HE WERE TO INSTEAD DIRECT HIS HOSTILITY TOWARDS ME, THE LEADER OF THE MATOBAS...
I would have no choice...
...but to crush him...
...as my enemy.
Considering that he has unmistakable talent...
...THAT WOULD BE A TERRIBLE SHAME.
...
THE MATOBAS SURE HAVE A LOT OF ENEMIES.
YES, BUT MOST OF THE HOSTILITIES ARE MERELY SMOLDERING UNDER THE SURFACE.

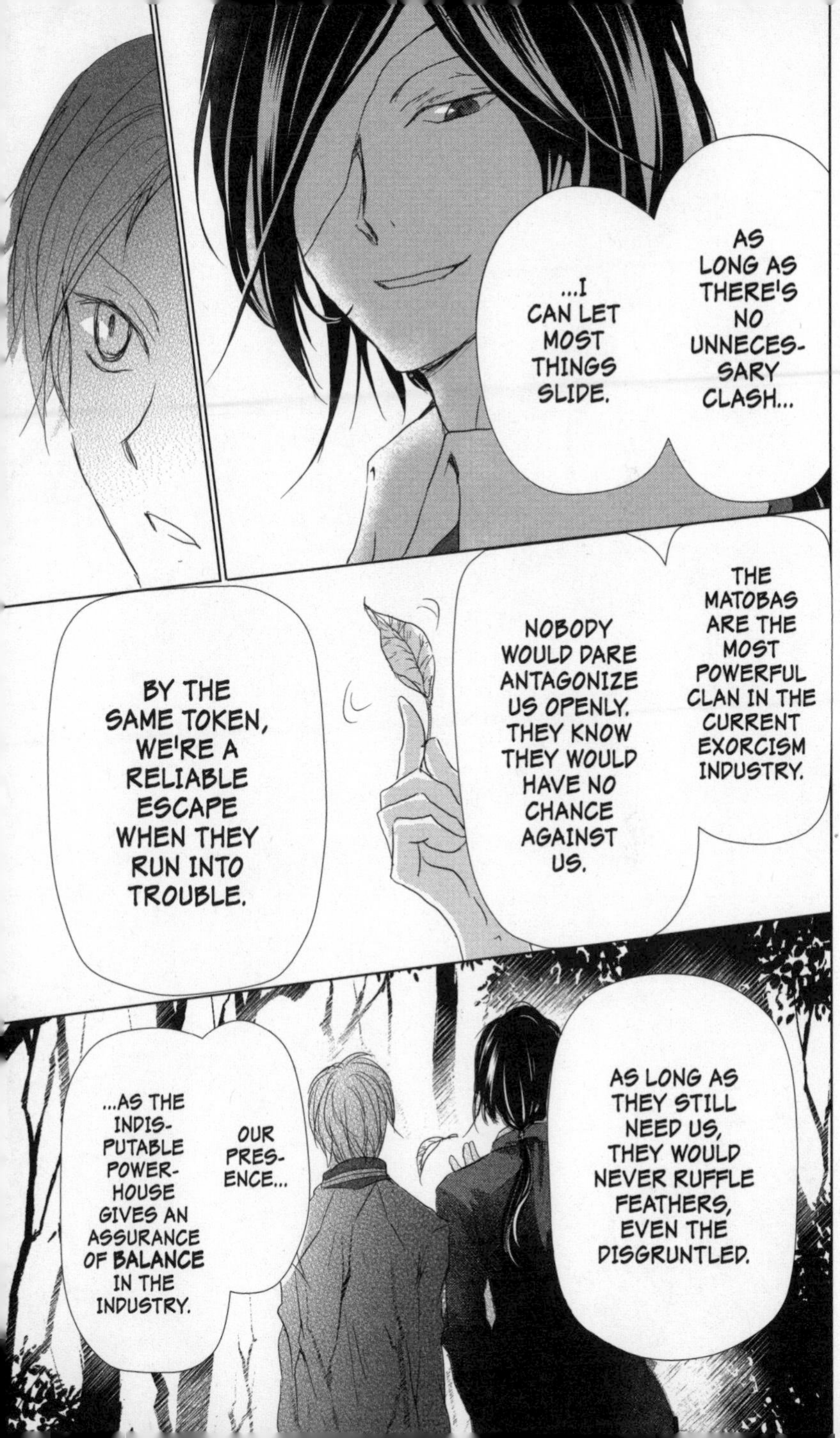
AS LONG AS THERE'S NO UNNECES-SARY CLASH...
...I CAN LET MOST THINGS SLIDE.
THE MATOBAS ARE THE MOST POWERFUL CLAN IN THE CURRENT EXORCISM INDUSTRY.
NOBODY WOULD DARE ANTAGONIZE US OPENLY. THEY KNOW THEY WOULD HAVE NO CHANCE AGAINST US.
BY THE SAME TOKEN, WE'RE A RELIABLE ESCAPE WHEN THEY RUN INTO TROUBLE.
AS LONG AS THEY STILL NEED US, THEY WOULD NEVER RUFFLE FEATHERS, EVEN THE DISGRUNTLED.
OUR PRES-ENCE...
...AS THE INDIS-PUTABLE POWER-HOUSE GIVES AN ASSURANCE OF BALANCE IN THE INDUSTRY.

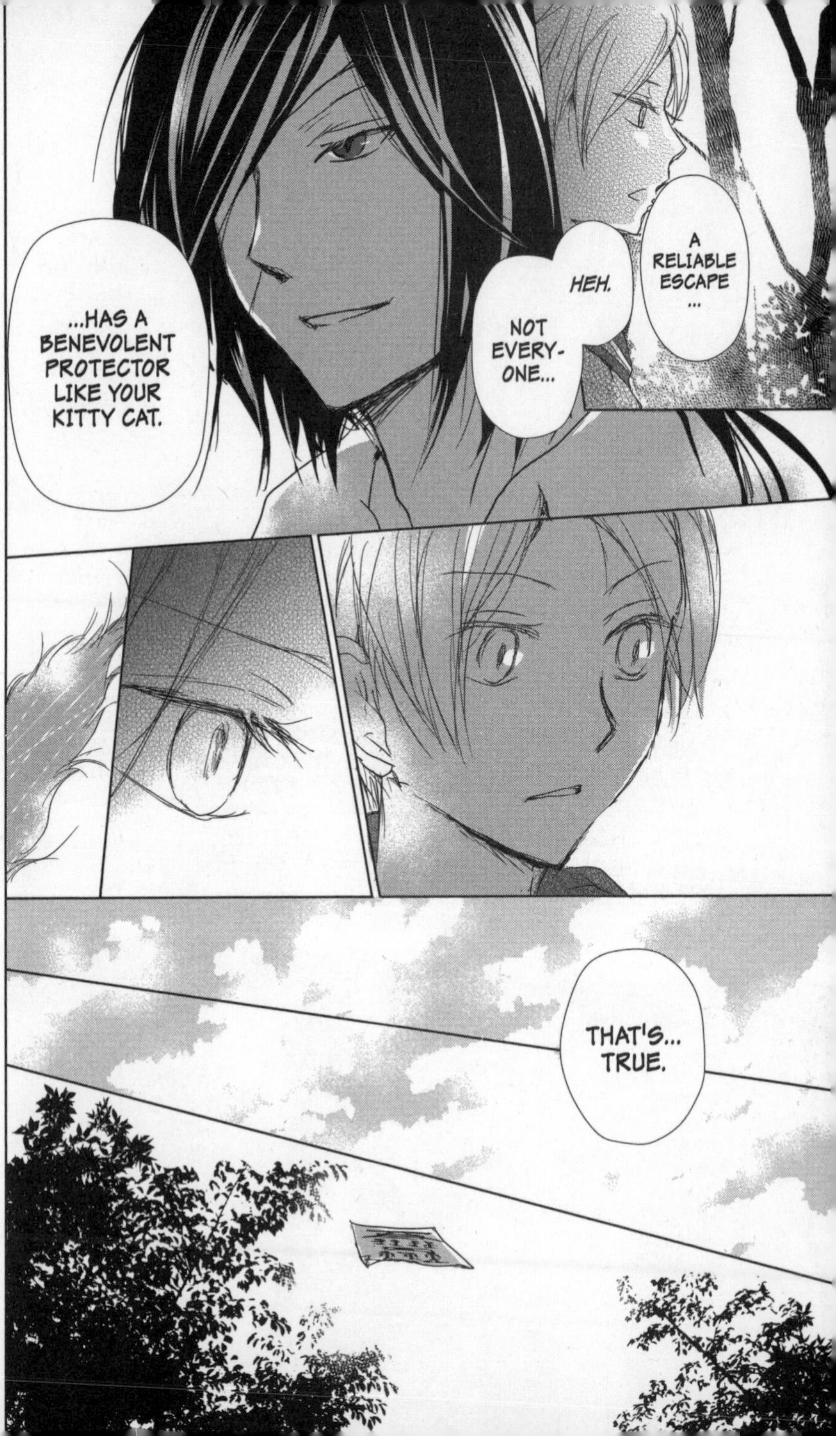
A RELIABLE ESCAPE ...
HEH.
NOT EVERY-ONE...
...HAS A BENEVOLENT PROTECTOR LIKE YOUR KITTY CAT.
THAT'S... TRUE.

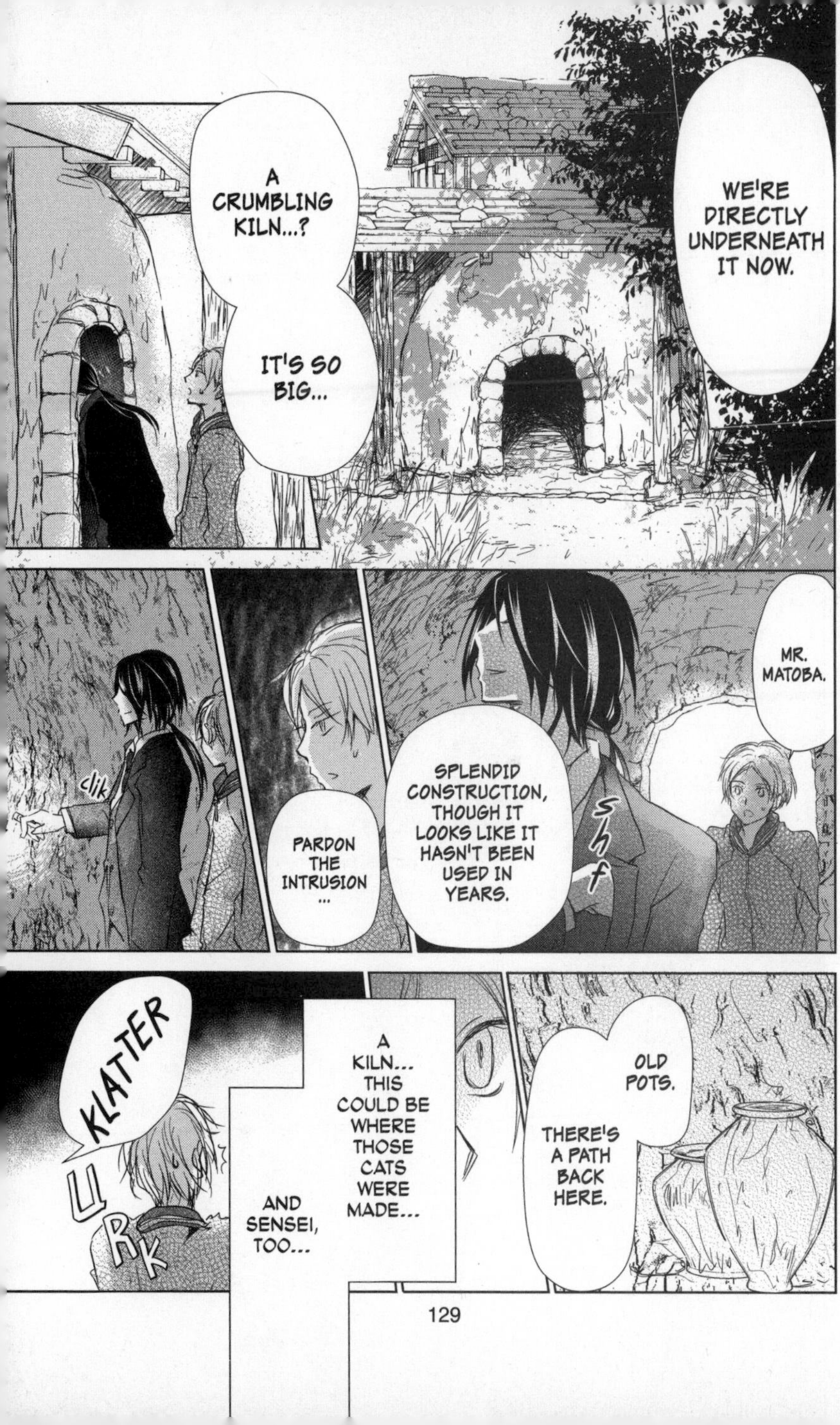
WE'RE DIRECTLY UNDERNEATH IT NOW.
A CRUMBLING KILN...?
IT'S SO BIG...
MR. MATOBA.
SPLENDID CONSTRUCTION, THOUGH IT LOOKS LIKE IT HASN'T BEEN USED IN YEARS.
shf
PARDON THE INTRUSION ...
clik
OLD POTS.
THERE'S A PATH BACK HERE.
A KILN... THIS COULD BE WHERE THOSE CATS WERE MADE...
AND SENSEI, TOO...
KLATTER
URK

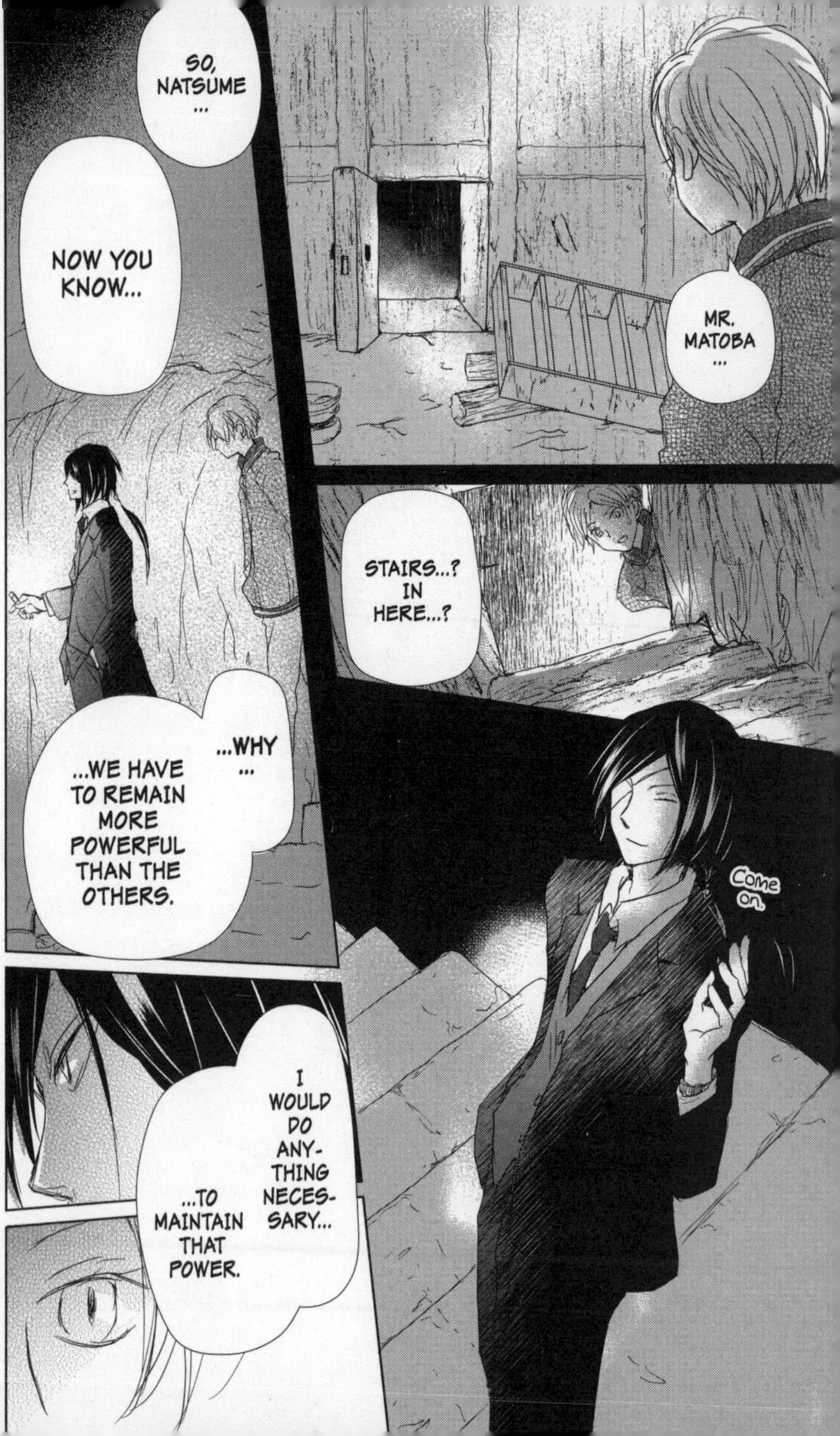
MR. MATOBA ...
STAIRS...? IN HERE...?
Come on.
SO, NATSUME ...
NOW YOU KNOW...
...WHY ...
...WE HAVE TO REMAIN MORE POWERFUL THAN THE OTHERS.
I WOULD DO ANY-THING NECES-SARY...
...TO MAINTAIN THAT POWER.

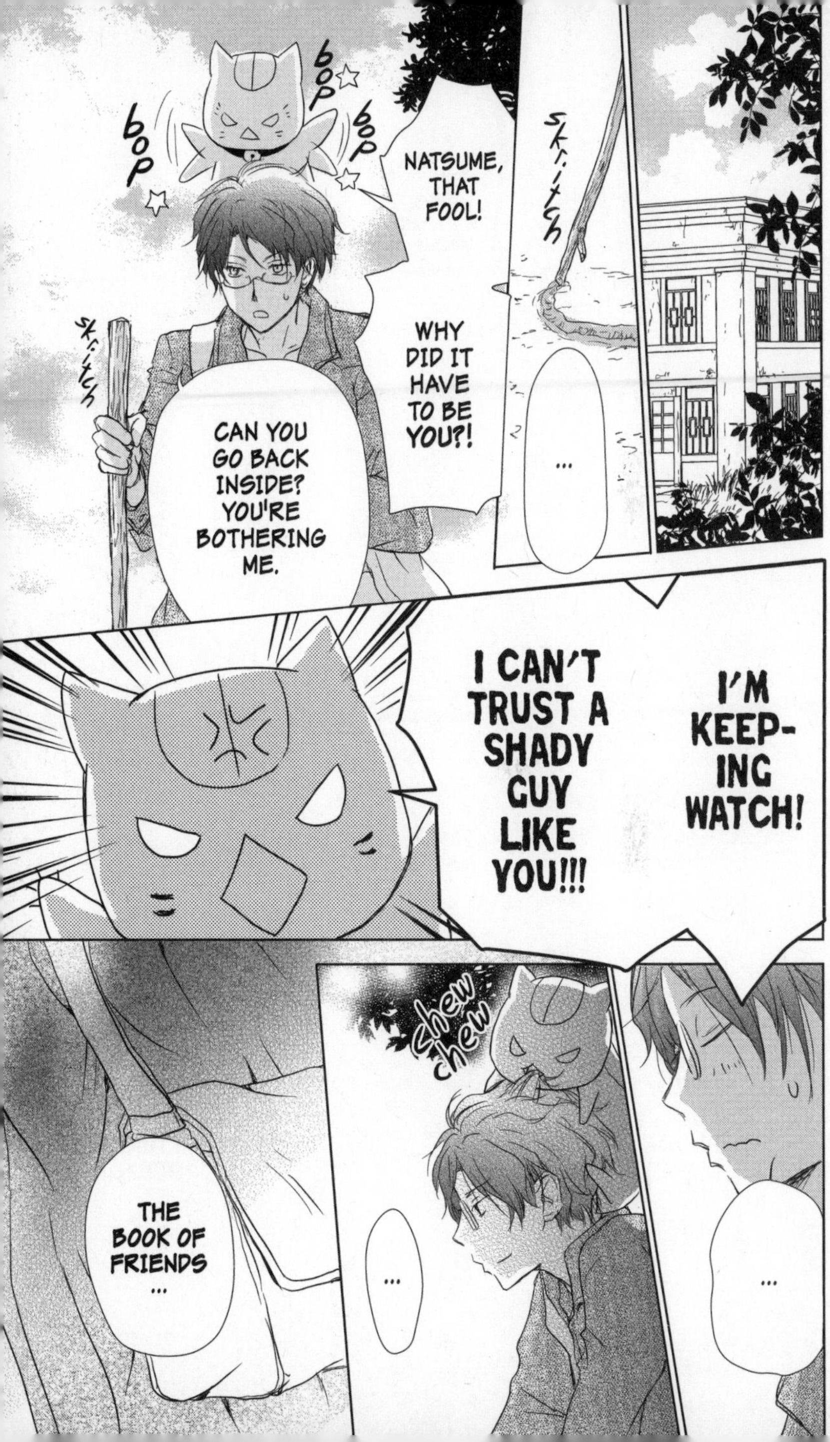
skritch
...
NATSUME, THAT FOOL!
WHY DID IT HAVE TO BE YOU?!
bop
bop
bop
CAN YOU GO BACK INSIDE? YOU'RE BOTHERING ME.
skritch
I'M KEEPING-ING WATCH!
I CAN'T TRUST A SHADY GUY LIKE YOU!!!
...
chew chew
...
THE BOOK OF FRIENDS ...

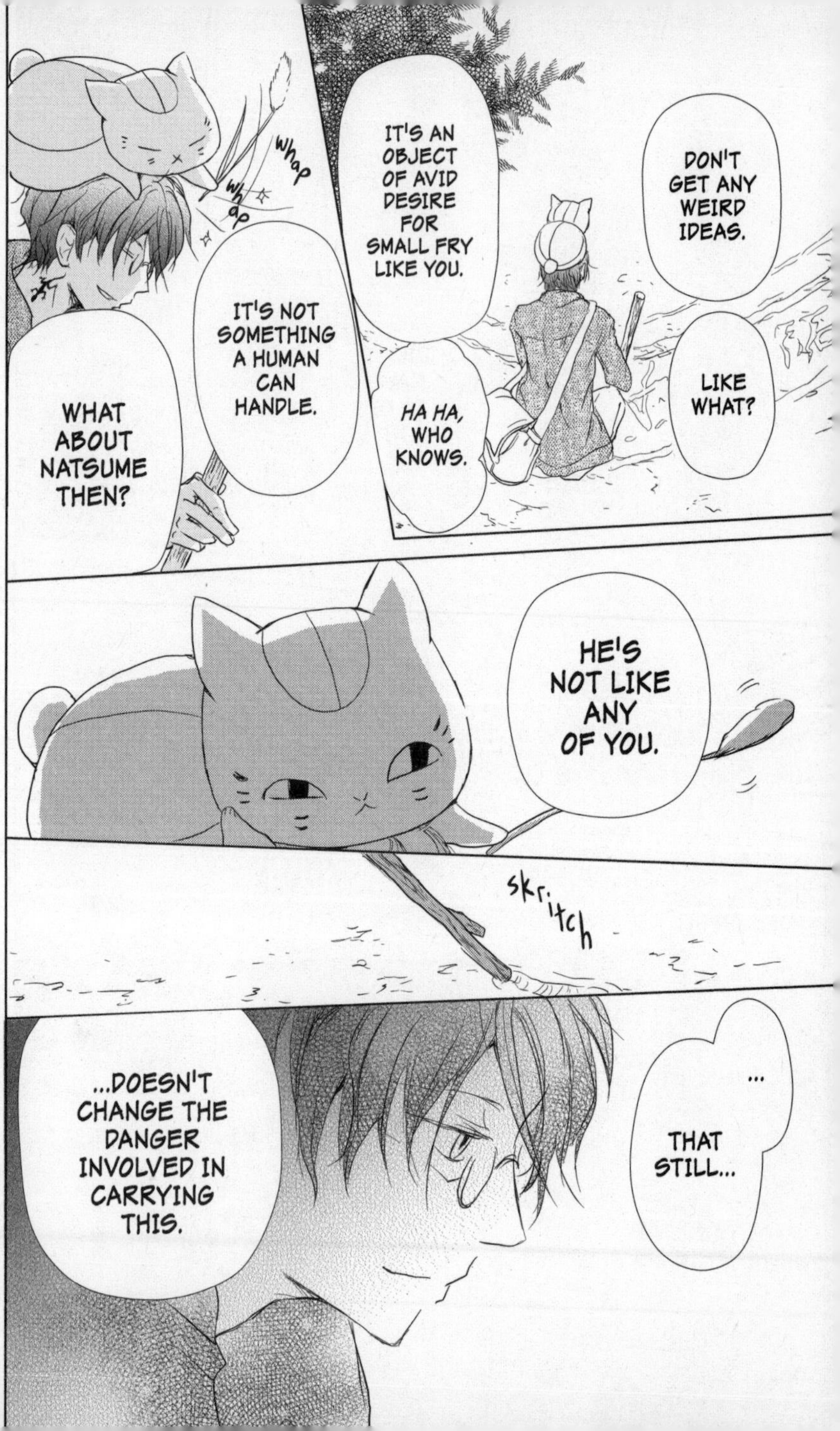
DON'T GET ANY WEIRD IDEAS.
LIKE WHAT?
IT'S AN OBJECT OF AVID DESIRE FOR SMALL FRY LIKE YOU.
HA HA, WHO KNOWS.
whap whap
IT'S NOT SOMETHING A HUMAN CAN HANDLE.
WHAT ABOUT NATSUME THEN?
HE'S NOT LIKE ANY OF YOU.
skritch
... THAT STILL...
...DOESN'T CHANGE THE DANGER INVOLVED IN CARRYING THIS.

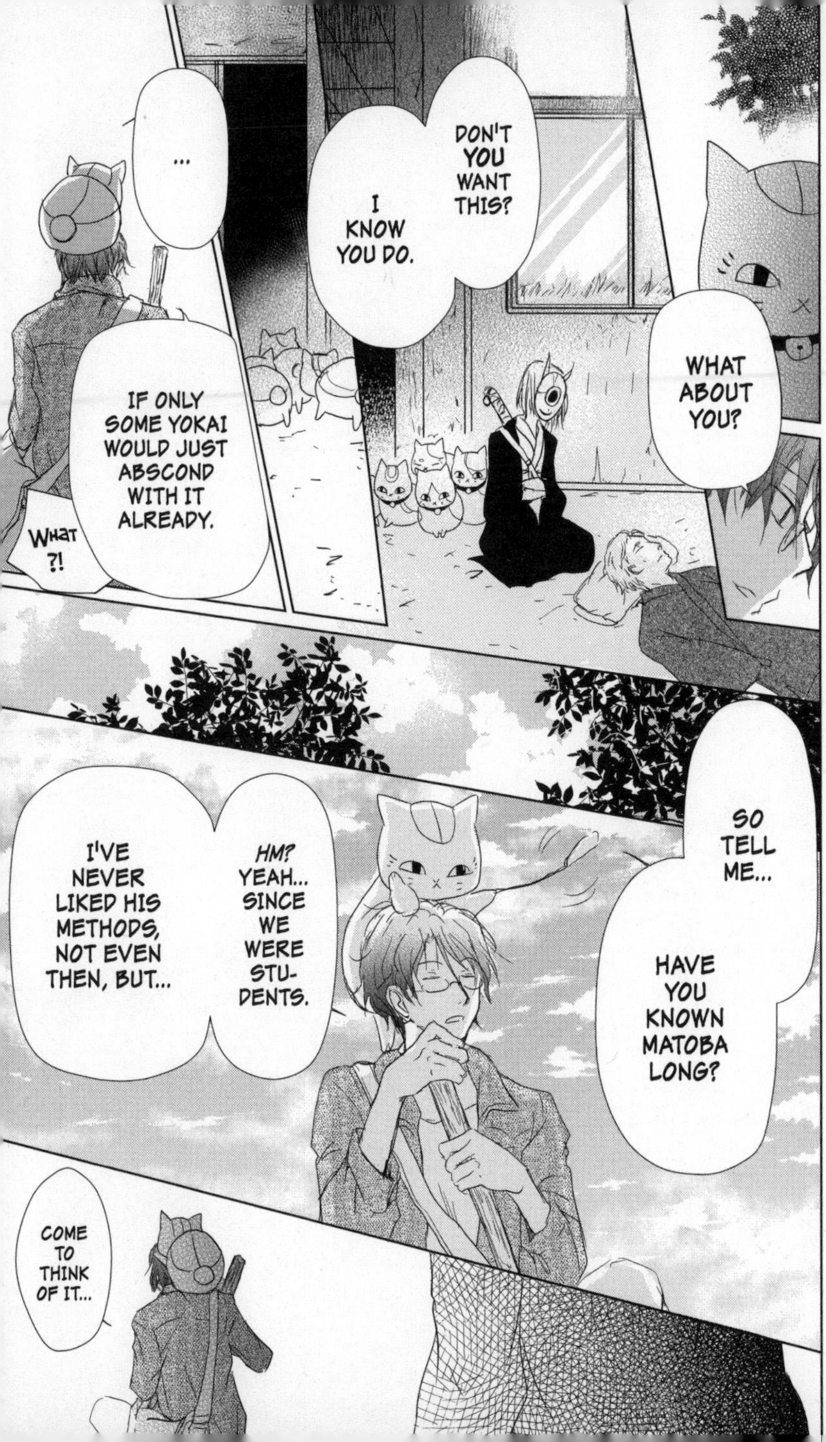
WHAT ABOUT YOU?
DON'T YOU WANT THIS?
I KNOW YOU DO.
...
IF ONLY SOME YOKAI WOULD JUST ABSCOND WITH IT ALREADY.
WHAT ?!
SO TELL ME...
HAVE YOU KNOWN MATOBA LONG?
HM? YEAH... SINCE WE WERE STU-DENTS.
I'VE NEVER LIKED HIS METHODS, NOT EVEN THEN, BUT...
COME TO THINK OF IT...

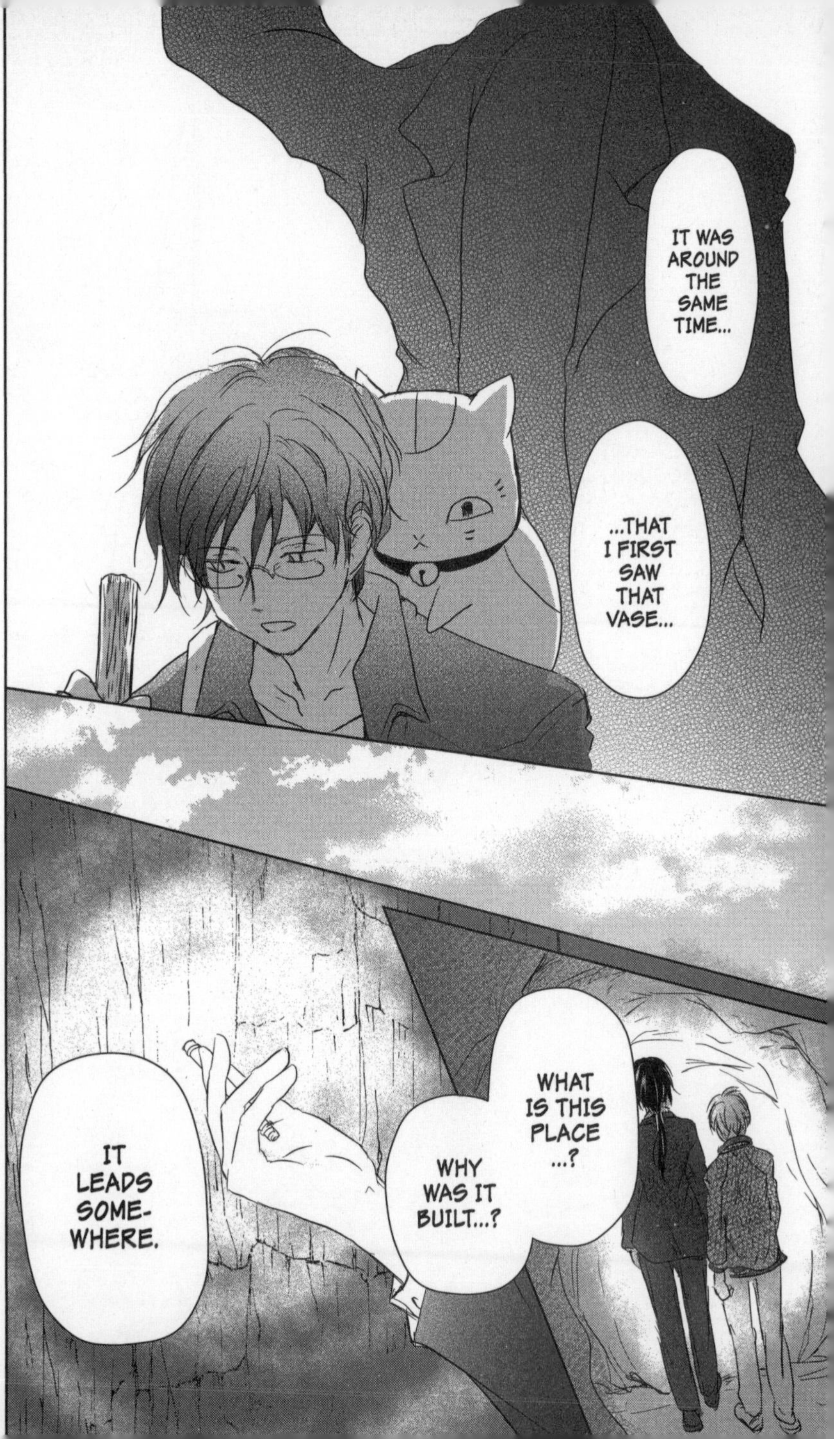
IT WAS AROUND THE SAME TIME...
...THAT I FIRST SAW THAT VASE...
WHAT IS THIS PLACE ...?
WHY WAS IT BUILT...?
IT LEADS SOME-WHERE.

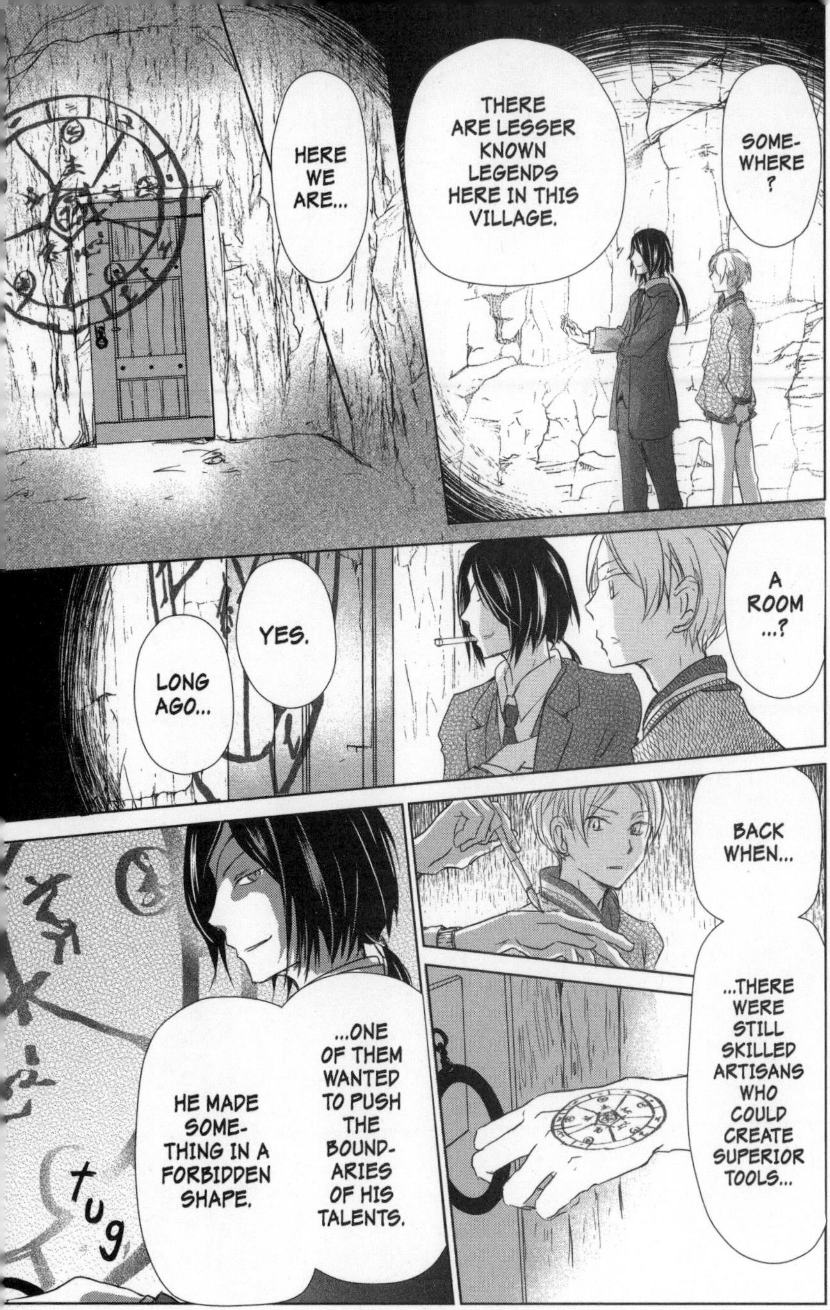
SOMEWHERE?
THERE ARE LESSER KNOWN LEGENDS HERE IN THIS VILLAGE.
HERE WE ARE...
A ROOM...?
YES.
LONG AGO...
BACK WHEN...
...THERE WERE STILL SKILLED ARTISANS WHO COULD CREATE SUPERIOR TOOLS...
...ONE OF THEM WANTED TO PUSH THE BOUNDARIES OF HIS TALENTS.
HE MADE SOMETHING IN A FORBIDDEN SHAPE.
tug

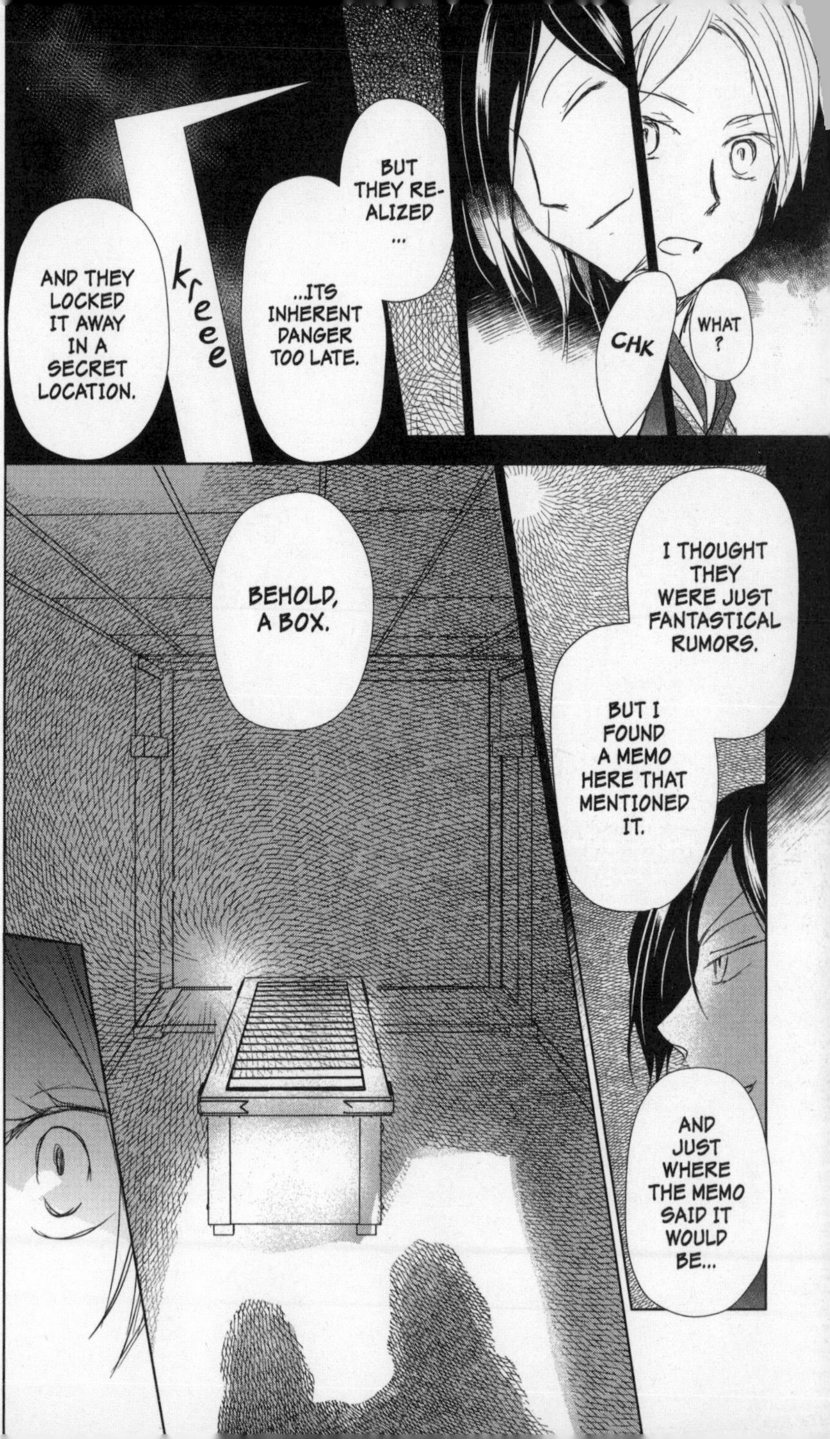
WHAT?
CHK
BUT THEY RE-ALIZED ...
...ITS INHERENT DANGER TOO LATE.
kreee
AND THEY LOCKED IT AWAY IN A SECRET LOCATION.
I THOUGHT THEY WERE JUST FANTASTICAL RUMORS.
BUT I FOUND A MEMO HERE THAT MENTIONED IT.
AND JUST WHERE THE MEMO SAID IT WOULD BE...
BEHOLD, A BOX.

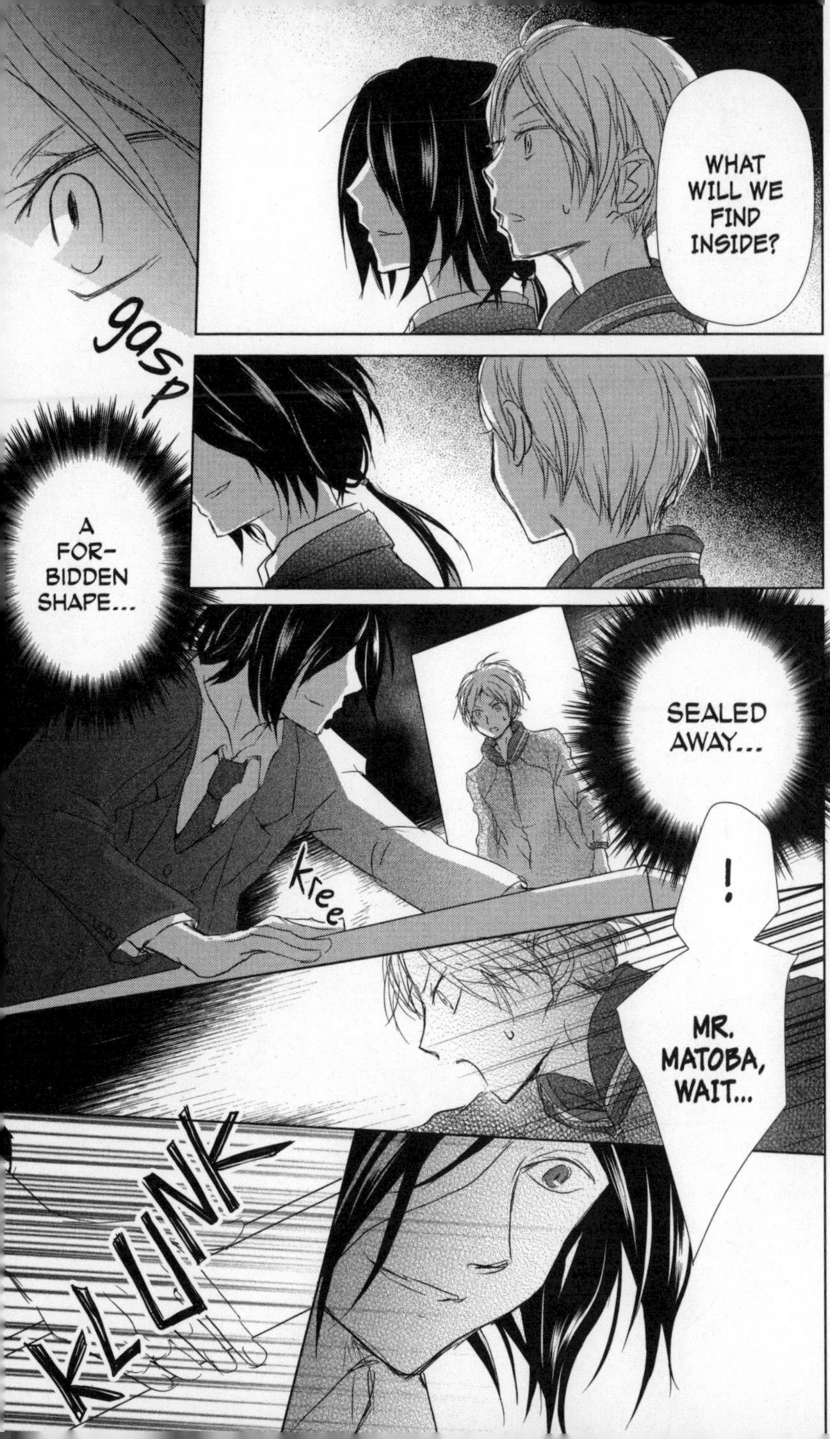
WHAT WILL WE FIND INSIDE?
gasp
A FOR-BIDDEN SHAPE...
SEALED AWAY...
kree
!
MR. MATOBA, WAIT...
KLUNK

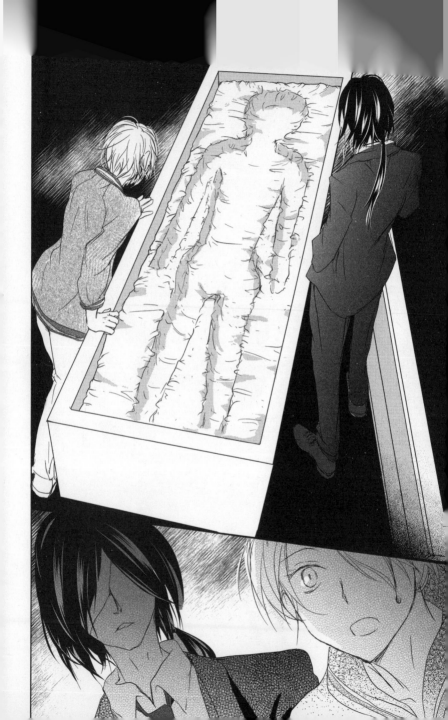

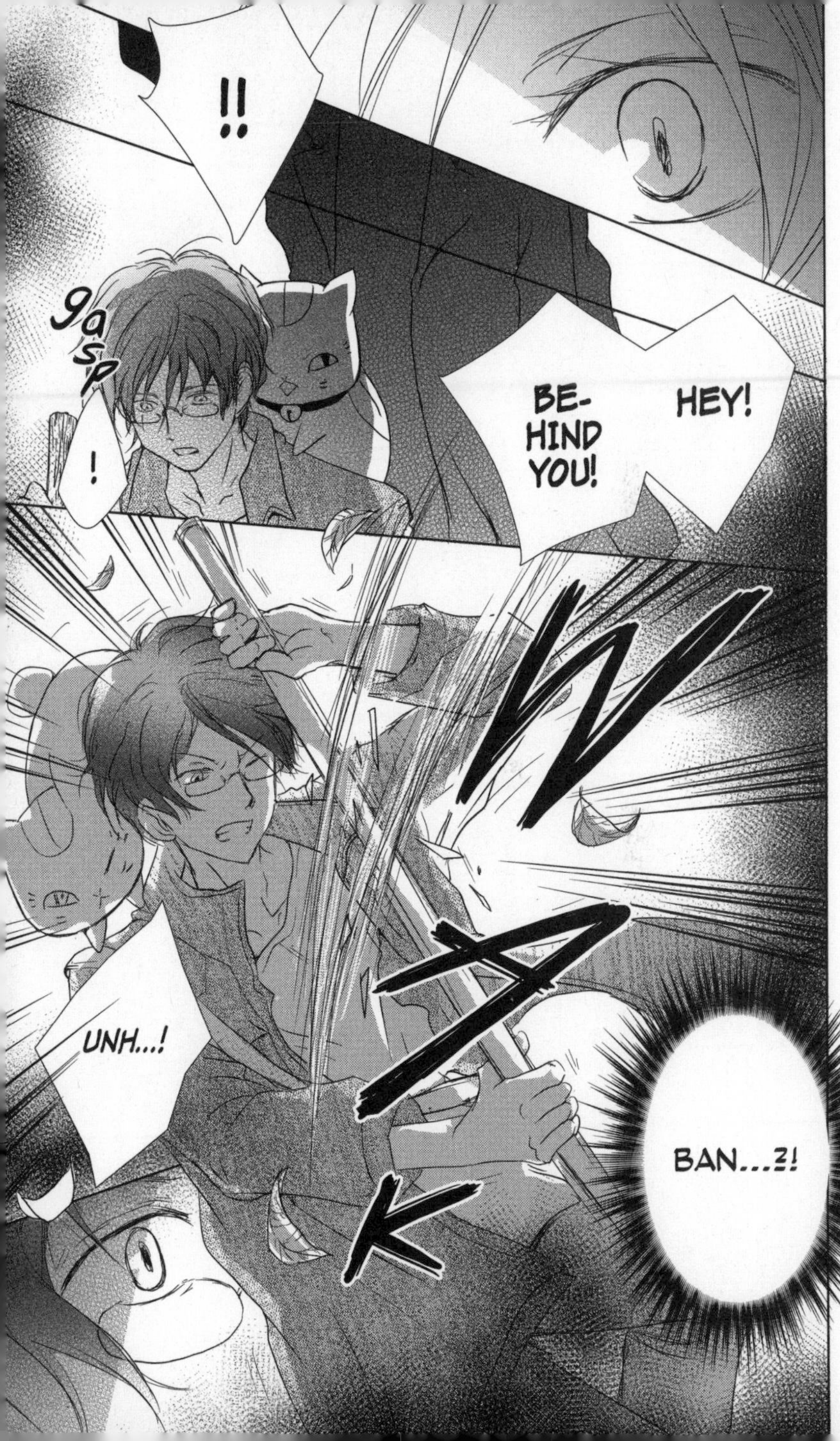
!!
HEY! BE-HIND YOU!
gasp
!
WAK
BAN...?!
UNH...!

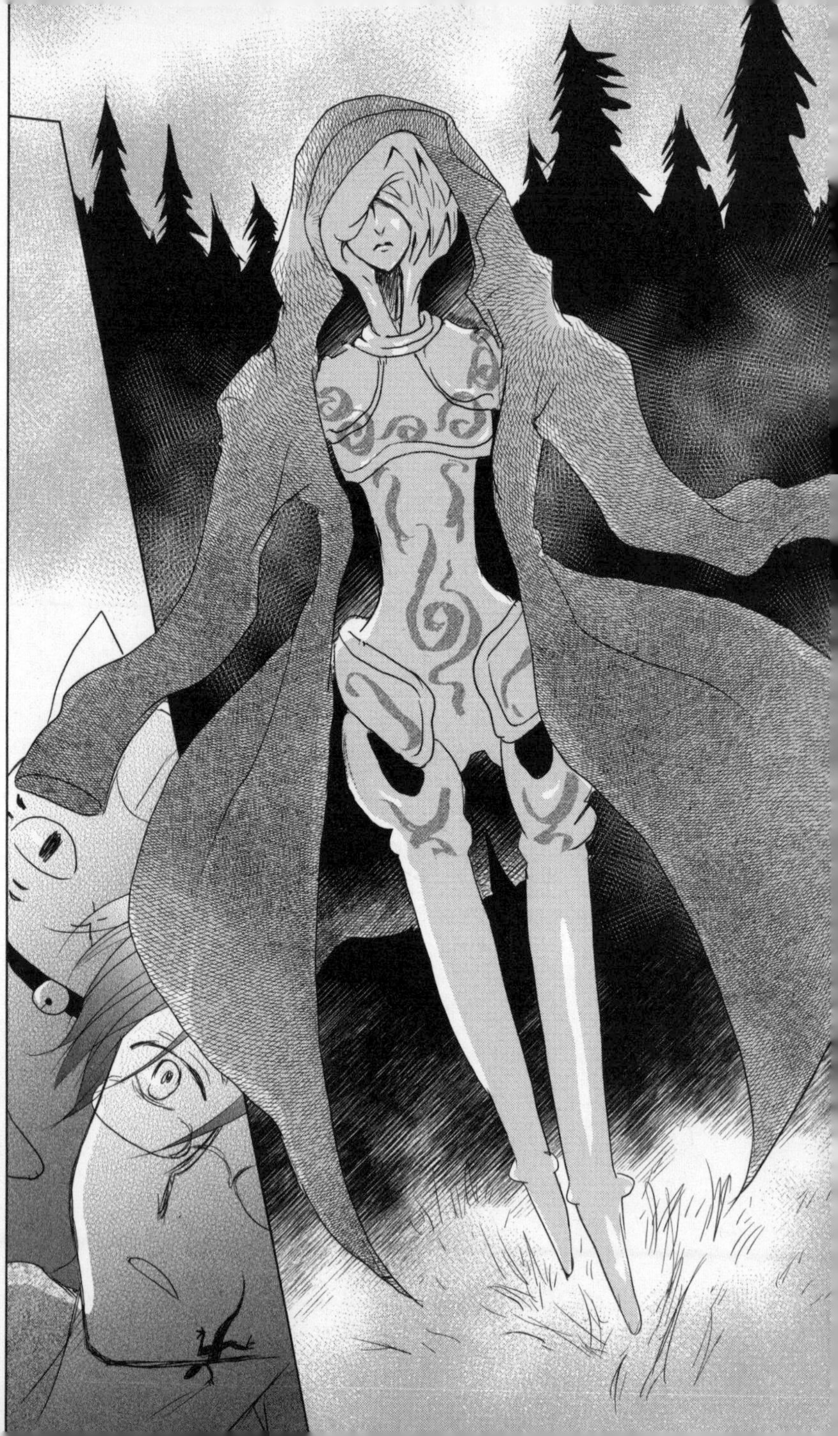

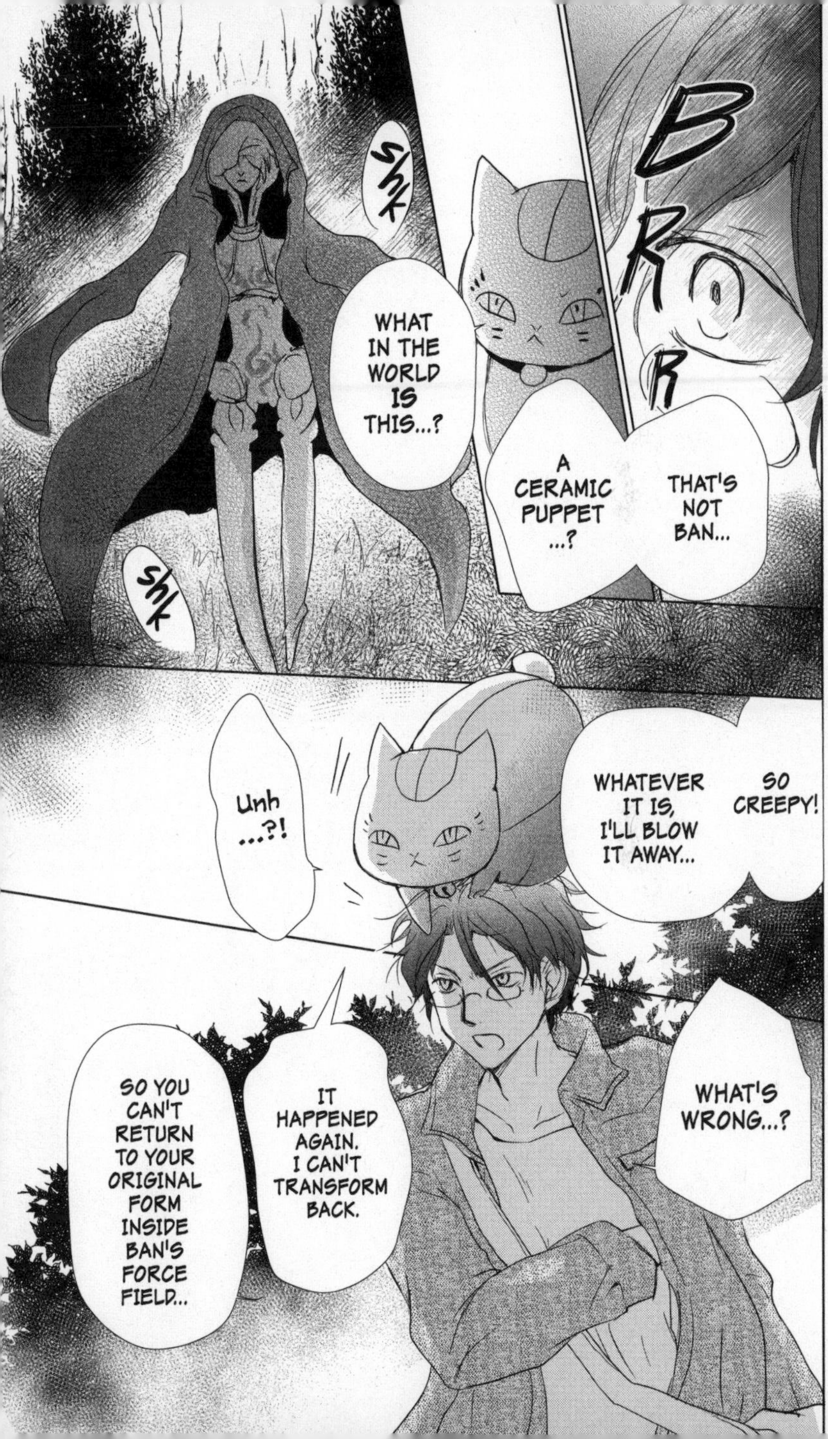
BRR
THAT'S NOT BAN...
A CERAMIC PUPPET ...?
WHAT IN THE WORLD IS THIS...?
shk
shk
SO CREEPY!
WHATEVER IT IS, I'LL BLOW IT AWAY...
Unh ...?!
WHAT'S WRONG...?
IT HAPPENED AGAIN. I CAN'T TRANSFORM BACK.
SO YOU CAN'T RETURN TO YOUR ORIGINAL FORM INSIDE BAN'S FORCE FIELD...

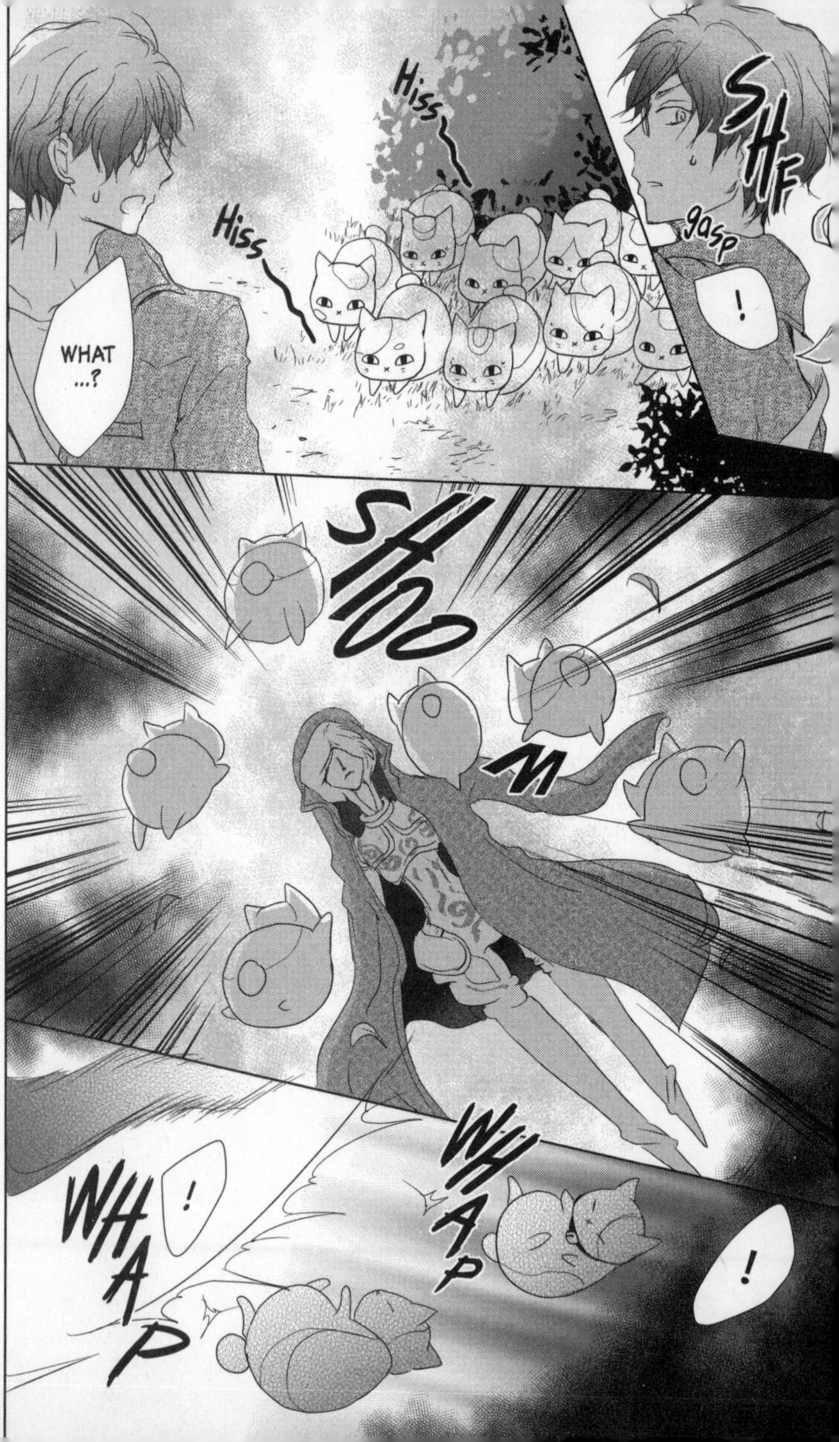
SHF
gasp
!
Hiss~
Hiss~
WHAT ...?
SHOOM
WHAP
!
!
WHAP

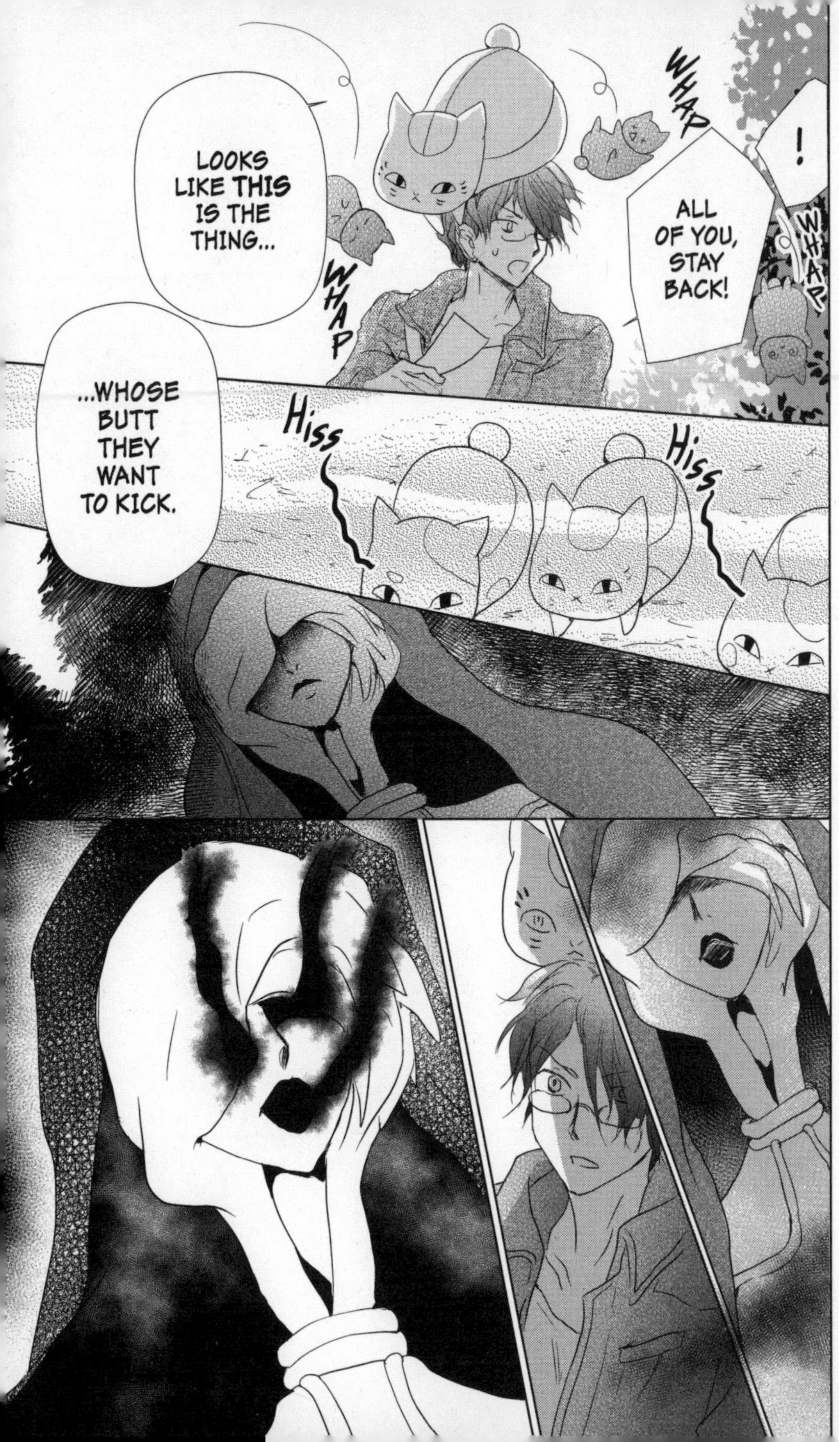

!
WHAP
ALL OF YOU, STAY BACK!
WHAP
LOOKS LIKE THIS IS THE THING...
WHAP
...WHOSE BUTT THEY WANT TO KICK.
Hiss
Hiss

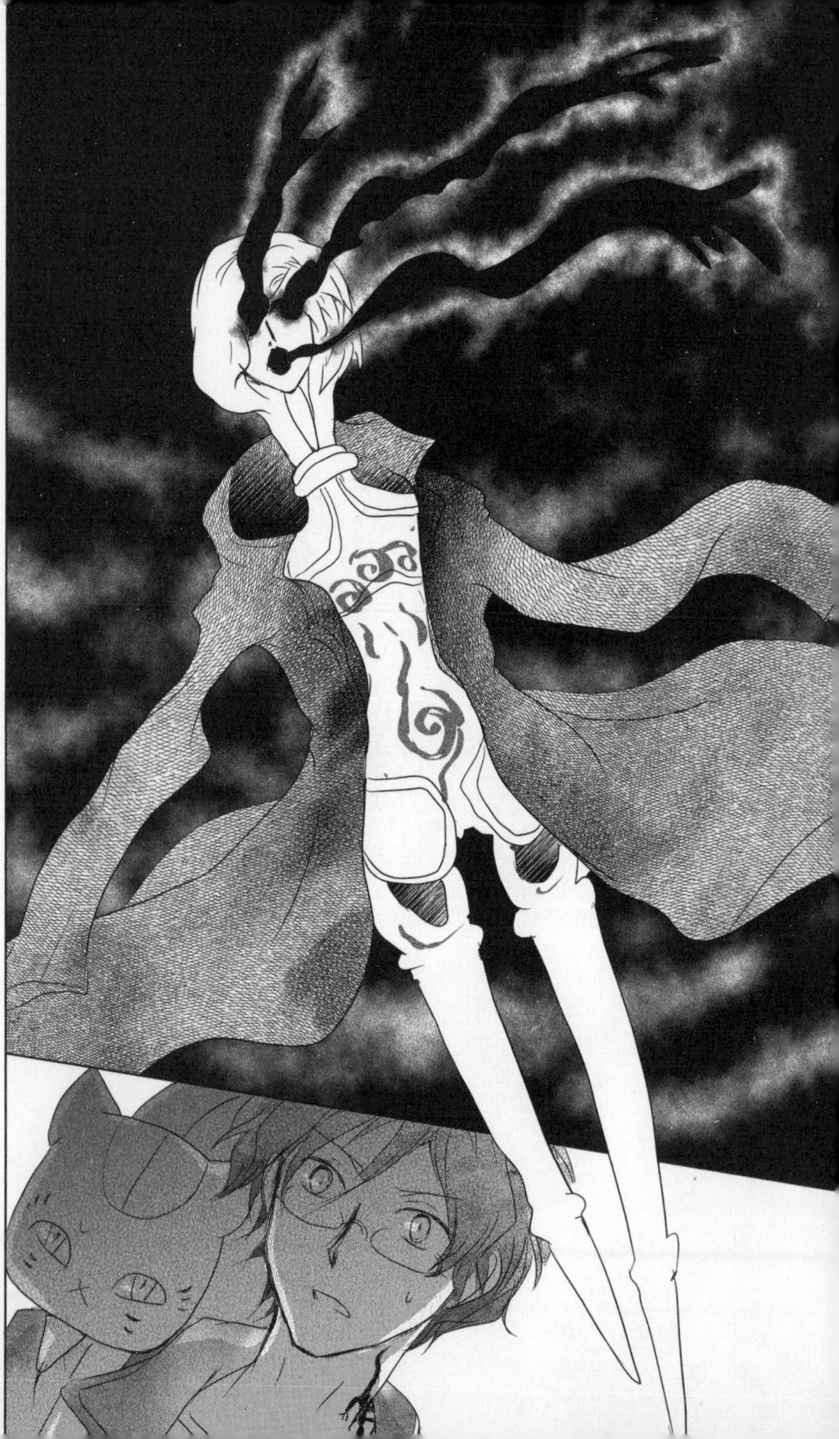

Hello, Midorikawa here. *Natsume's Book of Friends* has reached its 25th volume. No matter how many times it happens, I always feel nervous and ecstatic when a new volume gets published.

As always, it's a battle between the fun and difficulties of working on manga, but I'm going to keep working hard to make something my readers will enjoy reading. Please continue to give me your support!

The sidebars that I'm sure you're all used to are going away starting this volume. That's where advertisements are placed in the magazines, and I always struggle with where to place them in terms of timing and the flow of my scenes as I work on my rough drafts. But when the graphic novels are published, they offered memorable spaces where I can include greetings or messages of gratitude for which there were few opportunities.

✳ *CHAPTER 100*

Thanks to the longevity of the series, I was able to reach the 100th chapter. Thank you so much!

"Where Vessels Lie in Slumber, Part I" was the actual milestone, and to commemorate it, all the other manga artists drew a hidden Nyanko Sensei somewhere in their series' chapter appearing in that issue of *LaLa*. There were so many adorable Nyanko Senseis. My heart was full of gratitude toward them all, the editorial department who came up with the idea, and all the readers. That issue will be my cherished possession.

✳ *LETTERS*

Letters from my readers give me so much motivation. Whether they're cute drawings, wonderful anecdotes or heartfelt thoughts on my work, I cherish each and every one of them. I can't really send replies, but I'll keep working hard to provide entertaining stories.

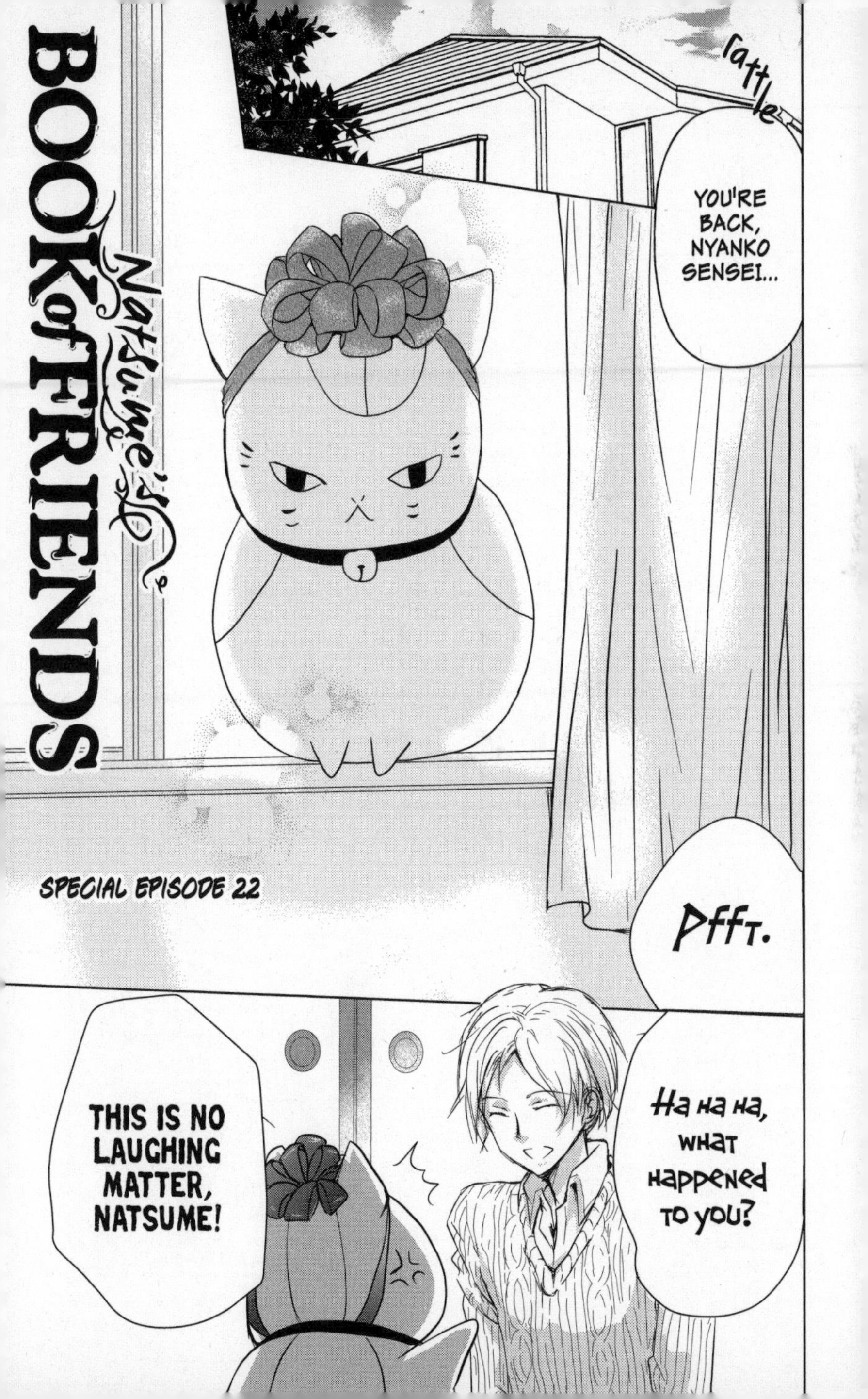

rattle
YOU'RE BACK, NYANKO SENSEI...
Natsume's BOOK of FRIENDS
SPECIAL EPISODE 22
Pfft.
Ha ha ha, what happened to you?
THIS IS NO LAUGHING MATTER, NATSUME!

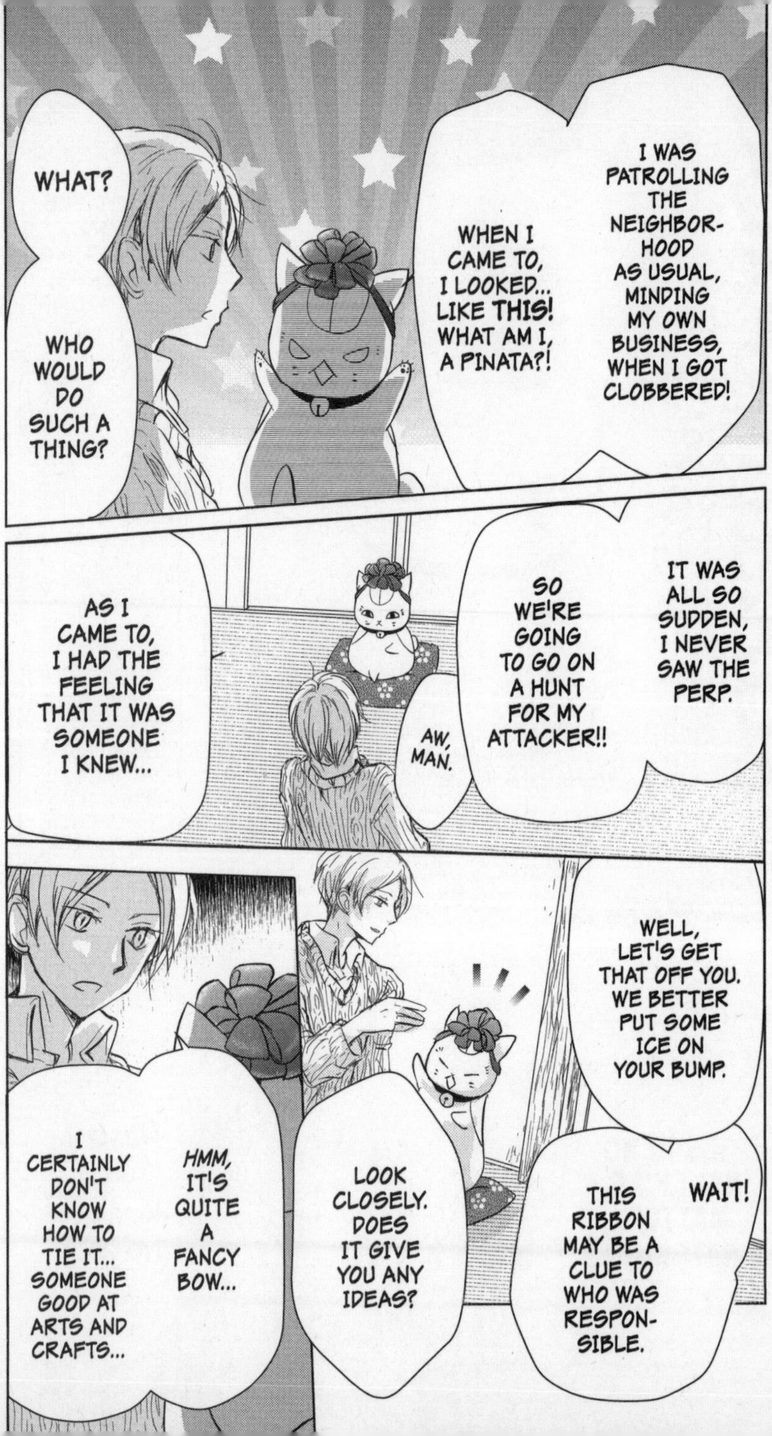
I WAS PATROLLING THE NEIGHBOR-HOOD AS USUAL, MINDING MY OWN BUSINESS, WHEN I GOT CLOBBERED!
WHEN I CAME TO, I LOOKED... LIKE THIS! WHAT AM I, A PINATA?!
WHAT?
WHO WOULD DO SUCH A THING?
IT WAS ALL SO SUDDEN, I NEVER SAW THE PERP.
SO WE'RE GOING TO GO ON A HUNT FOR MY ATTACKER!!
AW, MAN.
AS I CAME TO, I HAD THE FEELING THAT IT WAS SOMEONE I KNEW...
WELL, LET'S GET THAT OFF YOU. WE BETTER PUT SOME ICE ON YOUR BUMP.
WAIT!
THIS RIBBON MAY BE A CLUE TO WHO WAS RESPON-SIBLE.
LOOK CLOSELY. DOES IT GIVE YOU ANY IDEAS?
HMM, IT'S QUITE A FANCY BOW...
I CERTAINLY DON'T KNOW HOW TO TIE IT... SOMEONE GOOD AT ARTS AND CRAFTS...

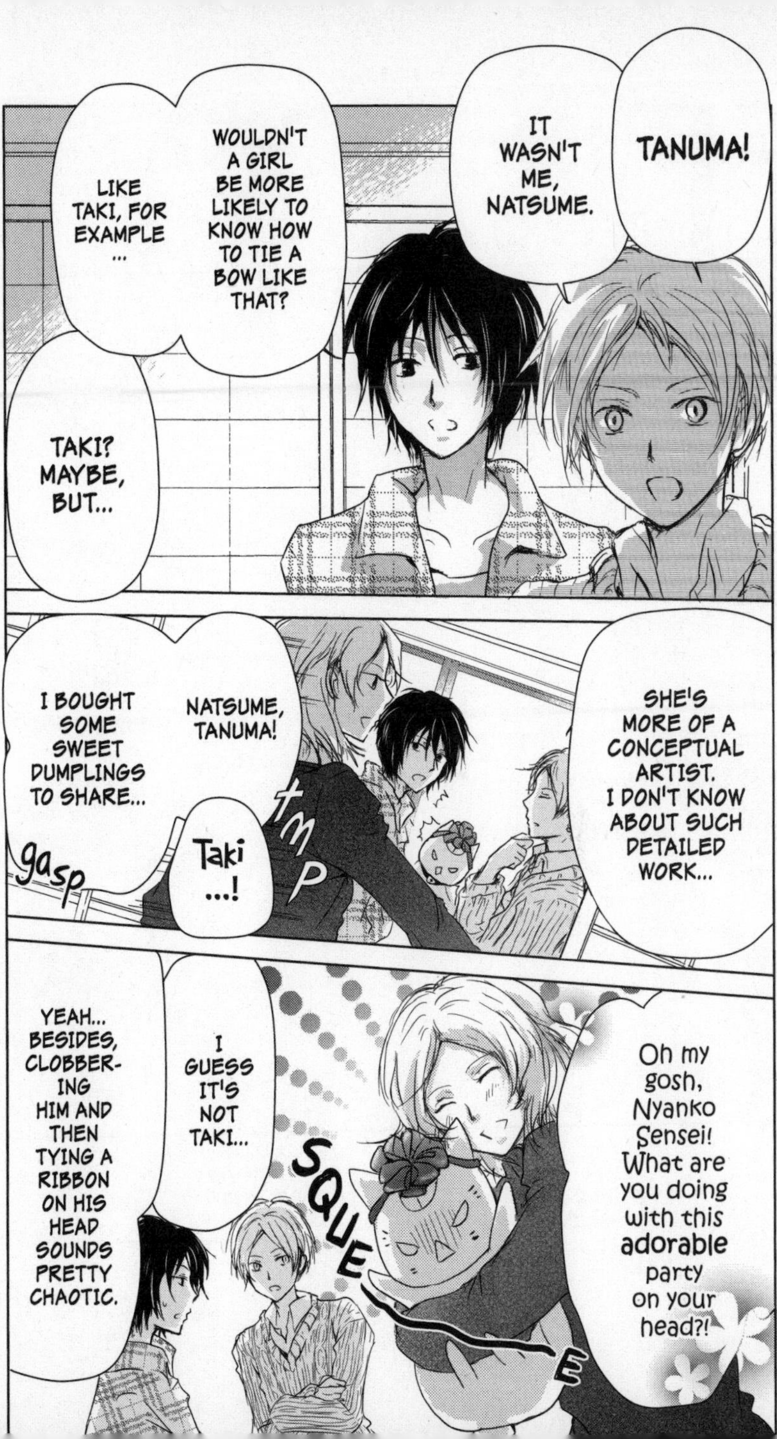
TANUMA!
IT WASN'T ME, NATSUME.
WOULDN'T A GIRL BE MORE LIKELY TO KNOW HOW TO TIE A BOW LIKE THAT?
LIKE TAKI, FOR EXAMPLE ...
TAKI? MAYBE, BUT...
SHE'S MORE OF A CONCEPTUAL ARTIST. I DON'T KNOW ABOUT SUCH DETAILED WORK...
tmp
Taki ...!
NATSUME, TANUMA!
I BOUGHT SOME SWEET DUMPLINGS TO SHARE...
gasp
Oh my gosh, Nyanko Sensei! What are you doing with this adorable party on your head?!
SQUEE
I GUESS IT'S NOT TAKI...
YEAH... BESIDES, CLOBBERING HIM AND THEN TYING A RIBBON ON HIS HEAD SOUNDS PRETTY CHAOTIC.

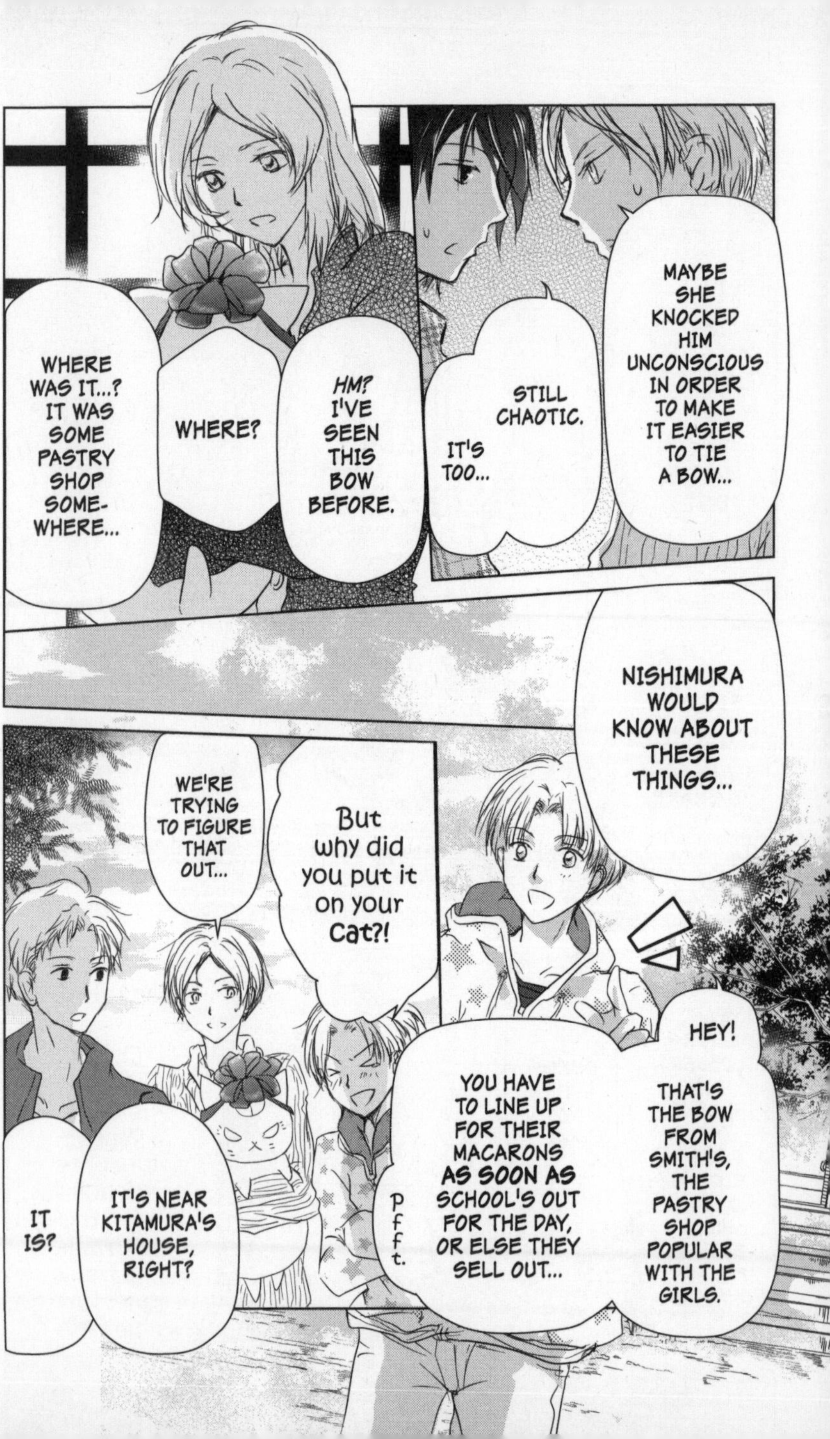
MAYBE SHE KNOCKED HIM UNCONSCIOUS IN ORDER TO MAKE IT EASIER TO TIE A BOW...
IT'S TOO... STILL CHAOTIC.
HM? I'VE SEEN THIS BOW BEFORE.
WHERE?
WHERE WAS IT...? IT WAS SOME PASTRY SHOP SOME-WHERE...
NISHIMURA WOULD KNOW ABOUT THESE THINGS...
HEY!
THAT'S THE BOW FROM SMITH'S, THE PASTRY SHOP POPULAR WITH THE GIRLS.
YOU HAVE TO LINE UP FOR THEIR MACARONS AS SOON AS SCHOOL'S OUT FOR THE DAY, OR ELSE THEY SELL OUT...
Pfft.
But why did you put it on your cat?!
WE'RE TRYING TO FIGURE THAT OUT...
IT'S NEAR KITAMURA'S HOUSE, RIGHT?
IT IS?

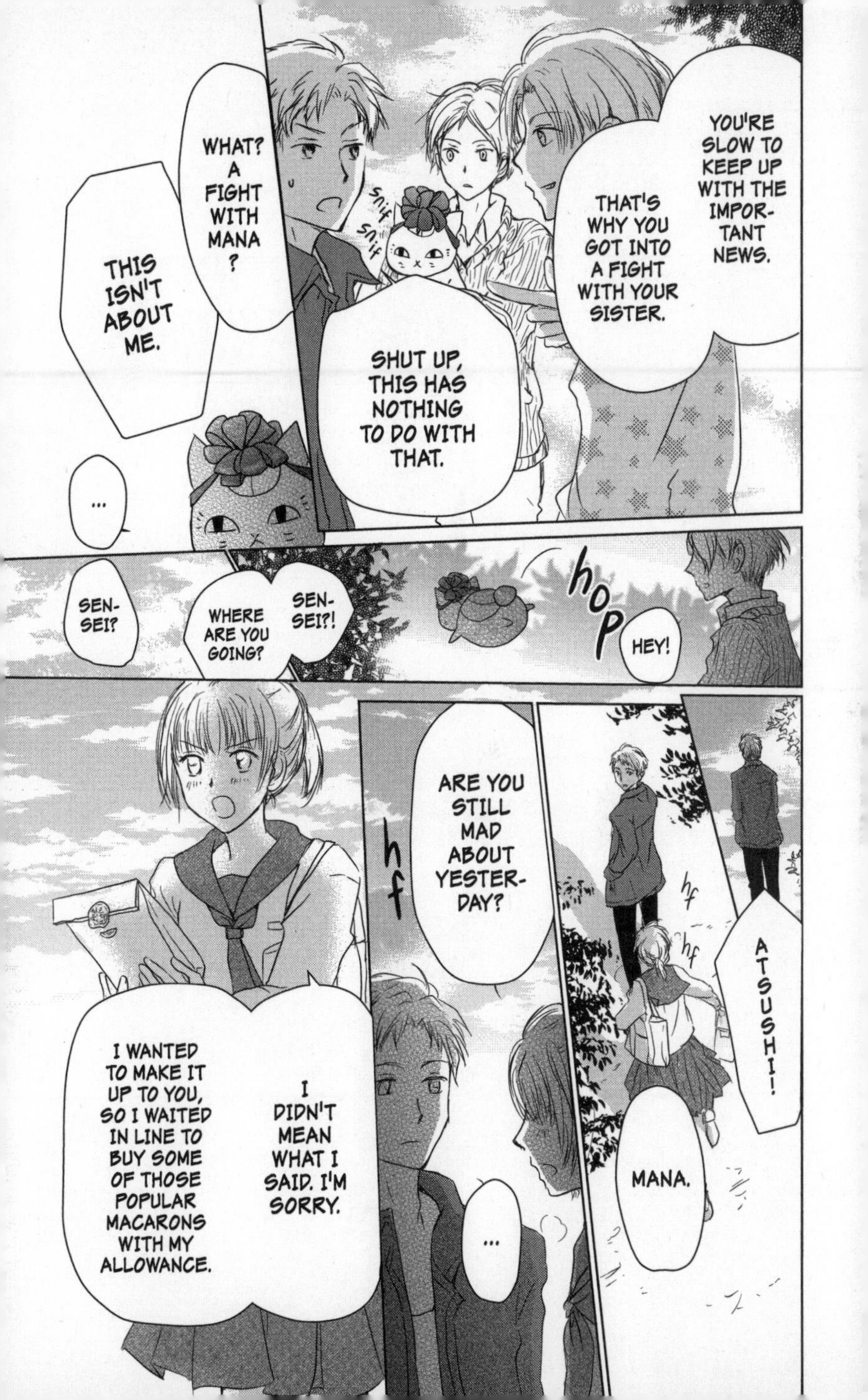
YOU'RE SLOW TO KEEP UP WITH THE IMPORTANT NEWS.
THAT'S WHY YOU GOT INTO A FIGHT WITH YOUR SISTER.
WHAT? A FIGHT WITH MANA?
SHUT UP, THIS HAS NOTHING TO DO WITH THAT.
THIS ISN'T ABOUT ME.
...
HEY!
hop
SEN-SEI?!
WHERE ARE YOU GOING?
SEN-SEI?
ATSUSHI!
hf
hf
MANA.
ARE YOU STILL MAD ABOUT YESTERDAY?
hf
...
I DIDN'T MEAN WHAT I SAID. I'M SORRY.
I WANTED TO MAKE IT UP TO YOU, SO I WAITED IN LINE TO BUY SOME OF THOSE POPULAR MACARONS WITH MY ALLOWANCE.

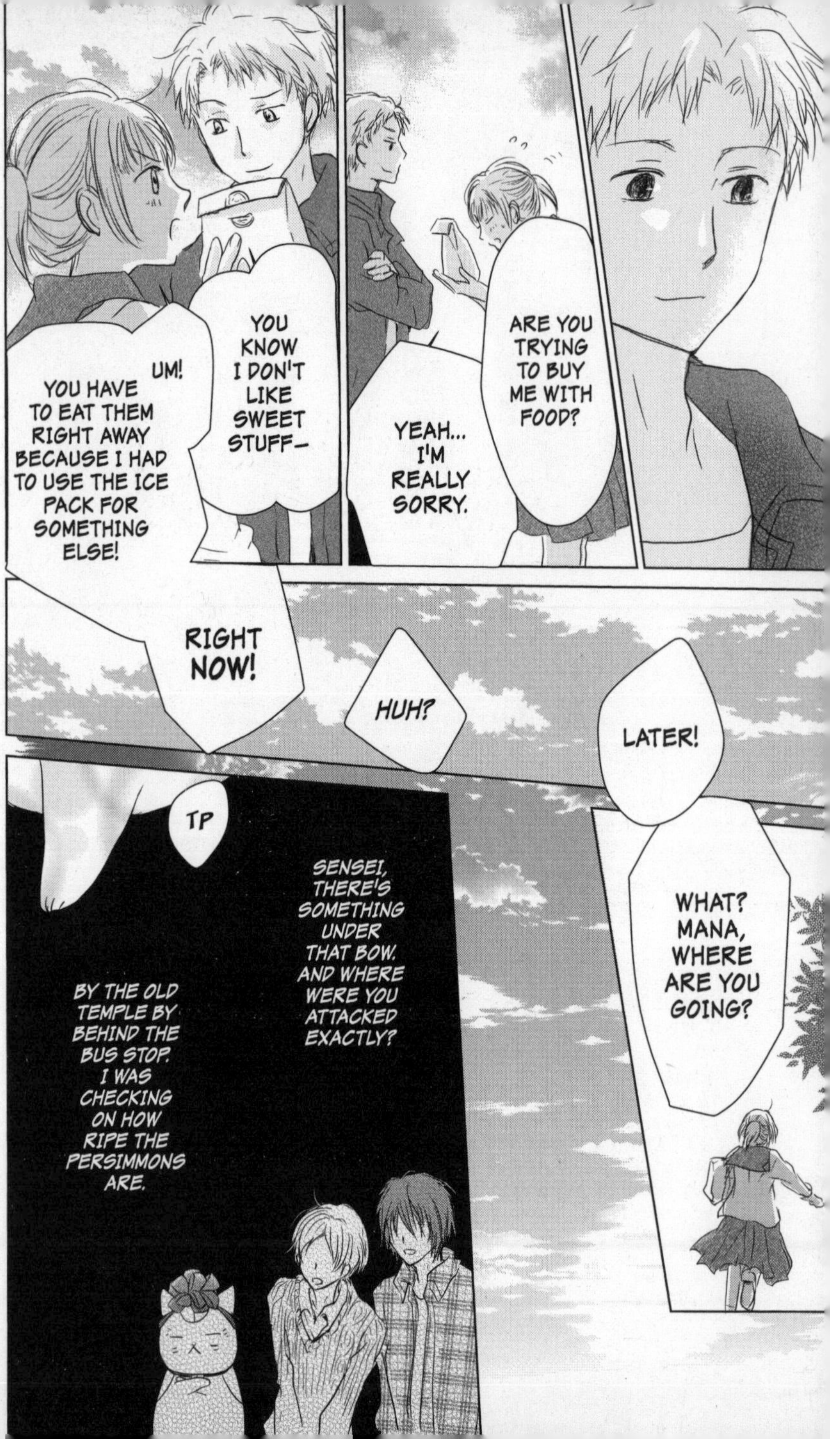
ARE YOU TRYING TO BUY ME WITH FOOD?
YEAH... I'M REALLY SORRY.
YOU KNOW I DON'T LIKE SWEET STUFF—
UM! YOU HAVE TO EAT THEM RIGHT AWAY BECAUSE I HAD TO USE THE ICE PACK FOR SOMETHING ELSE!
LATER!
HUH?
RIGHT NOW!
WHAT? MANA, WHERE ARE YOU GOING?
TP
SENSEI, THERE'S SOMETHING UNDER THAT BOW. AND WHERE WERE YOU ATTACKED EXACTLY?
BY THE OLD TEMPLE BY BEHIND THE BUS STOP. I WAS CHECKING ON HOW RIPE THE PERSIMMONS ARE.

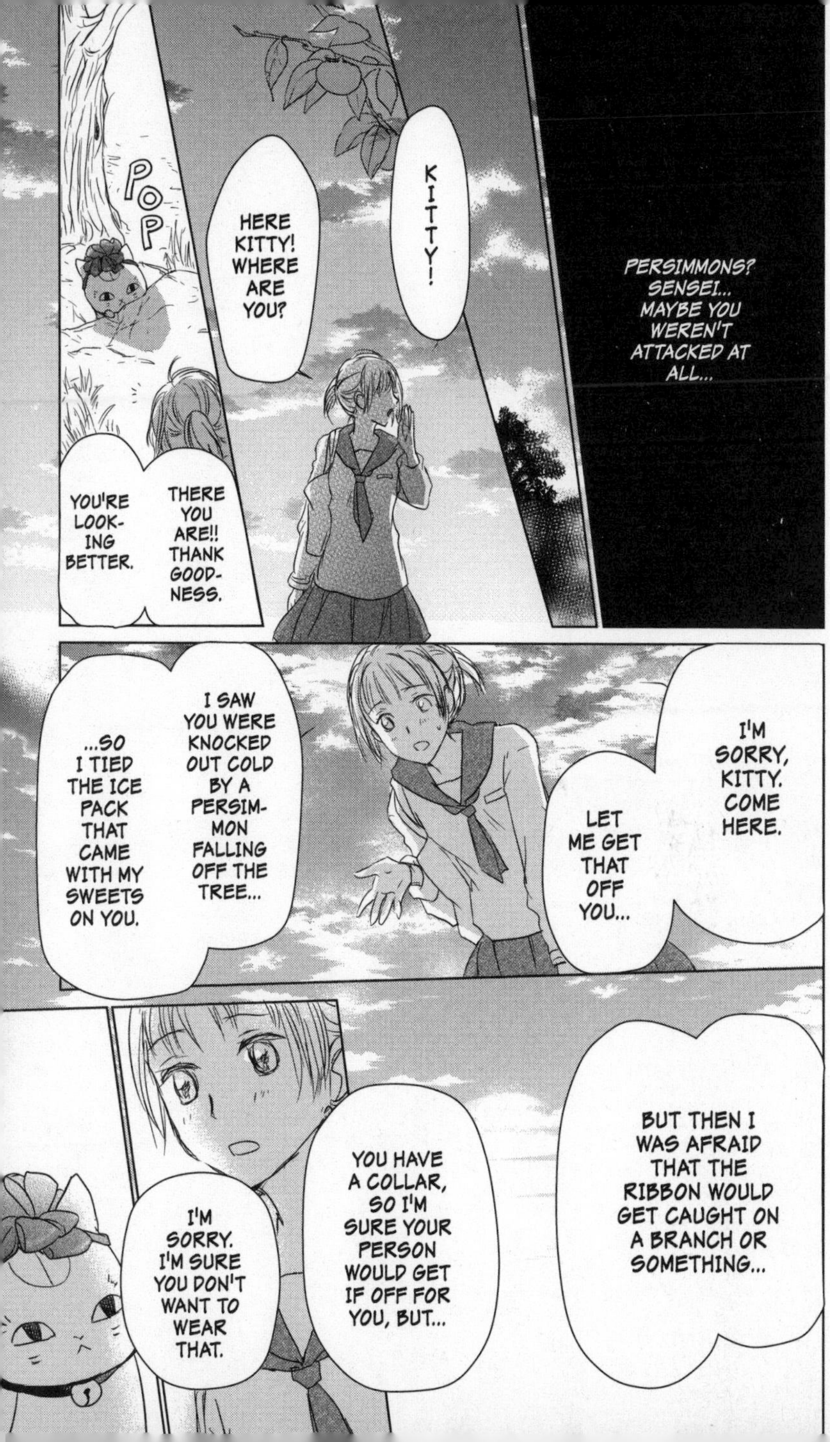
PERSIMMONS? SENSEI... MAYBE YOU WEREN'T ATTACKED AT ALL...
KITTY!
HERE KITTY! WHERE ARE YOU?
POP
THERE YOU ARE!! THANK GOODNESS.
YOU'RE LOOKING BETTER.
I'M SORRY, KITTY. COME HERE.
LET ME GET THAT OFF YOU...
I SAW YOU WERE KNOCKED OUT COLD BY A PERSIMMON FALLING OFF THE TREE...
...SO I TIED THE ICE PACK THAT CAME WITH MY SWEETS ON YOU.
BUT THEN I WAS AFRAID THAT THE RIBBON WOULD GET CAUGHT ON A BRANCH OR SOMETHING...
YOU HAVE A COLLAR, SO I'M SURE YOUR PERSON WOULD GET IF OFF FOR YOU, BUT...
I'M SORRY. I'M SURE YOU DON'T WANT TO WEAR THAT.

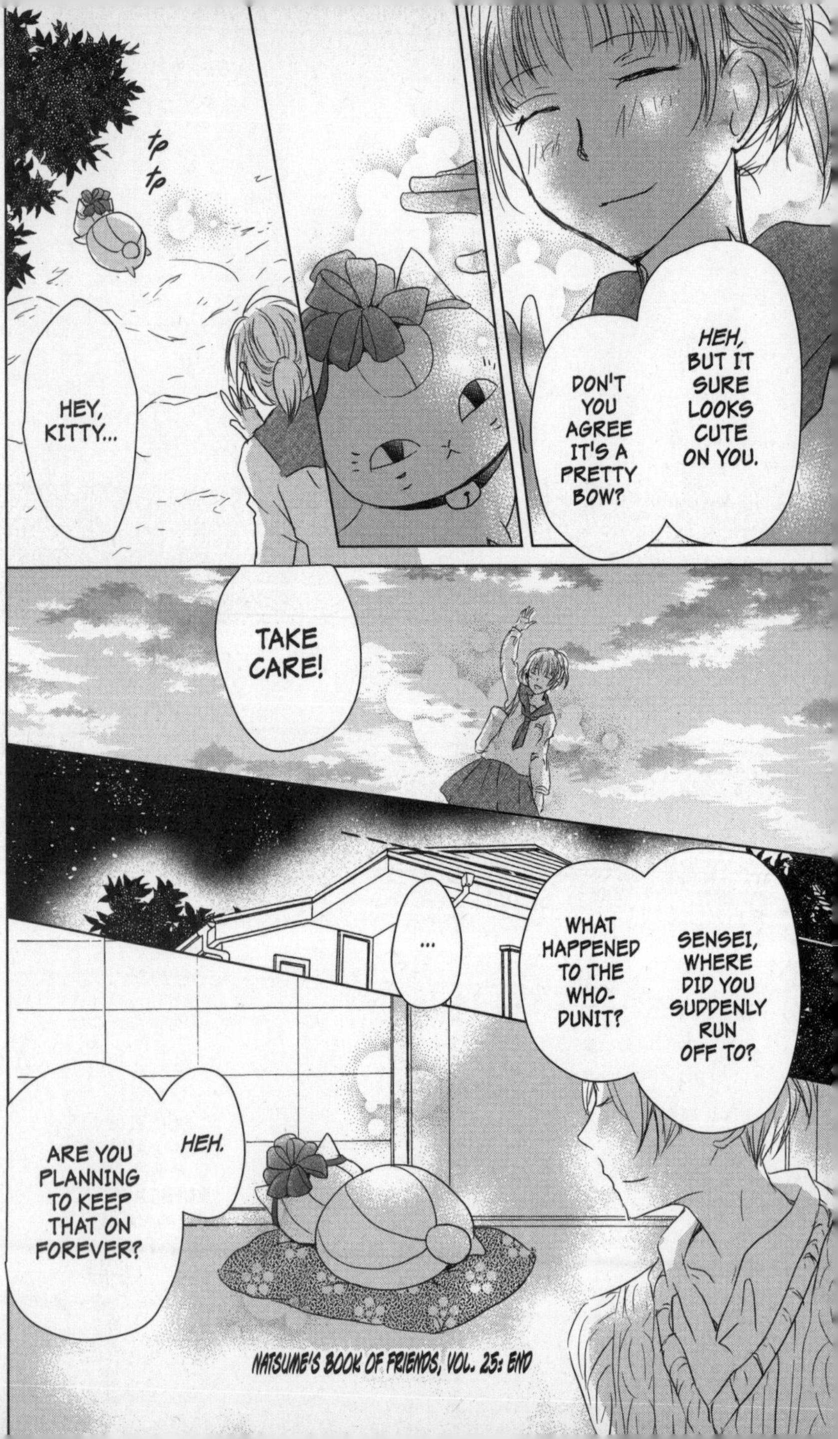
HEH, BUT IT SURE LOOKS CUTE ON YOU.
DON'T YOU AGREE IT'S A PRETTY BOW?
HEY, KITTY...
TAKE CARE!
SENSEI, WHERE DID YOU SUDDENLY RUN OFF TO?
WHAT HAPPENED TO THE WHO-DUNIT?
...
HEH.
ARE YOU PLANNING TO KEEP THAT ON FOREVER?
NATSUME'S BOOK OF FRIENDS, VOL. 25: END

AFTER-
WORD

Thank you for reading. To avoid spoilers, please read the entire volume before reading the rest of this afterword.

As the relationships between Natsume and his friends continue to change, I'm finally able, in the 25th volume, to publish stories I'd been planning since this series started. Even though I came up with the ideas ages ago, I couldn't fully visualize them with the way Natsume and Nyanko Sensei initially were, but now I'm starting to be able to work the ideas in. At the same time there are a number of moments I'm no longer able to include because relationships have moved on past those points. I'm a little sad that I can't use the stories that could only work when Natsume couldn't allow himself to be close to others, but I also know that that's a good thing. It's weird. I'll eventually work them in a different direction, in some shape or form.

SPECIAL EPISODE 21

I agonized over what to include in these 16 pages, but I wanted to focus on the weirdness of the fan club. Since the series has been running for a long time, sometimes I assign secret challenges for myself (for example, I banned the use of monologues in "Tsukihigui"). So since this episode was short, I banned the main character. But it turned out so insular without Natsume, and while it felt like a fresh twist, it reaffirmed my belief that the person who acts as a conduit between worlds is important.

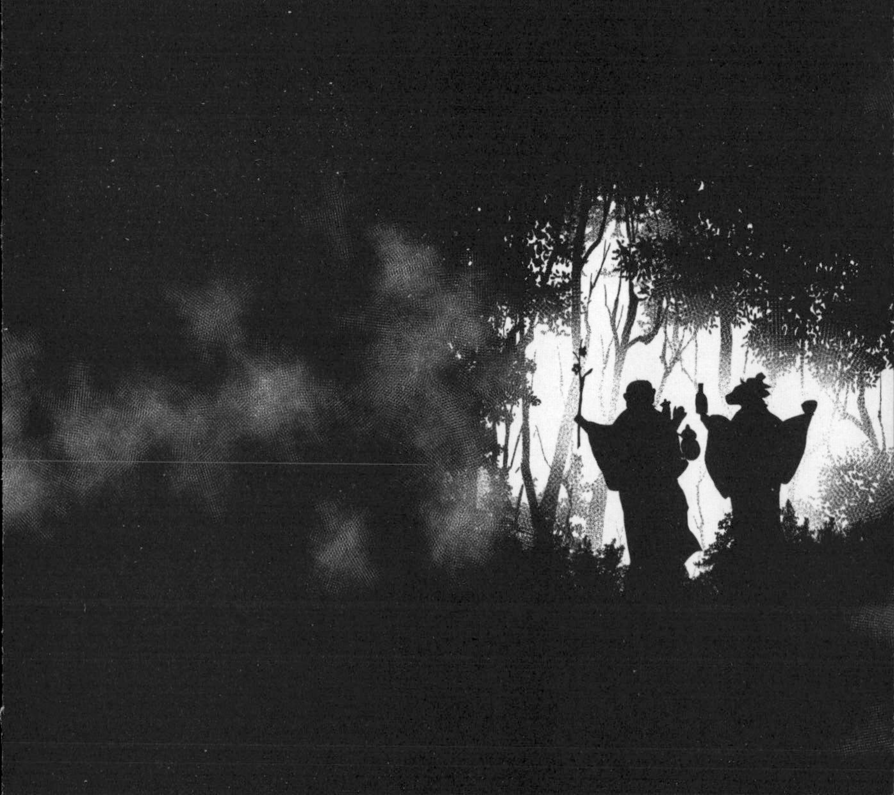

CHAPTERS 100-102 Where Vessels Lie in Slumber

Since it was the special 100th chapter, I talked it over with my editor and got them to approve a longer story. I was so happy to work with characters who usually go home as soon as they show up.

I was excited since it was a story I've wanted to work on since the beginning, but I was worried that some people would be shocked to see a field of roly-polies. Natsume can act natural when he's with Tanuma or Taki, but when he's with Natori and Matoba and they're on duty as exorcists, he tries to be strong. I felt that may expose an unexpected fragility. I hope you can pick up on the instability that happens through this growth.

SPECIAL EPISODE 22

I was given eight pages and I agonized over them. Since it was so short, I wanted to see if I could include as many characters as possible. So it was about them going around asking everyone something. Going on patrol is important!

I'm so grateful that I can continue working as a manga artist,
and that I can keep working on these characters. I would like to
thank my editors for brainstorming with me, my assistants for
lending me their skills, my family for struggling alongside me and
supporting me, and my readers.

I'll keep working hard to produce something you'll want to keep
picking up. Please continue with your support!

Thanks to:

Lulu Eijo
Sachi Fujita
Lido
My sister
Mr. Nakamura
Hoen Kikaku Ltd.

Thank you.